Posing a Threat

Flappers,

Chorus Girls,

Posing a Threat

and Other

Brazen Performers

of the American 1920s

Angela J. Latham

Wesleyan University Press
PUBLISHED BY UNIVERSITY PRESS OF NEW ENGLAND
HANOVER AND LONDON

Wesleyan University Press
Published by University Press of New England, Hanover, NH 03755
© 2000 by Angela J. Latham
All rights reserved
Printed in the United States of America
5 4 3 2 1

CIP data appear at the end of the book

Angela J. Latham, "Packaging Woman: The Concurrent Rise of Beauty Pageants,
Public Bathing, and Other Performances of Female 'Nudity,'" *Journal of Popular
Culture* 29.3 (Winter 1995): 149–67. Popular Press, Bowling Green State University.

Angela J. Latham, "Performance, Ethnography, and History: An Analysis of Displays
by Female Bathers in the 1920s," *Text and Performance Quarterly* 17 (April 1997):
170–81. The National Communication Association, Annandale, Virginia.

Angela J. Latham, "The Right to Bare: Containing and Encoding American Women
in Popular Entertainments of the 1920s," *Theatre Journal* 49 (December 1997):
455–73. The Johns Hopkins University Press.

Illustrations that are not otherwise credited are in the author's collection.

FRONTISPIECE: "Ziegfeld Girl." Culver Pictures.

In Memory of NELLIE M. LATHAM

A Teacher

Contents

4. The Right to Bare: Containing and Encoding American Women in the Popular Theater

5. The Transgressions of Ladies' Night

Illustrations

Acknowledgments

This work is a product of the affirmation and assistance of many people. I am especially indebted to Kathryn Oberdeck and Robert Graves, without whose objectivity and expertise I would certainly have been hostage to my own shortsightedness. Thanks also to Suzanna Tamminen and the fine staff at Wesleyan University Press/University Press of New England, who helped me refine and clarify my ideas and gave me the opportunity to present this work to a broader audience. Likewise, John Rouse and Paul Gray, who edited earlier sections of this writing, also deserve my sincere thanks, as do each of the anonymous reviewers along the way who have offered much invaluable advice. Jack Sharrar, whose fascination with American theater of the 1920s rivals my own, graciously shared his time and wisdom, not to mention his copy of *Gold Diggers*.

Archivists and library personnel have become some of my favorite people in this process, but I would be remiss not to mention by name Kathy Danner of the University of Illinois Library, Bud Michel of the Press of Atlantic City, and Scott Burgh, law librarian for the city of Chicago.

My fellows in the Program for the Study of Cultural Values and Ethics at the University of Illinois were a captivating group, and I thank them for their lively conversation and collegiality. I am grateful for the financial support of this fellowship program and that of the Graduate College at Illinois, which generously paid me to do what I wanted to do anyway but in so doing greatly affirmed the value of my work.

This book began during a period of considerable personal difficulty. My sincerest gratitude to family and friends, whose encouragement helped me see far enough down the road to want to keep moving in a forward direction, and to Braden, who made it worth the trip. Thanks most of all to Al, to whom transgressive femininity poses no threat.

July 1999   A.J.L.

Posing a Threat

Introduction

As his one-hundredth birthday drew near, a newspaper reporter asked my grandfather, Roy Latham, about the changes he had experienced during the course of a century. Born in 1896, he had witnessed such remarkable technological advances as the invention of automobiles, airplanes, radios, television, and computers. He had lived through two world wars and was a veteran of World War I. He had seen men walk on the moon. When questioned specifically about what events most intrigued him, however, my grandfather responded that when women began to wear short hairstyles he was quite taken aback. "When I was a boy, all the girls had long braids. . . . They had hair clear down to their waist. When girls had long hair, you knew you were kissing a girl. When they started to cut their hair, I said, 'Why, that's plum crazy!'"[1] In that he had been audience to some of the most astonishing achievements in the history of the human race, it indeed seems curious that women who "bobbed" their hair were so clearly foregrounded in my grandfather's memory. On the other hand, his reflections confirm what many others have suggested and what is in fact an implicit assumption of this book; that is, the ways in which female members of a society present themselves and the reactions to such presentations are among the most candid indications of the values and mores of a generation.[2]

My grandfather's protest was as specific as it was symbolic. What he did not mention in this interview was that his wife, Nellie Latham, had her own hair bobbed and wore it short throughout their fifty-three-year marriage. In the early 1920s, when she first had it cut, bobbed hair and the "flapper look" to which it alluded were not considered appropriate for young, female schoolteachers in the rural area of southern Indiana where she taught.[3] She cut her hair anyway and kept her long braid, which was, in its severed form, called a "switch." As it turns out, this nomenclature was quite apt, for she pinned the switch to her remaining hair before going to work, transforming her image to assume her public role of "schoolmarm." Of course, even this disguise was minor in comparison to when, after marrying, she posed as a single woman in order to keep her job. Not only in rural Indiana but throughout

America in the 1920s, female teachers were usually required to give up their profession when they married.[4] No doubt her subterfuge failed when the birth of the Lathams' first children, twins, appeared imminent.

Nellie Latham's carefully concealed opposition to unreasonable strictures that were intended to proscribe her most personal life choices was by no means exceptional. Many other women of the 1920s, keenly aware of the censure they faced, also attempted and sometimes succeeded in thwarting the impositions of a society that would have physically, emotionally, and spiritually restricted their rightful autonomy. Expected at least to conform in their appearance, whether to the mandates of a morality that judged character by hemlines and hairstyles or to the tyranny of the fashion system itself, many women achieved some measure of freedom by disguising defiance to look like conformity. Thus, a long braid of hair—a symbol of traditional femininity both within her social context and within her most intimate relationship— pinned carefully to her bobbed hair became Nellie Latham's secret emblem of self-assertion and independence.

This book examines performances by American women in the 1920s, including ones like my grandmother's that were quite subtle, even unacknowledged as "performances" by the actor or her audience. The specific performances featured here may be classified in two ways.[5] First, there are those internally monitored portrayals of self that occur throughout the ordinary moments of life. These performances are defined not by a particular activity but by the performer's *ambition* to present herself before others in a certain way, usually while engaging in a seemingly unrelated endeavor that in fact conceals her performative intentions. Certainly, fashion itself, part and parcel of the performance of identity, was and still is an obvious example of this type of performance. Indeed, the "flapper look" was as much a pose as it was a particular style of clothing that women wore.[6] Moreover, some flapper-era fashions seemed particularly to create a sense of the performative whenever they were worn. Women's "bathing costumes" of the 1920s are an especially vivid case in point and as such will receive particular emphasis here. Rather less apparently, however, my grandmother's efforts to fulfill the expectations associated with the role of "teacher" to students and employers, even to the point of deliberately deceiving them, are also an example of performances that are intended to look like anything but performances.

The second type of performance discussed here is overtly theatrical. Costumes are chosen or prepared specifically for an event that occurs before a defined audience. Such presentations occur in a place and time set aside for the occasion of the performance and involve the display of a performance-specific skill. This skill might be the ability to dramatically portray a fictional character, of course, but also to perform a stylized presentation of self. Thus inclusively defined, a woman in a Ziegfeld *Follies* revue who gracefully descended a long flight of stairs performed, even though she did not appear "in character." So, for that matter, did a "bathing beauty" contestant, who presented herself in a manner that idealized her own image. Although she performed on a boardwalk instead of a stage, she nevertheless did so in a conspicuously theatrical way, given her use of costume and the presence of an audience gathered at a time and place devoted to the occasion of her performance. Indeed, bathers' revue participants posed precisely (and literally) at the juncture between both kinds of performances defined here, and they therefore warrant and receive special attention. To be sure, the bathing beauty contestant differed performatively from her "merely" fashionable counterpart whose ostensible purpose was to swim. Whereas the latter generally hid her performative intentions, the former openly acknowledged hers. The act of parading down the boardwalk for all the world to see, in the context of a revue, clearly denoted entry into the realm of the theatrical, where audience and performer mutually acknowledge their reciprocal relationship.

Regardless of performance genre, live, not mediated, presentations comprise the major emphasis here. Although photographic evidence assists this inquiry in many ways, as does an awareness of the influence of film in 1920s American culture, the specific circumstances in which women performed are crucial to understanding the performances themselves; such media usually dislocate performance from context.[7]

Fashion and theater were among the most closely monitored and heavily censored sites of female performance in the 1920s. The sheer volume of discussion within popular publications of this decade that is devoted to controversial fashionable and theatrical performances by women well substantiates my claim. These published debates afford us a relatively clear impression of the ideological climate in which women enacted particular forms of resistance. For this reason, I investigated a variety of print media sources from the 1920s and present here my critique of this popular discourse as it pertains to the way in which women presented themselves to others, specifically with regard to the fashions they wore and the theater they helped to create.

To fully appreciate how American women in the 1920s transformed their lives through performance, however, a rhetorical survey of the ideologies they resisted is not enough. This is a point I will take up more fully in chapter 1; but for now, I must at least stress that it is essential as well to interrogate specific, locally situated instances in which performances occurred. Thus, for example, following my review of fashion debates, I explore individual acts of opposition to dress codes for what they reveal about both the cultural institutions that imposed such codes and the women who transgressed them. Similarly, after summarizing and analyzing theater debates, I assess the controversy surrounding the play *Ladies' Night in a Turkish Bath*. Reactions to the production of this play clarify particulars of the commercial appropriation and censorship of the female body.

I have organized this book in a way that I believe is consistent with the foregoing discussion. Specifically, in chapter 1, I pursue two primary objectives. First, I briefly describe certain aspects of the sociocultural context that was the American 1920s, in part by critiquing commonly held assumptions about this era. Second, I explain my methodological approach and its theoretical underpinnings. Chapters 2 and 3 feature contested performances of fashion by American women in the 1920s. In chapter 2, I describe popular women's fashions, but I also detail controversial aspects of these styles, in an effort to define the ideological as well as the material features of female attire. By centering on so fundamental a component of self-presentation as clothing, this chapter serves as a foundation for the discussion in chapter 3 of locally situated contests over fashions for women, in particular, conflicts about fashions in bathing costumes. Such costumes were among the most controversial and thus most emphatically censured of all women's fashions. Moreover, bathing attire was worn in situations that heightened a woman's sense of being "on display"[8] since, for most women, swimming was a public experience and one in which the woman wore less clothing than usual. Public bathing was also a context/ritual in which physical autonomy—that is, the sheer ability to move about freely—was an especially pragmatic concern for women.

This is not to say that other fashion controversies did not also include pragmatic appeals. The difficulty of wearing unnecessary or confining clothing while sunbathing or swimming, however, was central to most arguments about bathing costumes. Thus, these conflicts contain some of the most clearly articulated and boldly stated opposition to morality-based or other kinds of display censorship. Furthermore, the regulation of bathing costumes was often quite explicitly coded within certain communities and therefore affords the greatest opportunity to explore and compare legal and civic dimensions of women's performative displays. I also address how the performance of bathers' revues, especially the creation of the Miss America pageant, sanctioned otherwise contested self-presentations by women.

Chapters 4 and 5 feature controversial performances by women in popular entertainments of the American 1920s. In chapter 4, as in chapter 2, I emphasize the rhetoric of censorship more than its specific implementation. The 1920s were an extraordinary period, during which the American theater was repeatedly targeted by censorship efforts instigated by reformers both within and without the entertainment industry. Sexually provocative displays by women were commonly the object of censorship; this, despite the fact that the 1920s were also the heyday of the Ziegfeld *Follies* and its many imitators, shows whose appeal was based largely on the bared physiques of young "chorines." Florenz Ziegfeld's motto, "glorifying the American girl," which he and others used to defend norm-defying displays of female nudity, suggests that, then as now, the enterprising appropriation of youthful American beauty was its own justification. I situate the popularity of such revues and other venues that featured women's bodies within the broader context of theater censorship in this curious cultural climate of attraction and repulsion with regard to the staging of the bared female body. In these ways, chapter 4 contextualizes my analysis in chapter 5 of the censorship of A. H. Woods's Chicago production of *Ladies' Night in a Turkish Bath*.

By way of disguise, display, or a judicious appropriation of both, performance was a primary means by which women contested, affirmed, mitigated, and revolutionized norms of female self-presentation and self-stylization. I underscore here the contestation and censorship of women's performances with the understanding that such an emphasis effectively marks the idiosyncrasies of America's cultural ideals in this era. Moreover, I contend that, when we locate the ways in which cultural values were bodily inscribed for women in the 1920s, we thereby isolate crucial and historically specific variables in the developing iconicity of the female body.

Each of my particular objectives in writing this book is encompassed by my broadest hope, namely, that you may, as I have, develop a deeper appreciation of how performance, particularly the strategic performance of transgressive femininity, immeasurably enriched the era of history that is often recognized as the very threshold of American modernity.

FIG. 1. Flapper.

1 Starting Points

What We Have Been Told

Popular mythology holds that the 1920s were a historical milestone in American women's achievement of political and personal autonomy. Our collective imagination maintains a fixed place for the smiling, devil-may-care "flapper" who, while perhaps not politically conscientious enough to vote but certainly buoyed up by the authority to do so, puts a face on an otherwise ethereal "new woman" (figs. 1 and 2). Freed at last from the fetters of American Victorianism, she was unrestrained by trailing skirts, corsets, or old-fashioned notions of sex.[1]

The feminist historian Estelle B. Freedman some time ago expressed concern that scholars presumed too much about the lives of women of the 1920s based on popular stereotypes of flappers, bathing beauty queens, chorus girls, and other such alluring yet facile representations. It was unsatisfactory, in her opinion, that historians had "generally retained the notion of the revolution in manners and morals" in their characterizations of the post–World War I decade, although such a view was understandable given the abundance of evidence that would in fact suggest there was such a revolution. Freedman insisted, however, that one must question "[h]ow the social freedom in clothing, manners, and sex contributed to deeper social change." To portray the postsuffrage era as a time of "full equality, when in fact discrimination . . . was abundant, has perpetuated a myth of equality."[2] She maintained that this mythology could and should be dismantled through "[o]riginal and creative use of primary resources," through the process of reopening the countless stories of individual struggle that lie waiting to be exhumed.[3]

I undertake the writing of this book in wholehearted agreement with Freedman. Further, I contend that to identify *performance* clues, which are often embedded within these stories, is to perceive with special clarity the ways in which at least some women did exert autonomy and enact resistance. One important result of such an effort is, of course, that we thereby remediate the still-too-common monolithic historical assessments of women's

FIG. 2. The "New Woman." From "New Fashions for the Late Spring," *Delineator* 98 (May 1921): 79.

powerlessness throughout social history, a powerlessness often implied by the silence of women's voices in many archival and historical accounts. As Carroll Smith-Rosenberg states: "We are used to thinking of women as victims or as co-opted spokespersons for male power relations. This view of women . . . fails to look for evidence of women's reaction, of the ways women manipulated men and events to create new fields of power or to assert female autonomy."[4] Performance-centered scrutiny of primary sources from the 1920s clearly indicates that many women did react, sometimes violently, in their attempts to appropriate personal power.

At the risk of being obvious but reluctant to leave a crucial point to chance, I hasten to qualify the discussion to this point with the reminder that gender, in and of itself, is a terribly imprecise identity marker. No one woman of the 1920s—or today for that matter—felt exactly the same as another about issues of empowerment. After all, a woman often struggled alone to become empowered in her own way; indeed, empowerment was uniquely defined by each woman. Furthermore, other identity markers, such as age, race, ethnicity, and economic status, significantly affected a woman's view of power issues. White women and wealthy women faced dissimilar and usually fewer constraints than did minority and poor women. Young women were apt to prioritize issues differently from older women and thus found themselves frequently opposed by their seniors. In fact, some women achieved power by wresting it from the hands of other women. Certainly, I do not presume to speak for every woman of this era. In the attempt to responsibly negotiate these complex issues of identity, I must necessarily admit that no particular viewpoint or event fairly represents the opinions or experiences of all American women in the 1920s. I offer this caveat even as I insist in principle on the importance of the specific in understanding the whole.

The foremost symbol of woman's increasing influence in the American 1920s, her right to vote, must be considered in light of other features of American culture of that era. We need only recall that this decade in American history also included the Wales Padlock law, Prohibition, the "Red Scare," the Scopes trial, the Sacco-Vanzetti case, and a variety of new means of mass enculturation to know that this was a time when the American ideal of individual liberty was virtually under siege.[5] Writing in 1931, when such matters were still well in view, the historian Frederick Lewis Allen depicted the suspicion that permeated American society at the turn of the decade of the 1920s and concluded that "intolerance became an American virtue."[6] Battles over personal freedoms were fought on many fronts, but for most women these struggles, to no one's surprise, centered on issues of self-presentation. How long a woman's hair or skirt was, whether she spent her hard-earned money on cheap stockings or silk ones, or whether she wore stockings at all with her bathing costume were believed by some to be matters of great consequence, not only for the individual woman but for the nation as well.[7]

Although ostensibly about one woman or group of women, certain richly textured historical narratives do have a tremendous capacity to reveal the mitigated nature of personal liberty for *all* American women of the 1920s. Some accounts of specific enactments of resistance also suggest how the absence of a common political cause, that of suffrage, splintered the focus of the women's movement in the 1920s. Elaine Showalter, in fact, describes the 1920s as "feminism's awkward age" and notes.

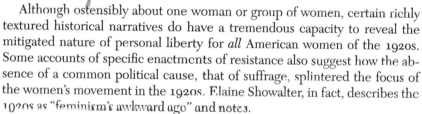

The collapse of the suffrage coalition, the factionalization of the women's movement into bitterly opposed parties, and the absence of a clearly defined female voting bloc contributed to the political decline. On the personal level, the difficulty of applying feminist theory to daily life in a society still organized on patriarchal principles, and the younger generation's disavowal of the ideals and goals of the women's movement, led to fatigue and withdrawal among former leaders.[8]

Nancy F. Cott describes the postsuffrage era similarly: "The uniting goal of the vote accomplished, women faced the difficult realization of the larger goals of Feminism: individuality, full political participation, economic independence, 'sex rights.'"[9] Revisionist efforts by Freedman, Showalter, Cott, and other historians enable us to see the 1920s more clearly for what they were: a time when women were apt to measure their progress from highly personal vantage points, within intimate relationships and immediate social circumstances. By identifying unique struggles over personal freedoms that women continued to face, such scholarship refines previously held notions of the ways in which women participated in society in America during the 1920s and contributes to a more nuanced understanding of the American postsuffrage era generally.

The significance of the 1920s to the increasing iconicity of the female body in American culture deserves particular emphasis. Some scholars have already wisely acknowledged this era as crucial to our understanding of the present exploitation of the female image. Lary May, for example, has appropriately addressed the impact of the motion picture industry on American culture from 1890 through 1929. He credits the influence of moviemakers in the "break from the asceticism of the past," both before and after World War I. He contends: "Yet after 1919, devotion to a large-scale political movement declined, and film makers like DeMille began to project even more radical changes within family and sexual life. Impulses for public duty waned, and reform would be focused within the private realm of manners, rhetoric, and taste."[10] More specifically and a point well taken here, May notes that, prior to World War I, motion picture heroines like Mary Pickford "still carried the temperance, suffrage, and moral impulses of nineteenth-century women." By the 1920s, however, "[m]otherhood, as an ideal which had lasted for a century, virtually disappeared from films as the main aspiration for women. Now heroines became flappers or erotic wives, like DeMille's major characters."[11] May's scholarship is a collage that makes meaning out of the interrelationships among a myriad of cultural forces in the 1920s, not the least of which was the motion picture industry.

Similarly, Lewis A. Erenberg appraises the transformation of American culture between 1890 and 1930 through the lens of performance, namely, the popular entertainments that flourished in New York during this period. He notes the impact of film in creating influential female "types," especially the "woman as plaything" mentality that emerged early in the century.[12] Focusing primarily on live performance venues, Erenberg offers abundant evidence as to the ways in which women's bodies were appropriated in amusements such as cabaret revues, vaudeville, and burlesque. He contends that the popular image of the chorus girl was considerably revised in the late teens and early twenties and suggests, as do I, that Florenz Ziegfeld Jr. was largely responsible for promoting this transformation. "Prior to Ziegfeld, chorus women in burlesque were picked for their bulk rather than their skill. . . . Under Ziegfeld, the chorus developed from a static and inactive picture to a dynamic and well-precisioned ensemble."[13]

The regulation of the female body, for entertainment purposes or otherwise, has long been contested and remains a highly volatile subject of debate, whose intensity is increased by the association of this issue with questions of dominance, violence, economics, self-determination, and morality. An interrogation of proscriptions against body display and the controversy they engender is positioned at the intersection of several fields of inquiry. Theater historians, performance theorists, anthropologists, sociologists, and feminist scholars, to name a few, understandably concern themselves with the interplay between social context and self-presentation, inspecting relations between human beings, given a particular cultural milieu. One primary goal for many scholars at present is to determine more specifically the impact of gender and sexuality on the presentation of self, especially the way in which the body—according to the historian Joan Wallach Scott, "notoriously and ubiquitously associated with the female"—is central in the "reproduction and transformation of culture."[14] Many have, in fact, contributed to what has now become an extensive scholarly discourse about the human body as cultural signifier.[15]

Susan R. Bordo explains what may be the key point of consensus that frames this larger conversation: "The body is not only a *text* of culture. It is also . . . a *practical*, direct locus of social control."[16] This idea, when applied to and examined within historical contexts, is particularly intriguing. Indeed, retrospective analyses of body-presentation dilemmas are, I believe, an unusually persuasive means by which to show that the body *inevitably* functions as a site where cultural values are displayed, contested, negotiated, and ultimately transformed.[17]

Coming to Terms

In addition to contextualizing this work historiographically and thematically, a brief explanation of the methodological and theoretical strategies employed here is also warranted. As I mentioned previously, in order to assess the authorization or censorship of performances by women in the American 1920s and to determine how these processes were transformed, we must first acquaint ourselves with the ideological landscape of American culture as it existed at that time. As the anthropologists John and Jean Comaroff contend, "Improperly contextualized, the stories of ordinary people past stand in danger of remaining just that: stories. To become something more, these partial, 'hidden histories' have to be situated in the wider worlds of power and meaning that gave them life." Moreover, the Comaroffs assert, "there is no reason to assume that the histories of the repressed, in themselves, hold a special key to revelation . . . the discourses of the dominant also yield vital insights into the contexts and processes of which they were part."[18] In keeping with this idea, I carefully surveyed extant popular discourse about contested female performances of the 1920s—much of which was originally distributed nationally or circulated within large metropolitan areas. My critique of this discourse highlights what I feel are the most relevant as well as the most typical features of the ideological environment in which American women enacted their lives.

The anthropologist James C. Scott, like the Comoroffs, distinguishes between multiple social discourses. Scott, however, stresses the significance of the *interplay* of these discourses—by which he refers to many forms of social interaction—and how this interplay signals power relations within a society. He states that discourse of the socially dominant, what he describes as the "official story" or "public transcript," is a key means by which to determine dynamics of power within a culture. He similarly advises that "the public transcript is not the whole story" and is in fact an "indifferent guide to the opinion of subordinates." Sensitive to the "theatrical imperatives that normally prevail in situations of domination," Scott argues that subordinate groups usually find it to their advantage to produce "more or less credible performances," that is, ones that appear to be of a piece with the public transcript. Therefore, "[i]n ideological terms the public transcript will typically, by its accommodationist tone, provide convincing evidence for the hegemony of dominant values, for the hegemony of dominant discourse. It is in precisely this public domain where the effects of power relations are most manifest."[19]

In that unempowered groups are to some extent coerced into performing the values of the dominant, an analysis of power relations within a society that is based exclusively on the public transcript in which the former participate will likely lead to the inaccurate conclusion that "subordinate groups endorse the terms of their subordination and are willing, even enthusiastic, partners in that subordination."[20] Scott insists that, to comprehend the range of power dynamics within a culture, one naturally must attend to the discourse of the dominant as enacted by both empowered and unempowered groups. But one also must look closely to find what is revealed behind this "official story." Although such information is usually hidden, accessible primarily to members of subordinate groups, it does occasionally become "public" or may be otherwise accessed if one is sufficiently innovative. Indeed, in his book *Domination and the Arts of Resistance*, Scott explores at length the ways in which the "hidden transcripts" of cultural subordinates may be identified.

Scott's theoretical approach is quite useful to a culturally contextualized analysis of power relations, and I invoke his work here to the extent that it explains and enables my own. I too investigate hegemonic discourse, scrutinizing it against a backdrop of subversive discourse, and vice versa, in my efforts to discern multiple and complex strategies by which American women of the 1920s were oppressed. After all, vague terms such as "society," "patriarchy," and the like do not unmask women's oppressors. The thwarting of female power came in the form of highly nuanced ideologies, many of which were imposed by women on themselves and each other as well as by other culturally subordinate groups. My approach here, I believe, also effectively reveals the sophisticated means by which women sometimes resisted oppression. The "discourse" I examine in order to identify the specificities of hegemony and women's responses to it includes a wide range of social interaction, verbal as well as behavioral, most of which is, in any case, fundamentally performance.

Part and parcel of the theoretical rationale I have just outlined is a methodological approach I refer to as *historical performance ethnography*. To investigate performances of the past by means of ethnography, as I purport to do, seems oxymoronic at first glance. The anthropologist John Van Maanen noted, for example, that, as a method of research, ethnography usually denotes the fieldwork done by an investigator "who 'lives with and lives like' those who are studied."[21] Similarly, Dwight Conquergood, an early proponent and practitioner of ethnographic research in performance studies, contrasts the "participatory" and "open air" methods of ethnography with the "'arm chair' research of more sedentary and cerebral methods."[22] Both scholars implicitly define ethnography as an endeavor in which a researcher physically resides and participates in the culture under investigation. This view, while commonly accepted and rightly so, has been expanded by others, who would use the methods of ethnography to explore cultures not traditionally within its purview.

Advocates of just such an expansion, the Comaroffs approach history from an ethnographic perspective. Conversely, their ethnography is informed by a keen sense of history. They insist that "[e]thnography surely extends beyond the range of the empirical eye; its inquisitive spirit calls upon us to ground subjective, culturally configured action in society and history—and vice versa—wherever the task may take us." Addressing the limitations of fieldwork, particularly the improbability that an outsider might experience another culture in any but a fragmentary manner, the Comaroffs reveal the relative artificiality of the presence-as-practice standard of ethnography.[23] And while no one would deny the advantages of presence and participation as aids to cultural understanding, it seems reasonable nonetheless not only to acknowledge the viability of ethnographic techniques but to apply them even when the remoteness of a culture is a matter of time rather than place. In that one important aim of much historical research, like that of anthropology, is the "recovery of meaningful worlds," the methods of ethnography are, I submit, potentially invaluable to historians, even if difficult to employ comprehensively.[24]

Other anthropologists, of course, have attempted to enlarge the scope of fieldwork ethnography. Victor Turner's work was a prominent example of this. In particular, Turner advocated performance as a means of extending the range of ethnography. In the process, he implied the potential value of a performative emphasis within historical studies by admonishing that "[w]e have to try to re-experience in performance . . . as best we can, the socially bequeathed sparks of lives now biologically extinguished."[25] Turner also described the "anti-temporality" of performance and suggested that history is composed essentially of a variety of rituals and other cultural performances that "deny quotidian systems of measuring or reckoning the passage of time any existential grounding."[26] I contend that such cultural performances, in that they are antitemporal, are indeed a cultural gateway of sorts, a primary point of cultural entry for the historical ethnographer. Performances within culture(s) of the past, such as those by American women of the 1920s, are sites at which history may be most accessible in that they enable an understanding of human experience beyond that which is merely visible and immediate, while yet enhancing historic vision and immediacy.[27]

To proceed in this method, we must try to identify to the fullest extent possible the sensory experiences represented in the archives of history.[28] This effort is in many ways analogous to that of the ethnographer whose fieldwork provides a sense of the smells, sounds, sights, and movements of a culture and its people. The "ethnograph[er] of the archives" must also aim for a virtual kinesthetic understanding of the cultural world explored.[29] Granted, the "distance" at which the passage of time places us from the culture we seek to understand is a handicap for which we can never completely compensate. For this very reason, however, I believe a distanced ethnography that is performance-centered may be among the most fruitful means of recuperating historical lives and societies. The performative aspects of a historical culture—or any culture for that matter—are highly saturated with sensory clues. When examining these clues closely, observing costumes, props, settings, movements, and the like, we become privy to information about the larger social situation in which they are presented. On the other hand, having also carefully explored the ideological climate of a culture, in this case within discourse about women's fashionable as well as theatrical performances, the artifacts of performance may themselves become more meaningful. Nellie Latham's braid, for example, is a conundrum apart from knowledge of both the connotations of "bobbed hair" in the American 1920s generally and an understanding of her unique personal and professional context.

A great deal of historical evidence is, of course, structured as narrative. Diaries, news reports, and personal interviews, for instance, are essentially the *stories* of history. Historical performance ethnography assists our critique of historical narratives in that we are compelled to attend to the performative dimensions of such accounts, the aspects that in fact make them most vivid. The following story by Crystal Eastman, published in 1926, illustrates my point.

> I was a ringleader in the rebellion against skirts and stockings for swimming. On one hot Sunday morning the other fathers waited on my father and asked him to use his influence with me. I don't know what he said to them but he never said a word to me. He was, I know, startled and embarrassed to see his only daughter in a man's bathing suit with bare brown legs for all the world to see. I think it shocked him to his dying day. But he himself had been a swimmer; he knew he would not want to swim in a skirt and stockings. Why then should I?[30]

Examining this narrative, we notice quickly that, rather than presenting a specific display by Eastman, this account attests to an ongoing practice of display behavior, verified by her "brown," that is, suntanned legs. Eastman immediately claims her role in this scenario as "ringleader," a position substantiated by the fact that her father was the one to whom the fathers of her cohort appealed. The patriarchy portrayed in this instance is literal. Neither the "rebellious" young women nor their mothers attend this meeting, and indeed, the content of the discussion is never even revealed to Eastman. On the other hand, Eastman clearly appreciates that her own father does not acquiesce to the wishes of her friends' fathers. Although he never openly endorses her behavior—and she in fact assumes he is quite taken aback by it—her father's fairmindedness seems to be one of the most meaningful points of this story for Eastman.

Other details intensify the sensory as well as the emotional aspects of this event. It is hot and it is Sunday. Our awareness of the heat increases our sensitivity to the injustice of wearing unnecessary and constraining clothing. The fact that it is Sunday brings to mind the prospect of two potentially conflicting behavioral agendas—one leisurely, the other moralistic. The words Eastman selects to portray the emotions associated with this experience are graphic; her father is "startled," "embarrassed," and "shocked." She is his "only daughter," a factor accentuating the embarrassment he must have felt when seeing her not in merely functional swimwear but in a man's bathing suit. She has broken not only the usual norms of modesty but is cross-dressing as well. Costume is a key component of the many-layered conflict briefly represented here.

A worthy analysis of such display-related narratives usually requires the aid of many kinds of collateral resources where possible. As the Comaroffs advocate, we must keep in mind that we "work both in and outside the official record, both with and beyond the guardians of memory," the prerequisite for source viability, its potential to "tell us something of the way in which personal acts become social facts."[31] For example, in the Eastman story, location, date, and if possible, the names of other people involved should be identified. It is then more feasible to reconstruct with some measure of precision, by means of related sources, the nature of the controversy involved, the values represented in the debate, and intervening circumstances. Often, accounts of controversial displays by women in the 1920s appeared in local newspapers. This is especially true of displays that involved arrests and/or well-known persons. Reports like these help us begin to piece together the details of particular displays and the emotions they aroused, and they often direct us as well to other kinds of information, ranging from local weather reports to politics to city ordinances.

Without purporting to be comprehensive, the use of a wide variety of sources nevertheless enables a broader historical perspective while yet permitting idiosyncrasies of the archival record a valuable part in indicating larger sociocultural transformations. Specific discoveries implicate rather than prove the larger realities to which they refer and are not generalizable in a formulaic way. Rather, as Yvonna S. Lincoln and Egon G. Guba state in their extensive work *Naturalistic Inquiry*, "[l]ocal conditions, in short, make it impossible to generalize. . . . Constant flux militates against conclusions that are always and forever true; they can only be said to be true under such and such conditions and circumstances."[32] When it comes to stating conclusions, the humble demeanor of the cultural "outsider" is thus as appropriate to the ethnographer of the archives as it is to the field investigator. A research method attuned to performances that transform, whatever the place, time, genre, or status of the performer, powerfully amplifies the collective voices of a culture, not just those of the empowered elite. In this way, historical performance ethnography allows one to "listen" to the voices of another generation—voices that may never have been truly attended to before.

With considerable faith in performance as a responsive and reliable ethnographic technique, Conquergood confirms: "The performance paradigm privileges particular, participatory, dynamic, intimate, precarious, *embodied experience grounded in historical process*, contingency, and ideology."[33] This lavish summation describes performance as the ethnographic resource par excellence. Its usefulness within historical research in general and within this particular study are implied by Conquergood's words as well. Even without the advantage of attending the original performances, historical performance ethnography enables one, in a manner of speaking, to exhume from the archives the performing bodies of women engaged on numerous fronts in contests over personal liberty. As such, it helps to recuperate the "embodied experiences" of women so frequently absent in the chronicles of American history, and thus it participates fully in ongoing attempts to recover ways in which "[h]egemony . . . has its natural habitat within the human frame."[34]

More significantly perhaps, this method helps reveal precisely how performative behaviors themselves may simultaneously comply with as well as resist such hegemony and, specifically, how performances by women in the American 1920s usually comprised overlapping strategies of display and disguise in which defiance was embedded within apparent compliance.

2 Fashionable Discourse

Mary had a little skirt,
The latest style no doubt,
But every time she got inside,
She was more than halfway out.[1]

In his sermon on 26 June 1921, Rev. John Roach Straton, pastor of New York City's Calvary Baptist Church and an outspoken advocate of theater reform in the 1920s, recited not the exalted poetry of the Psalms but this trite doggerel instead. Straton and many other morality crusaders seemed transfixed by what they perceived to be the unprecedented depravity of a generation. These reformers zealously warned others of the evils of the day and were especially ardent when calling attention to issues that they felt reflected badly on the character of women. Although F. Scott Fitzgerald, Dorothy Parker, and other popular writers created heroines who were nonchalant about their own virtue, real women who conveyed such an attitude were generally considered to be a social threat and thus inspired virtually endless commentary.[2]

Straton, for one, was alarmed by what he felt new styles in women's clothing indicated about female morality or, more precisely, immorality. A woman's legs, once carefully shielded from public view, were now flagrantly if self-consciously displayed. Although fashionable skirt lengths had varied for a few years and still rose and fell depending on the formality of the occasion, the fact was that women had apparently determined not to return to the ankle- or floor-length styles their mothers and grandmothers had worn (fig. 4). In point of fact, however, it seemed that the length of women's skirts was actually less worrisome to would-be dress reformers than the manner in which women wore them. The "flapper look" suggested far more than fashionable, if immodest, taste in clothing. It comprised a pose, a posturing, a contrived

18

FIG. 3. Flapper Jokes. From A. Russell, "The Modern Girl," *Atlanta Sunday Constitution Magazine*, 8 January 1922, p. 10. Courtesy of the Library of Congress.

19

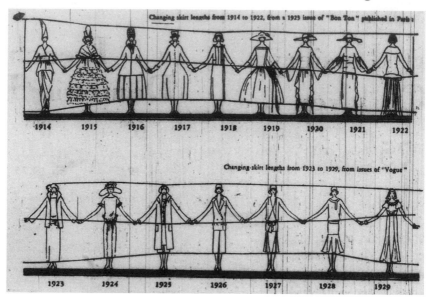

Changing skirt lengths from 1914 to 1922, from a 1923 issue of "Bon Ton" published in Paris

1914   1915   1916   1917   1918   1919   1920   1921   1922

Changing skirt lengths from 1923 to 1929, from issues of "Vogue"

1923   1924   1925   1926   1927   1928   1929

FIG. 4. Changing Skirt Lengths, 1914–1929. From "I Will Wear the New Clothes as They Are Meant to Be Worn," *New York Times*, 29 December 1929. Courtesy of the Library of Congress.

demeanor—in short, a performance. As Bruce Bliven described her, "Flapper Jane" was "frankly, heavily made up, not to imitate nature, but for an altogether artificial effect—pallor mortis, poisonously scarlet lips, richly ringed eyes—the latter looking not so much debauched (which is the intention) as diabetic. Her walk duplicates the swagger supposed by innocent America to go with the female half of a Paris Apache dance."[3]

Although Bliven pushed his point rather past the mark, flapper-style fashions were indeed associated with a distinctive mien that was itself a common source of criticism (figs. 5 and 6). A photograph issued by the YWCA as part of their "campaign against certain modern tendencies," for example, features two young women who are dressed almost identically, beneath which a caption reads "Proper and Improper Way to Dress." The "proper" woman stands erect, both feet planted squarely on the floor, while the other woman stands slouching, hands on hips, feet at awkward angles (fig. 7).[4]

An unnamed writer for *Good Housekeeping*, also concerned about postural tendencies among the readership of the magazine, warned that bad posture led to a "defect of figure," that is, the problem of an enlarged hip, which was "nearly always the outcome of a bad habit of sitting, standing, leaning, or

All of a piece, including posture

FIG. 5. Caricature of Flapper Posture. Illustration by Ralph Barton for
Hazel Rawson Cades, "Good Looks: 'What Men Don't Like,'" *Woman's
Home Companion* 51 (October 1924): 42. University of Illinois Library.

walking in a manner that naturally throws the hip out."[5] Miss E. K. Bertine,
who supervised the exercise program at a women's health center in New
York, complained, in fact, that young women had gotten the wrong idea
about what it meant to be beautiful. Their posture, a "lop-sided" stance characterized by "sunken chests and round shoulders," suggested fatigue, rather
than beauty.[6] Whether tired, provocative, energized, or indifferent, however,
the fashionable flapper was correctly perceived to present a serious challenge
to the tenacious influence of American Victorian traditions of feminine behavior and display (fig. 8).

The "challenge" to gender and sex codes that had been handed down from
the nineteenth century came in many forms, not just via the so-called rebellion of would-be flappers.[7] Certainly, discourse *about* fashion was also central
to the process by which some women, as well as men, consciously distanced
themselves from what came increasingly to be viewed by them as a repressive,

FIG. 6. Posing Flapper. Cover illustration, "Too Many Parties and Too Many Pals," sheet music (New York: Leo Feist, 1925).

"hand-me-down" moral and behavioral tradition.[8] This discourse was multifaceted. Although, like Straton, many argued about women's dress from primarily a moral standpoint—to be sure, this preoccupation surfaces in most antifashion discourse—there were several other considerations expressed as well. Medical and economic questions, for example, frequently arose in these debates. Aesthetic arguments were used to condemn as well as condone new fashions. The variety of opinions expressed on these matters seems infinite. Young, old, male, female, sanctimonious, or irreverent, scores of people troubled to announce publicly what they felt women should and should not be allowed to wear. Unfortunately, racial and ethnic diversity were not fairly represented in most discourse, certainly not in the most widely distributed magazines. When not simply ignored, minority groups were generally featured in these publications in unflattering ways; often they were quite blatantly portrayed as "exotic other" in the attempt to show "foreign" influences on women's fashions and behavior (fig. 9).

Women themselves were also quite divided in their opinions about what constituted appropriate self-display. Although by no means neatly categorized in their views according to age groups, younger women were more likely to embrace fashion trends associated with the "new morality" which, as Christina Simmons states, "proclaimed the existence and legitimacy of female desire."[9] Older women, some of whom had been prominent members of the nineteenth-century woman's movement, were perplexed at best but often chagrined that younger women considered such "trivial" matters as their appearance worthy of feminist zeal.[10] This was not to deny that members of the woman's movement had themselves helped to instigate dress reform. They had argued, however, that women's health and physical autonomy were compromised by nineteenth- and even early-twentieth-century clothing styles.[11]

"PROPER AND IMPROPER."

This picture, under the title "Proper and Improper Way to Dress, has been widely circulated by the Y. W. C. A. in its educational campaign against certain modern tendencies.

FIG. 7. Anti-Flapper Propaganda. Illustration for "Is the Younger Generation in Peril?" *Literary Digest* 69 (14 May 1921): 1. Courtesy of the Library of Congress.

FIG. 8. Flapper Cartoon. Cover illustration, *Life* 87 (18 February 1926). Courtesy of the Library of Congress.

FIG. 9. Flapper as Appropriation of "Primitive Other." Cover illustration, *Life* 88 (15 July 1926). Courtesy of the Library of Congress.

Pragmatic considerations, while not ignored in the 1920s debates about women's fashions, did not seem any longer to be of central concern. One student editor of a college newspaper wryly observed: "The hobble skirt . . . long-ago brought a cry for dress reform. What have the reformers to say about the modern knee-length, kid-glove-fitting gown, with abbreviated top and bottom, to say nothing of the short-sleeved or sleeveless waists which accompany these modern 'creations.' The bathing girl of to-day is merely a foresight of the average girl of to-morrow, it would seem, from the trend of modern feminism toward elimination of essential apparel."[12] Some people clearly felt that the right to move about freely had become a moot point in dress reform; so-called fashion freedom now merely abetted the shallow, sex-based impulses of young women in the 1920s.

Dorothy Dunbar Bromley, writing for *Harper's* magazine in 1927, discussed the divergent strains of modern feminism in considerable detail. She pointed to the wide range of opinions women held when it came to the subject of their rights, including their right to dress themselves in more revealing styles. She contended that the term *feminism* had itself become opprobrious. Young women in their twenties and thirties typically associated this word with the "old school of fighting feminists who wore flat heels and had very little feminine charm." Although she might admire these "pioneer feminists" for their courage—even while she "judges them for their zealotry and inartistic methods"—the modern young woman did not, according to Bromley, wish to "wear their mantle." Nor did the young feminist moderates wish to emulate the "second generation of feminists" who, although the "worst of the fight is over," yet had the "battle cry still on their lips."[13] That Bromley, in her attempt to explain the diversity of feminism in the 1920s, so frequently referred to clothing in both literal and metaphorical ways is itself quite telling.

Nancy Cott states that it was characteristic of new generations of feminists, in both the 1910s and 1920s, to give less than full credit to their forebears when it came to questions of female "sex rights." Just as feminists of the 1910s failed to acknowledge "free lovers, radicals, and sex hygienists" of the late nineteenth century, so also the younger feminists of the 1920s "looked across the generational divide and saw Victorian sensibilities, as though the venturesome Feminists of the 1910s had never existed." Had they looked closely, these young women might have seen that "the restless Feminists of the 1910s had led the way for the heterosexual claims and behavior of the postwar generation."[14] Clearly, in their ideas about what, in fact, it meant to be liberated as women, as well as in their views of feminism itself, women were all but united. As often as not, women's ideological differences in these matters were generationally configured and were signified by the very clothes on their backs.

1920s Fashion in Perspective

In *Fashion, Culture, and Identity*, Fred Davis describes the workings of the fashion cycle and how this cycle has accelerated in recent decades. According to Davis, the rapid turnover of women's styles, common in the late twentieth century, was not typical earlier in the century, certainly not in the 1920s.[15] A lawsuit against a vaudeville actress in Chicago in March 1922, however, suggests that Davis's claim may warrant qualification. More significantly, however, this fashion-related legal drama illustrates how variables like fashion, economic privilege, the performance of gender, and many other factors are densely interwoven in the structuring of social power.

Morris Kutock, a tailor employed by Frances Kennedy, an actress, sued Kennedy for payment for services rendered. He had made for her, at her request, a $175 gown that she then refused to purchase. Kennedy argued that her gown was to have been completed by February 5 but was not. She left Chicago for her performances in New York on February 6 and, since the gown was not ready, had to quickly arrange for another one. By the time she returned to Chicago, she refused to buy the gown from Kutock since, as she noted in her court testimony, "dresses go out of style about every three weeks."[16]

To illustrate her point about the rapidity with which women's fashions changed, Kennedy's attorney and husband, Thomas J. Johnson, took three gowns out of a suitcase the couple had brought to court with them and held the dresses up as "evidence" to be inspected by the judge and jury. It was noted that the most recently purchased gown was "distinctly longer" than either of the other two. Doris Faulkner, a model, also verified Kennedy's claim, testifying that "styles change weekly sometimes and that, of course, an actress couldn't be expected to wear a gown four weeks behind the style." A costumer, a designer, and even Robert D. Boniel, a critic for the *Dramatic Mirror* made similar statements.[17] Following such "expert testimony," the jury, a group of six women between the ages of eighteen and twenty-two, took only three or four minutes to deliberate, then announced their verdict: that Kennedy should not be required to pay Kutock, as they concurred that it was true that dress styles could change in four weeks' time. Upon hearing their verdict, Kennedy reportedly hugged and kissed the jurors, invited them to her show, and distributed autographed pictures of herself.[18]

Ostensibly inconsequential incidents even indirectly related to the ways in which women in the 1920s presented themselves were linked with crucial issues of empowerment. Not only did *Kutock v. Kennedy* raise questions about the foibles of fashion, for example; it also, unfortunately, increased opposition to women's participation in the legal system itself. Kennedy, for her part, was portrayed in newspaper accounts as artful and coy in the courtroom. Asked about her age, she reportedly "cast down her eyes, toyed with a fold of her mink wrap and looked desperately at her husband." At last she said that she could never remember how old she was and had often relied on her sister for this information. However, since her sister too had forgotten it, Kennedy's age was not forthcoming in her court testimony. When jurors decided promptly in Kennedy's favor despite the implausible content of some of her testimony, another Chicago-area judge, not connected with these proceedings, complained: "A jury of women is illegal. That judge ought to be impeached. The grand jury's going to hear about these goings on."[19] The proceedings themselves apparently were so raucous that one police officer reported the attendant loud "feminine laughter and the excitement" to Chicago's chief of police, who then decided that the room in City Hall where the case was heard would no longer be offered for use as a courtroom.[20]

The timing of this case was especially inopportune in that residents of Illinois had begun to consider whether to allow women the right to serve as members of juries. Many people were as yet unconvinced that women could handle this responsibility. A day or so earlier, Chicago newspapers announced that a woman named Florence Sullivan had been mistakenly summoned for jury duty on the assumption that Florence was a man's name. When the error was discovered, she was excused from duty "on legal grounds" by the presiding judge. She meekly noted that she was willing to be a juror but preferred not to as she did "not think the Criminal court [was] the place for women to serve."[21]

Less than two weeks later, as part of the legal maneuvering on behalf of Illinois governor Len Small, who had been charged with conspiracy to defraud the state of Illinois, Small's attorneys attacked the legality of the jury venue on grounds that women had not been considered as potential jury members. Women in Illinois had been given "full rights as voters and citizens," but as one of Small's attorneys, Werner W. Schroeder, suggested, although other states had begun to permit women on juries, Illinois had not officially done so.[22] Another report noted the difficulty that the presence of women on a jury would create, given that female jurors would, presumably when sequestered, share quarters with men on the third floor of the courthouse in a room that was filled with cots but no partitions.[23]

In any case, the juncture of these events, which directly and indirectly challenged a woman's competence to participate in the Illinois jury system, foregrounds several issues. Women had only recently been granted the right to vote, and there was still considerable uncertainty about what other aspects of American citizenship they should be entitled to. Reluctance toward female entitlement was fueled by doubts about whether women were indeed prepared to handle the rights of "full" citizenship. The behavior of the women involved in *Kutock v. Kennedy*, at least as portrayed in the press, did not alleviate these concerns. Given the amount and kind of attention this litigation received, some people surely remained unconvinced that women could be trusted with weighty matters of state when they so blithely and indecorously handled "their own" affairs. More admirably portrayed was the compliant attitude of Florence Sullivan, who politely declined to serve on the jury to which she had been erroneously appointed.

Interpreted in light of related incidents and situated within a broader understanding of the local and national context in which it occurred, this episode vividly illustrates that the performance of "appropriate" femininity was the necessary prerequisite to female empowerment. Kennedy was, unflattering press notwithstanding, empowered by her "feminine wiles" routine. Kutock, a dressmaker, could hardly have been considered uninformed about fashion trends. He was clearly no match though, for those perceived to be the final authorities on fashion—women. Moreover, Kennedy's machinations were of a piece with long-held assumptions about femininity in that she was "properly" concerned with the minutiae of fashion. She deftly managed these assumptions to her advantage. After all, as an entertainer—or as a woman for that matter—was she not obliged to create a pleasing appearance? So it would seem.

The unprecedented and "illegal" participation of females on a jury, rather than serving as a model of a new, more equitable system of justice, merely highlighted the sexism underlying not only this case but the judiciary process itself.[24] Such sexism also was underscored, albeit less dramatically, when Florence Sullivan declined to participate in a criminal proceeding where women did not "rightfully" belong. She was graciously thanked for her willingness to serve, quickly relieved of her duties, and warmly represented in the press. On the other hand, when Governor Small raised the question about women serving on his jury, his query seemed insincere—just a delay tactic. Besides, women on juries were, quite simply, inconvenient. Not surprisingly, Small's request to have women as well as men on the jury that deliberated in his case was denied.[25] The role of "femininity" ascribed to women was still, essentially, a "bit part" within the larger scheme of things. Regrettably, the performances of Kennedy and her jurors, as mediated by the press, likely delayed the process of change.

On the face of it, the verdict in *Kutock v. Kennedy*, suggesting that women's clothing styles were even then part of a rapidly changing fashion cycle, is somewhat confusing. Fashion historians generally regard the 1920s as a relatively stable era of fashion history. As Fred Davis contends, "Neither in women's nor men's dress today can a single fashion come to rule the roost as was the case with, for example . . . the flapper dress. . . . Nor do fashions today seem capable of enforcing uniformlike compliance throughout society and across all class and status groupings."[26] Paul H. Nystrom, whose extensive work *The Economics of Fashion* was published in 1928, explains the seeming discrepancy between Davis's views of 1920s fashions and the verdict in *Kutock v. Kennedy*. Nystrom noted that fashions in scarves, jewelry, and other accessories did last only briefly, perhaps one season. Fashions in silhouettes, the general outline of garments, however, usually lasted for several years.[27] Probably the women involved in this case were responding to subtle gradations in style, not to more pronounced changes that were, as both Nystrom and Davis suggest and as many primary sources from the 1920s also show, slower in coming.[28]

The following advice excerpted from *Vogue*, one of the foremost sources of fashion information in the 1920s, also explicates the "look" of women's clothing at that time and indirectly reveals as well the growing emphasis on fashion itself within American culture.

> The "ideal" modern figure, from a fashion point of view, will be found to fulfil[l] the acrobat's dream of fitness. A rolling body gathers no fat. . . . A really supple and muscular young body, with no spare flesh on the well-made frame, will be neither board-like nor "lumpy." A flat abdomen is the surest guarantee, both of healthy living and of good dressing; if you have it, you are living right, if you have it, you may dress well. If you have it not—go get it. The hips, too, no longer bulging with evidences of a sedentary maturity, need not be matchboarded to hide their natural curves. Their curves are right. The dressmaker needs them.[29]

These comments are exemplary, though not exceptional, in that the author melds issues of both fashion and figure, essentially prescribing that a woman's body fit popular fashions rather than vice versa and clearly stressing a woman's obligation to find ways to fit the mold of fashion if her own body naturally falls short of this aim. This fashion imperative also alludes to several issues that became prominent points of contention in clothing debates of the 1920s. First of all, it exemplifies what was to many the tyrannous hold of fashion, which women were thought too willing, even eager, to accept. It also specifies youthfulness and slenderness as exclusive requirements for membership among the fashionable (fig. 10). Further, it links fashion, health, and an active lifestyle to the highly contingent visual appeal of the "natural" body.[30]

In his classic study *The Psychology of Clothes*, published in 1930, the psychologist J. C. Flugel noted primary implications of the fashions of the decade just ended. He discussed the "vicissitudes of fashion" and stressed that the fashions of his female contemporaries were characterized by an emphasis on youthfulness and body display.

> At the present time interest has departed from the trunk and is cent[e]red on the limbs. Sleeves must be either altogether absent, or else tightly fitting, in

Modish Lines are Lines of Youth

And, to achieve these youthful lines, the brassiere or bandeau is as important as the corset itself. Warner's Brassieres and Bandeaux Brassieres include models for the fuller figure, as well as those of lighter design for the average and slender types.

The Brassiere or bandeau is part of one's corseting today— and there is a Warner model for every figure.

Warner's

Brassieres and Bandeaux Brassieres

FIG. 10. Achieving the Fashionable Silhouette. Advertisement for Warner's brassieres, *Delineator* 98 (May 21): 60.

order that the long lines and graceful contours of the arm may be fully appreciated. Legs have emerged after centuries of shrouding . . . in the last year or two, [a woman's] ankles, calves, and knees (all the more dazzling in their suddenly revealed beauty after their long sojourn in the dark) have been her chief erotic weapons. In this accentuation of the limbs, we can see a natural concomitant of the idealization of youth.[31]

Robert S. Lynd and Helen Merrell Lynd documented the prevailing look of women's fashions in the American 1920s in their still highly respected sociological study, *Middletown*, published in 1929. They noted that "[a]mong

women and girls . . . skirts have shortened from the ground to the knee and
the lower limbs have been emphasized by sheer silk stockings; more of the
arms and neck are habitually exposed; while the increasing abandonment of
petticoats and corsets reveals more of the natural contours of the body."[32]
Although the Lynds, Flugel, and the unidentified writer for *Vogue* assessed
women's fashion from diverse perspectives, their descriptions render a remarkably consistent and relatively detailed image of the fashionably dressed
woman of the 1920s. Notably, each source also clearly implies the significant
departure these fashions represent from past styles in clothing for women.
Taken together and in light of broader social ramifications of fashions for
women as illustrated by *Kutock v. Kennedy*, these fashion experts provide an
ideal vantage point from which we may assess not only the material but also
the ideological features of women's fashions in the American 1920s.

Dame Fashion as Tyrant

> Curiously enough, women fear being called original or individual, but
> never hesitate to make fools of themselves in following the latest fash-
> ion. A woman will submit to any torture, any ridicule if she believes
> she is worshiping that absurd goddess, Fashion.[33]

Critics repeatedly indicted women throughout the 1920s for their alleged
subservience to fashion. What lends peculiar irony to the scornful rebuke
above, however, is that its source was one of the most famous French fashion
designers of all time, Paul Poiret. Moreover, the excerpt cited here comprised part of his preface to ten fashion "precepts" of Poiret's own to which
women were to adhere.

Hugh A. Studdert Kennedy, comparatively benevolent toward women and
the fashions they selected, was, in fact, brusquely rebuked when he defended
women's clothing choices, by none other than Carrie Chapman Catt, noted
feminist and president of the International Woman Suffrage Alliance.[34] Acknowledging Kennedy's "gallant defense" of current fashions as part of an
overall trend toward greater autonomy among women and noting as well
opponents' views of these styles as immodest, Catt vetoed both positions,
claiming instead that "pro and con supporters have overlooked the fundamental fact that women do not wear short skirts or bobbed hair by their own elec-
tion . . . but in obedience to the dictum of fashion."[35] Catt's ire was aroused by
a new round of speculation, common throughout the 1920s, that a campaign
for superfluous fashions was being waged by that presumed archenemy of
women's sartorial freedom commonly known as "Paris." Of all the antifashion
sentiments expressed throughout the 1920s, diatribes against the authority of

fashion in general and Paris in particular came closest to rivaling, in both frequency and intensity, the attacks against immodesty.[36] Indeed, many popular women's magazines of the 1920s, as well as many publications not geared primarily to women, protested that "Dame Fashion" was no less than a tyrant. On the other hand, many more women's magazines further reinforced the authority of Paris styles. The *Delineator*, for example, a popular monthly published and distributed nationally by Butterick, a producer of clothing patterns, boasted that "the line of Paris, the finish of Paris, the charm of Paris, may be had in any home," although formerly the designs of Paris had been available only to "those rich women whose dress allowance reached to Paris itself."[37]

One of the most influential forces in women's fashion was the French designer Gabrielle "Coco" Chanel. By the 1920s her influence rivaled even Paul Poiret's. Chanel was largely responsible for the popularity of the simple, rather boyish look that became a staple of women's fashions at this time, first in France and subsequently in the United States.[38] In an article Chanel wrote for the already well-established mainstream women's magazine, *Ladies' Home Journal*, she generally assumed an admonishing tone toward her readers but frequently lapsed into outright bossiness. For example, in reference to beach apparel, Chanel wrote: "Don't wear picture hats or picturesque costumes; their fussiness, their absurdity, inevitably keep their wearers out of the water. . . . Don't wear materials that water makes transparent and clinging. . . . Do not attract attention by such vulgar means, but be at your ease, be comfortable, swim and splash, wrap yourself up in a thick bathrobe and do not try to confuse your seashore background with a scene from a musical comedy."[39]

Delivered in no less strident a timbre than that of moralists who attached global and eternal significance to the choices women made about their apparel, Chanel's edicts reveal how women were, quite simply, harangued about the manner in which they publicly presented themselves. Those who cautioned women against blind obedience to fashion's proscriptions— not the least of whom, like Chanel and Poiret, themselves comprised the fashion system—spoke in tones laden with certainty, reproach, and superiority. Words like *must, ought, should, never,* and *always* were the common vocabulary of fashion experts. Much fashion advice was harsh at best, hostile at worst. Granted, accusations of fashion hegemony were not unwarranted and were, in fact, underscored by the very discourse that claimed to challenge fashion's hegemony, a discourse that appeared as much within as outside the fashion industry.

The subtitle for an essay in *Good Housekeeping* suggests an additional line of attack often employed by writers more harsh than hostile: "Know Yourself —Make the Best of Your Good Lines But Do Not Fail to Correct Your Defects."[40] This warning, in both substance and attitude, indicates the double bind in which a woman found herself if she attended to fashion authority, and it reveals the razor-thin line that fashion has always marked between display and disguise. The message is clear: bodily imperfection necessitates subterfuge. Thus, to "know yourself" had nothing to do with meaningful reflection but instead meant a curious sort of hide-and-seek a woman played by and with herself, carefully searching her physical attributes to determine what best to keep hidden away from the all-too-watchful eyes of others.

An especially rich source for what I consider hostile fashion advice is a beauty manual entitled *The Well-Dressed Woman,* written by Anne Rittenhouse, a fashion columnist in the 1920s. She preached a fashion code whose major incentive was guilt evasion. Moreover, she impugned personal goals that might rival a woman's primary obligation to create a pleasing appearance. Rittenhouse declared: "It is the way of laziness and self-deception to place the responsibility for ungracious and inadequate clothes on the pursuit of self-styled 'higher occupations.'"[41] Her credo, presented in the last chapter of the manual, echoed a comment in the foreword that "it is wise for the woman who boasts that her clothes are ill-chosen because life is filled with better things, to mend her ways and speech."[42] This grim introductory threat proceeded, rather illogically as it turns out, from Rittenhouse's claim that "[clothes] do not express moral qualities." Perhaps not, but readers, if they took the rest of Rittenhouse's manual seriously, could surely never say that a woman's *attention* to her clothes was not a moral issue. Rittenhouse's appeals were heavily cloaked in language more suitable to the pulpit than to the fashion text. Note, for example, the biblical allusions within the following:

> The mistake made by the majority on the subject of clothes is to think that good taste is a gift or that the right choice of suitable raiment is a birthright. Rid their minds of that error and light breaks in; an optimistic struggle to attain the desired goal begins. The essentials to victory in this struggle are observation, imitation, calculation. Salvation is not wholly from within.[43]

Indeed, much like a "fire-and-brimstone" evangelist, Rittenhouse also resorted to "crisis conversion" stories to get wayward "dowds" to "repent." She wrote of one "not well dressed" woman who, wearing an "unforgivable" hat, entered a dressmaker's house and asked if she might have a light-blue, satin evening gown made for herself. Noting the dressmaker's surprise, the woman explained that her son had been a soldier in France during the past two years but had been wounded and was coming home within the week. His mother admitted that, even as a boy, he had loved for her to wear pretty clothes and wanted her to dress up for company in light colors, especially blue. She now regretted that she had refused to oblige his wishes, but she wanted to "please and surprise him by wearing the tone of blue he likes" for his homecoming. Rittenhouse concludes her maudlin anecdote by quoting the dressmaker's assurances that the mother would look "perfectly beautiful" after the latter plaintively asked, "Do you think I am too old, too wrinkled, too sad and worried-looking?"[44] So-called fashion experts like Rittenhouse often skillfully employed such emotionally manipulative tactics in their efforts to control the women who looked to them for fashion guidance.

Even—perhaps especially—women's rights proponents like Catt and Gilman spoke as though they too had the authority to command the choices of other women in matters of dress. And although these activists' social reform agenda was invaluable in most regards, occasionally the more moderate and merciful tones of outsiders to the woman's movement softened their seeming hostility toward other women less politically or socially conscientious than they. As noted earlier, Hugh A. Studdert Kennedy, for one, astutely reminded Catt and readers of the *Woman Citizen*, once an important forum for the suffrage movement, that "of course, short skirts, bare arms, bare knees and bare backs are only a few, out of many outward and visible signs, of that inward and spiritual grace seen operating so vigorously today in the movement in which Mrs. Catt has taken so prominent a part." He contended that, for all her fashion consciousness, "[t]he flapper is *hard at work* . . . interested in many things, where her sister of twenty or thirty years ago was interested in very few and her sister of a hundred years ago in but one."[45] Not only was this an apt rejoinder to Catt, a member of the editorial staff of the *Woman Citizen*, but surely his words also helped to check the influence of those like Rittenhouse who indeed seemed to believe that a woman had no more pressing an obligation than to attend to her appearance.

In her essay "We Needn't Be Robots in Our Dress," the wife of the playwright and novelist Booth Tarkington stressed instead a woman's responsibility to choose clothes that served personal needs, not those of fashion designers. Tarkington encouraged women to suit popular fashion trends to their own tastes and disdainfully noted: "I don't like bobbed hair or short skirts or tiny, tight-fitting hats or the straight up-and-down silhouette that spells present-day smartness. Sometimes I feel as though we were all robots, cut from the same universal pattern, with no minds or personalities of our own."[46] Curiously, "Mrs. Booth Tarkington," as she is referred to throughout her article, seems not to notice the inconsistency of her own obeisance to another kind of fashion authority. She confessed, for example, that "[b]lack is always smart, of course, but my leaning to this color is chiefly, I admit, a concession to Mr. Tarkington's taste. Every so often he says to me: 'Why don't you get a black velvet dress?' So I dutifully go forth and purchase one. He thinks black velvet is the most beautiful thing there is."[47] Thus, while Paris did not hold much sway with her, nor perhaps did the advice of fashion evangelists, "Mr. Tarkington" certainly did.

Mary Alden Hopkins, a popular essayist who was featured in "These Modern Women," a series for *Nation* magazine, consciously set out to examine women's motives for adopting certain styles of clothing. Her essay, more upbeat than many that addressed this question, ultimately defended a woman's desire to dress fashionably. Hopkins declared: "Votes and jobs and citizenship have not lessened for women one jot of the importance of clothes. Because women find them important, because they are an expression of her sex, her clothes are her second self."[48] As to the role of fashion in a woman's life, including how it absorbed her time, money, and energy, Hopkins interviewed several "well-known psychologists." Dr. Caroline F. J. Rickards blithely responded: "The streets are gayer when women turn out in bright hats and clever little frocks. A well-dressed woman literally gives happiness to those she meets, even though they are hardly conscious of her presence. A group of daintily gowned women spread[s] a holiday air in the dreariest neighborhood." In addition to the decorative function of women, Rickards also explained that she felt fashion was necessary, after all, since the "surplus of sex energy" that women channel into their appearance "might otherwise do actual harm."[49]

This conspicuously Freudian view of the female psyche was also expressed by others whom Hopkins interviewed. Some felt that subconscious motives, especially the desire to attract attention, caused women to don outlandish fashions. Hopkins herself mused: "When dainty Myrabel tiptoes like a disgusted pussy along a sloppy pavement, we are more likely to notice her if she wears thin-soled high-heeled pumps than if she splashes along in sensible overshoes. Better be censured than ignored, is Myrabel's unconscious motto."[50] Hopkins may well have been right about "Myrabel"—certainly attention-getting performances by women routinely elicited some degree of censorship.

All things considered, the so-called tyranny of fashion in the 1920s is difficult if not impossible to isolate. After all, women themselves were obviously highly engaged in the fashion system, if not, in exceptional cases, empowered by it.[51] And whether through the propaganda of the fashion industry itself, or through the influence of those closest to her, a woman's apparel choices ultimately represented the influence of many interrelated processes, social as well as personal, conscious and perhaps subconscious. Fashion itself was a highly charged arena of struggle, where power over women's choices was appropriated, usurped, and exploited by contestants on all sides. Not remarkably, the power contested involved large amounts of money. The economic factors at play in the grand dispute over women's clothing in the American 1920s warrant particular scrutiny.

A High Price to Pay

Strictly factual data about economic variables such as the price of particular clothing articles or other information about the manufacture and sale of apparel items in the 1920s are fairly simple to compile. More problematic is to detect the subtle ways in which economic considerations were strategically employed within controversies about the clothes women actually chose to wear.[52] When fashion detractors complained about women's clothing from a financial perspective—and they often did—they generally argued that women spent to excess on their appearance and/or that the particular clothing for which they spent good money was a poor investment. As I will show, however, these seemingly straightforward complaints masked a host of other agendas; indeed, the "economics of fashion" was a sizable soapbox. This point is especially well illustrated in essays by Carrie Chapman Catt, noted earlier for her disdain of the authority the French fashion industry exerted.

Catt believed that underlying the fashion edicts of French designers there was no real concern for women, only greed. In her essay "How Many Yards in Your Skirt?" Catt essentially claimed that the yardage in the skirts of American women was precisely as much as France needed to sell in order to pay her debts.[53] Catt challenged women to dress independently and, in a word, patriotically. She explained—with no small measure of suspicion and contempt— just how profitable it was to France's economy for American women to adopt new fashions, impractical and tasteless, in her opinion, as such fashions often were. She reported on a recent campaign to bring back "elegance" to women's fashions. This effort was instigated by the French minister of commerce and staged at elite social gatherings where models paraded in honor of the "return" of dresses conspicuous for elaborate trimmings and abundant fabric. In Catt's view, "[t]he obvious aim of these demonstrations has been to win the approval of the rich and socially prominent women visitors, the world-around correspondents and the diplomats of many lands."

Obvious though the ploy may have been, it even more obviously failed with Catt, who apparently attended such "demonstrations" herself. She described pleas "on behalf of the suffering unemployed girls of Paris who made trimmings and flowers" as "touching." Catt spurned as naive the added hint by another speaker that for American women to abandon the so-called simple and severe look for the more "decorative and feminine" would make it easier for France to pay her debts. She was equally snide about the "ostrich men" of South Africa who had purportedly visited Paris again and successfully convinced others that their only hope of survival was "more feathers worn by women."[54]

According to Catt, the clothing purchases of American women were

ECSTASY

*A new hand made chemise of
lace and indestructable
voile . . . $16.50*

Sax-Kay

1426 Wash. Blvd.

FIG. 11. Chemise Advertisement. *Playgoer* 3
(31 March 1929): 33.

largely responsible for France's economic advances. In her essay "The Chemise Problem,"
she assumed her typical anti-French and essentially antifashion stance out of concern for
the effects women's clothing purchases could
have on the U.S. economy. She envisioned an
economic "war" between France and the
United States fought with weapons of commerce: tariffs, embargoes, and "economic es-
pionage."[55] At issue in this war, Catt claimed,
was the chemise, the "oldest female garment,"
one which, in all probability, "Eve designed
. . . as her 'going away' costume when she de-
parted from the Garden of Eden." Although
for centuries the chemise had been a carefully kept secret by women who hid it amid
their laundry and talked of it only in whispers
between themselves, advertisers had created
a "female blush felt 'round the world.'" Now
the chemise was displayed in shops, no longer
made of "chaste and simple white." Instead,
it came in several colors—and in silk, no less.
Its trimmings were of lace and roses and even
butterflies (figs. 11 and 12). Women's response
to all this? Catt replied that they "blushed and
bought, blushed again and bought more."
The chemise, so cautiously guarded for centuries by modest women, had become a
"source of profit to bold, unmodest men."

And whose chemises were the advertisers
and shopkeepers now selling? France's, of
course. Catt presented the mathematics involved: "[France] was pushing
hard to pay her debts. If forty million American women and girls would buy
a French chemise at a profit of one dollar each, France would be enriched
by forty millions of dollars." Ultimately, Catt surmised, the United States lost
this economic war, after a great deal of political posturing on both sides of the
Atlantic to secure the greatest possible economic advantage by means of this
"one-time badge of woman's modesty."[56]

The magazine in which Catt expressed her beliefs on these economic matters, the *Woman Citizen*, was characterized not only by its feminist stance but also by its social reform agenda. In April 1920, for example, the magazine contained a report about deplorable conditions in which many items of clothing were made. Disease infested tenements where many garments were constructed—even posing a health threat to buyers—but also, "tenement house work" was, simply, an inhumane occupation, given the drudgery of the work and its meager rewards. Moreover, children were employed in large numbers in this kind of work; they comprised 12 percent of employees whose responsibility it was to transport items back and forth between home and factory. The most "abominable" feature of tenement work was that workers were paid so little, certainly not enough to remove them from their horrible conditions, while those higher up within the hierarchy of the fashion enterprise clearly profited from their victimization. The writer observed: "In view of the high cost of all wearing apparel to the consumer, there is something so sinister . . . about this catalogue of underpay. . . . The prating of high cost of labor on the extravagantly high cost of women's clothes comes down to this sickening array of disease, filth and starvation."[57]

The crusade this unidentified writer for the *Woman Citizen* waged against the injustices of the tenement work system, as well as Catt's goadings to "buy American" were not, of course, concerns peculiar to the 1920s. Indeed, these were longtime complaints of Progressive-era feminists.[58] To recognize the historical significance of such labor-specific, antifashion arguments, however, helps to account for tensions between older and younger feminists in the 1920s. Presuffrage

FIG. 12. Silk Fabric for Homemade Undergarments. Advertisement for Skinner's silk, *Delineator* 98 (May 1921): 97.

Skinner's *for wear*

Camisoles
Kniekers
Boudoir Caps
Negligees
Petticoats

*T*AKE the dainty things you wear out of the luxury class—make them of Skinner's All-Silk Satin.

Lovely, soft, intimate garments of satin, so dear to a woman's heart—yet so often a luxury because an inferior quality won't stand the wear, become practical for everyday use when made of

Skinner's

ALL-SILK SATIN
(36 inches wide)

Frilly petticoats, combinations or bloomers of Skinner's stand up almost as sturdily as their cotton sisters. Boudoir caps, night robes, camisoles, all so simple to make, will not only give you pride in their beauty, but will astonish you week after week by the way they *wear* and *wash*.

Ask your favorite store for Skinner's "404" All-Silk Satin. It comes in ninety different shades. "Look for the Name in the Selvage"—none genuine without it.

WILLIAM SKINNER & SONS

Manufacturers also of Skinner's Pure-dye Taffetas and Skinner's famous Lining Satins

Mills, Holyoke, Mass.
New York   Established 1848   Chicago
Boston   Philadelphia

LOOK FOR THE NAME IN THE SELVAGE

feminists, schooled in a tradition of social reform, could not take lightly what they viewed to be younger women's crass consumerism, especially since it represented such injustices as tenement work and child labor, not to mention a lack of patriotism. Furthermore, in spite of the sudden notoriety of the "new" brand of feminism—the kind that the feminists of the woman's movement generation regarded as self-absorbed—the outspokenness of women like Catt reminded everyone that she and others of her ilk were still a force with which to be reckoned.[59]

At age forty-two, only three years after suffrage had been granted to American women but long since her days as a "ringleader" in the bathing suit rebellion noted in the previous chapter, Crystal Eastman reflected on the status of the woman's movement. She observed: "Today . . . there is no longer a single, simple aim and a solitary barrier to break down." Instead, she continued, "there are a hundred different questions of civil law, problems of . . . moral and social custom to be solved before women can come wholly into their inheritance of freedom."[60] Clearly, however, deciding which problems to solve, not to mention defining just what the problems were, were hotly contested issues.

Fashionable clothing was, in fact, expensive, not only relative to the wages of those who made it but also proportionate to the incomes of many women who purchased it. Still, it would seem that most women were determined to clothe themselves stylishly even if they could not well afford to. For this they were relentlessly criticized. Not surprisingly, young women were particularly susceptible to these attacks. A few, however, spoke out to the effect that, although young women sacrificed significantly for the sake of their appearance, their investment was reasonable. Instead of scorning the extravagances of the "young working girl," these sympathizers seemed concerned with finding ways to empower young women by helping them learn to manage their finances more capably. For example, in the *Survey*, a reform-oriented periodical that featured sociological studies, Hattie E. Anderson, a staff member of the Milwaukee Vocational School, reported on the findings of a survey she had coordinated. Questionnaires had been distributed to 1,318 young women who attended her school, the responses to which were used to evaluate their clothing expenditures.

Anderson began her discussion in this way: "Volumes have been written about the working girl, her wages and her standard of living. She has been pictured as a poor, worried creature hurrying to the sweatshop, or as a 'flapper' painted and powdered and reckless. Obviously much that has been written comes from unreliable sources and is not founded on facts." Anderson detailed her own findings, apparently in hopes that results based on the extensive sample of young women who responded to the Milwaukee survey would help clarify the record. Among the most significant data she and

Created especially
        to wear with short skirts

This new chiffon hose . . . silk from toe to narrow garter hem $1 00

FIG. 13. Advertisement for Silk Hosiery. *Saturday Evening Post* 199 (24 July 1926): 62.

her colleagues accumulated was the discovery that, on average, the young women surveyed spent 46.3 percent of their income on clothing.[61] Anderson seemed even more surprised by the "striking revelation" that the girls bought an average of 15 pairs of silk hosiery per year, and one young woman reportedly admitted to buying an "almost unbelievable" 122 pairs.

Although plain cotton hosiery was sold by mail-order through companies such as Sears, Roebuck for as little as three dollars for six pairs and silk hosiery cost around a dollar or more per pair, fancy styles of hosiery purchased in department stores could cost six dollars or more per pair (figs. 13 and 14). Even so, Anderson reasoned that "hosiery is one of the most important articles of feminine apparel in these short-skirted days." She kindly

The text within the advertisement image:

FRENCH HOSE

...CLOCKED *the*

PARIS WAY

The Parisienne insists upon hose of an enchanting, misty sheerness for the elaboration of her formal costumes. Hudson's has imported these hose —delicately lace clocked the Paris way—faintly tinted with opalescent hues—nacre violin (orchid), argent (silver), nacre mouette (lavender), nacre chartreuse (cream silver), and peche (peach). $6 pair

THE HOSIERY SHOP
FIRST FLOOR - FARMER

HUDSON'S

FIG. 14. Advertisement for Fancy French Hosiery. *Playgoer* 2 (19 February 1928): 4.

added: "The working girl, approaching the age of eighteen, should be intensely interested in her clothing, and much that might, at first glance, seem frivolous is really a natural expression of her desire to look her best."[62] Anderson concluded her report by discussing how the Milwaukee Vocational School had utilized the findings of this survey to teach students financial management skills. She also suggested that other educational institutions do the same.

Anderson's findings are especially valuable because they represent such a large sample population. Her report is also remarkable in that she did not criticize the young women surveyed, even though she acknowledged the difficult position they might be in were they to continue to devote so much of their incomes to their apparel. While the survey Anderson conducted was unique in these ways, the purchasing habits of young working women fairly often formed the subject of serious inquiry. A writer for the *Literary Digest* reported on another investigation of the spending patterns of working-class young women. The group studied in this instance lived and worked in New York City and, depending on income, spent between 18 and 26 percent of their earnings for clothing, those in the higher-paying income brackets corresponding with the higher percentage bracket of financial outlay for clothing.[63] Professor Lillian H. Locke, instructor in household arts at Columbia Teachers College, was quoted in the *Digest* as saying: "Girls between the ages of eighteen and twenty-five have a right to look forward to matrimony. . . . Clothes go a long way to help her, and I'm afraid if she looks too dowdy in this day, she will never get there."[64] Another source noted in this article claimed that, in fact, it was inaccurate to classify the cost of a single young woman's clothes as a "living expense" but as a sort of business outlay, the price of eventually securing a husband. At the very least, her clothing was essential to the business of getting and keeping employment.[65]

The Religious Education Association also published a fairly comprehensive report, based on a study of the lives of young working women. In this report as well, clothing expenditures among the women studied reflected a substantial sum in light of actual income.[66] From the findings of these kinds of studies we can reasonably conclude that clothing was one of the most significant economic investments made by young women in the 1920s. While they may have been justified in such expenditures, it is easy to see as well how detractors could use such information against them.[67]

Instead of speaking plainly against what they perceived to be sheer and unwarranted extravagance in a woman's clothing, given her actual economic status, some critics merely ridiculed the very thing such a woman might have been trying to disguise—her lack of economic privilege. The following account is exemplary in this regard. It appeared in an article written by Henriette Weber, tellingly entitled "Silk Stockings and Sedition:"

"How they do it, I don't know, but they *do* do it," said an observant woman, watching two gum-chewing young flappers gaily striding along Fourteenth Street. There they were in tight fitting, black satin coats; of a dubious quality to be sure, but satin for all that, and with a bit of dead white cat about the neck. Smart little felt hats topped off their perfectly correct bobs—the hats imitations of Paris's latest cry, but costing, at the most, about one-tenth of what an "original French model" would bring. And there was a long expanse of slender leg encased in silken stocking, nothing less."[68]

Unlike reformers who railed against the injustice of the fashion system or who were in some cases genuinely concerned about women's financial welfare, this anecdote depicts yet a third reaction—one of class prejudice—that often surfaced in fashion debates of the 1920s. Some detractors obviously placed undue emphasis on fashion as a signifier of class standing and disparaged fashion trends that did not clearly mark socioeconomic status. Indeed, as Weber's story suggests, such people worried that poor women might appropriate fashions that falsely implied an advanced social standing.

Although speaking more impartially, as an economist, Paul H. Nystrom agreed that "wealth and the possession of wealth are important determining factors in the field of fashion," but he asserted as well that "it may be assumed that the fashion, whatever it may be, must demonstrate the presence of possession of that wealth."[69] Nystrom acknowledged that such a demonstration may in fact disguise the wearer's lack of wealth or privilege, suggesting, for example, that fashions might—and to succeed, should—imply that the wearer does not have to perform labor. The desire to portray, even pretend, to others that one leads a life of comparative leisure was, according to Nystrom, the reason women wore high heels, tight shoes, and makeup, the latter of which he claimed "would be disgusting and demoralizing if the person were engaged in manual labor of a degree causing profuse perspiration."[70] Clearly, and to the disdain of some truly privileged fashion consumers, the makers and marketers of fashion studiously avoided classism and thereby succeeded in reaching a much broader clientele. Moreover, as noted earlier, even women who made their own clothes had the latest styles available to them (fig. 15).

Ironically, early in the decade, when short skirts were still newly fashionable, a writer for the reformist publication *Outlook* claimed that long skirts were worn primarily by women of the "prosperous class" and short skirts by the women of the "wage-earning class." Generally coinciding with Nystrom's theory, clearly derived from Thorstein Veblen, the writer predicted that once it became clear that "the short skirt impl[ies] a weekly envelope . . . , its day in America is done."[71] Plainly, this writer was mistaken. Undoubtedly, what largely altered the formula on which this fashion forecast was based was the unprecedented growth of advertising, which burgeoned when radio and

New Styles for this Winter

By Martha Evans Hale
DRAWINGS BY
ERNEST KNOWLES

Dress 9814

Misses' Dress 9815

GRACEFUL side drapery and a smart little overblouse distinguish frock No. 9815. Charmeuse, chiffon, taffeta or satin would lend their soft draping qualities to this particular style and would make a very charming afternoon frock. The separate guimpe, with long sleeves, is of sheer material like georgette or chiffon. This misses' or small women's dress is designed for 16, 18 and 20 years. 16 size requires four yards and one-half of 36-inch figured material, with two yards and three-quarters of 27-inch plain material.

Waist 9807
Skirt 9818

Dress 9796

Waist 9810

FIG. 15. Dressy Clothes to Make at Home. From Martha Evans Hale, "New Styles for This Winter," *People's Home Journal* 35 (November 1920): 47.

other developing forms of mass communication became technologically feasible.[72] And of course, the appearance of wealth remained an important marketing strategy by which to reach all consumers, not just those who were in fact wealthy. Indeed, one common method of advertising new trends in women's clothing styles was to have them modeled by popular stage or screen actors, who were naturally perceived to be wealthy by the time they found themselves posing in the pages of popular fashion magazines. According to

Mary Alden Hopkins, the theater was itself utilized by the "leading modistes" to show the newest fashions, a claim with which the jury in *Kutock v. Kennedy* readily agreed.

Privilege, notoriety, wealth, and the advertising industry itself notwithstanding, the dominant force that compelled fashion in the 1920s was ultimately the working-class woman. As Hopkins also contended, "Fashions in this country are no longer ruled by a few leaders of society. They are determined by the purchases of several million working women, each of whom buys a pleasing dress, puts it on immediately, soon wears it shabby, and buys another. The girl with the pay envelope sets the style for the women who dressmake at home." To underscore her point, Hopkins recalled a conversation between a "haughty and experienced saleslady" from one of New York's "exclusive" Fifth Avenue shops and her employer. The former had been reprimanded for not "moving the stock" and in self-defense replied, "How can I sell these styles? The flappers won't buy them."[73]

By the end of the decade many people still worried that women would be persuaded, after years of comparative freedom, to return to more restrictive styles in clothing simply because they were said to be "in style." Just as many people believed that women would do no such thing. The essayist Ann Devon, for one, smugly observed that "each year woman grows a trifle more complacent about wearing what she likes and what she will. The designers and fashion dictators are now powerless to force her, as they once could, to gush about every innovation."[74] Incidentally, Devon also observed: "There is a tendency on the part of many women of unlimited income to patronize the less exclusive and expensive shops for many of their gowns."[75] Merely a passing reference within her essay, her observation yet seems an ironic footnote to Henriette Weber's tale of catty asides about "gum-chewing flappers."

The point that Devon as well as Weber made was, in fact, much the same: by the late 1920s "Dame Fashion's" influence on American women was strangely altered. Some women, naturally, remained quite willing to spend their hard-earned money on overpriced and impractical fashionable clothing or fabrics. Fashion was still much debated and much abused, still regarded by many as an enemy to women's personal and economic autonomy as well as to American economic supremacy. There could be no doubt, though, that in spite of economic forces that made it more profitable to dress women in as much and as costly yardage as possible, women's own wishes in this matter generally held sway throughout the decade. Moreover, not only wealthy women but less wealthy ones too might participate in the fashion system if they so desired. Indeed, the young working-class woman became more influential in this system than her older, wealthier counterpart. In addition to the power of her paycheck, she possessed the increasingly essential attribute of a fashionable appearance—youth (fig. 16). And although fashions would con-

FIG. 16. Young Flapper.

tinue to fluctuate and female autonomy would remain widely contested, women in the 1920s were at least recognized as an economic force with which to contend—no small step on the road to personal liberty.

Fashion and Morality

Fashions for women in the American 1920s generated heated controversy and obsessive concern about what the world was coming to, and dress re-formers took aim at fashion from several vantage points. No misgivings were more frequently expressed, however, than moral ones. Moreover, no aspect of fashion so kindled the fury of moralists as short skirts. I noted previously that early advocates for women's dress reform focused largely on health issues. They opposed, for example, the tight lacing of corsets. Some also argued that long, trailing skirts were unsanitary and debilitating.[76] But to the moralists who led the assault on fashion in the 1920s, health was at best an ancillary issue. In fact, these reformers insisted that women wear long skirts for the sake of modesty; that is, they contested stylish shorter skirts on moral grounds despite the enhanced mobility these skirts provided.

In May 1921 the lead article in the *Literary Digest* posed the troubling question "Is the Younger Generation in Peril?" and therewith launched a lengthy, detailed presentation of the many facets of immorality believed to be rampant among America's youth, particularly its young women. The article identified a number of dress reform efforts already underway, including those of the YWCA, the Women's Auxiliary of the Episcopal Church, and various state legislatures. Concerning the latter, the report noted the introduc-tion of several bills intended to govern women's dress. A bill proposed in Utah, for example, would fine and even imprison women whose skirts were more than three inches above their ankles. An Ohio bill reportedly declared that the skirts of any female over fourteen years of age should reach her instep. Bills proposed in as many as twenty-one states likewise attempted the ex-traordinary task of measuring modesty by the yard and, as would be expected, yielded results that were anything but consistent. The *Digest* quoted the New York *American*: "[I]t would seem that, were these to become laws, the dress with its four-inch-high skirt which would be moral in Virginia would be im-modest in Utah, while both the Utah and Virginia skirts would be wicked enough in Ohio to make their wearers subject to fine or imprisonment."[77]

The skirt debates were as enduring as they were confusing, however. Even several years later these arguments continued, as reported again in the *Liter-ary Digest*, 29 January 1927. Siding with Pope Pius's recent appeal to stem "what is held to be an increased immodesty in women's fashions," the author agreed that women's fashions had indeed played a key role in the "decay of morals and the downfall of nations" and contended as well that the "terrible potentialities" of women's dress were still present. Women's clothing did not "possess static qualities," and women forgot "that a passing wind, or sudden movement of the wearer, is sufficient to change their position. In cutting our garments, as well as in other things of life, we must allow for emergencies. To keep a skirt at a certain level in emergencies, it must drop considerably below that level normally."[78] Moral remonstrances were often paired in this way with other sorts of appeals—in this case one of prudence—to influence women's standards of dress.

One disgruntled reader of the opinion magazine the *Nation* complained in a letter to the editor about the flippant tone an author had adopted toward female modesty in dress. By way of rebuttal he claimed that "[c]iviliza- tion thrives in climates which require covering most of the year." Further, he layered what was initially a moralistic complaint with other rationales, in- cluding the ever-popular appeal to "good taste," something for which, in his opinion, contemporary fashion and even writers for the *Nation* showed "lit- tle reverence."[79] Similarly, one report detailing the recent dress reform ef- forts spearheaded by "Mrs. John B. Henderson" of Washington, claimed that "society women" from all over the United States were banding together "to condemn such vulgar fashions of women's apparel that do not tend to culti- vate innate modesty, good taste or good morals."[80] In a questionable attempt to add humor on this point, Reese Carmichael sardonically observed: "Were all women perfectly proportioned, fashion's problems would be solved by one-half. Were all women endowed with accurate taste, the other half of fashion's problems would be solved, and there would be no grotesquery, no immodesty, none of the funny figures that now form part of the feminine pageant."[81]

Most moralistically inclined dress reformers saw nothing humorous at all in fashion trends. Many, in fact, equated attractiveness with virtue and pon- derously attempted to convince others of the same. These calls for modesty in dress, coupled with harsh criticisms of unattractive and/or "tasteless" ap- pearance, essentially told women that to create a pleasing appearance was their moral obligation. Stern warnings about the consequences of inadequate concern for personal appearance often accompanied propaganda about a woman's responsibility to look attractive. In his article entitled "How I Like a Woman to Look," Frank Crane, for instance, told of a woman who was asked why she did not keep up her looks to "please her husband." Why, "there was no sense in continuing to run after you had caught the train!" she had replied. Crane then observed, ominously, "Later she found that husbands are not like trains. They don't always *stay* 'caught.'"[82] Small wonder that women worked vigilantly to upgrade their looks—even while they pretended not to. If con- spicuously concerned with her appearance, a woman was judged immodest by some critics, shallow by others, extravagant by still others, self-absorbed and lacking in good taste by all.

In addition to their trademark strategies to induce fear and guilt among women and thereby influence fashion, moralistic dress reform advocates also tried regularly to shame women into compliance with more righteous standards of dress. Remarks by Helen P. McCormick, president of the Catholic Big Sisters of Brooklyn, exemplify the distinction, albeit a subtle one, between the shaming tactics and the closely related fear and guilt rhetoric that moralists measured out in large doses. McCormick, whose position, curiously, was depicted as "not one of sour grapes," vitriolically objected to fashion trends from sleeveless dresses to the "lack of suitable and essential under-things." The "bathing girl" of 1924 McCormick bluntly described as "hideous, perfectly horrid." This "Big Sister," believing that the newer styles revealed bodily imperfections, advised: "Don't try to dress the way they do in revues. It can't be done in one case out of a thousand."[83] Although there are clear moral undertones to her diatribe, potentially evoking a myriad of feelings within her audience, certainly shame was a natural response for some who attended to McCormick. Her insistence that most women do not "measure up" to beauty standards the exacting ones to which McCormick herself apparently subscribed—surely intensified the embarrassment felt by those who were already insecure about their personal appearance.

Hugh A. Studdert Kennedy, in his thoughtful and expansive essay inadequately entitled "Short Skirts," explored the relationship between immorality and shame and suggested that the former was largely determined by sizable doses of the latter. Kennedy noted examples of fashions that would have been shunned as wanton nakedness in earlier eras but were largely taken in stride by 1926. Noting that one "Prince of the Church" recently decried the "unparalleled depravity of woman's dress," Kennedy retorted, "The lack of morality is not in the nakedness but in the shame, and the shame grows less day by day."[84]

Unfortunately for those who fought for dress reform, the short skirt was hardly the only "depraved" fashion women wore. Corsets, about which women's health advocates had complained for years, also troubled moralists, who wished all women would wear them. According to a report in the *Atlanta Constitution*, for example, there was a public outcry when uncorseted young women attended dance halls. Dancing was, understandably, a far more sensual experience without the "armamentation" of a corset. The Atlanta report also cited problems in Detroit, where church leaders were now convinced of the evils of modern jazz dancing, particularly the variety associated with the removal of the corset. The executive secretary of the Council of Churches in Detroit, Dr. M. C. Pearson, explained: "Young men like to have the girls remove their corsets. . . . This makes dancing a thing of passion. Corsetless dancing is nothing but passion" (figs. 3 and 17).[85]

Prunella: YOU USED TO WEAR CORSETS. WHY DID YOU
GIVE THEM UP?
Priscilla: I HAD A COUPLE OF COMPLAINTS.

FIG. 17. Corset Cartoon. *Life* 88 (9 September 1926): 8. Courtesy of the Library of
Congress.

In contrast to these barbs against the corrupting influence of 1920s fashions for women, there was, of course, some praise for the new styles. Fashion's advocates, perhaps with less to prove, given the overwhelming popularity of the "flapper look," were not usually as vitriolic as fashion's critics. Mary Gray Peck, however, more heavy-handed than some, unabashedly accused moralistic fashion opponents of hypocrisy, barely stopping short of accusing the pope himself.

> Particularly, Catholic ecclesiastics have thundered at young women to clothe themselves more seemly. The ideal of feminine apparel that pervades these moralists seems strongly influenced by the nun's garb. Their views on masculine attire are distinctly more liberal, as witness the splendor of texture and color worn by the Princes of the Church as they mass in religious ceremonies. It would seem somewhat inconsistent for bishops and cardinals to adjure young women to dress soberly, but they don't see it.[86]

Mary Alden Hopkins, never at a loss for words, described the beauty of the "silly little flapper" and, perhaps also not without risk of scandal, asserted: "I enjoy their round, firm bodies; their pretty, much-shown legs." She affirmed young working women who defied the "grouchy, prosperous employers" bent on suppressing all attractiveness in the dress of their female employees for fear that it might divert the attention of the young men in the offices where they worked. Directing her attack against not only "this present wave of firing for bobbed hair and general grouching over girls' naughty clothes," Hopkins also speculated about what she believed to be the real reasons behind employers' discomfiture over women's apparel. She accused bosses themselves of impure intentions, saying that most "feel more comfortable about a girl with thin hair and big teeth, who forgets to powder her nose" because, presumably, she thinks more about her work. Hopkins archly asks, "How the dickens does he know what she is thinking about? What he really means is that she doesn't tempt even his unconscious mind to amorous thoughts. He feels safe with her. Safe. Safe."[87]

Some moralists depicted women's employment as anything but a realm of safety for many of the same reasons Hopkins mentioned. In *Christ and the New Woman*, Clovis G. Chappell portrayed the office environment as one where a "young girl of charm and beauty is often brought into contact with a man without scruples." The two were thus thrown together, and because of economic necessity the young woman felt pressure to "keep her place" in unethical ways, possibly even becoming a "gold digger." According to Chappell, the young woman "finds a way to dress well while she works little and thus ends in moral bankruptcy."[88] Chappell's explicit concerns about what he perceived to be the ethical dilemmas endemic to the workplace ineffectively camouflaged commonly held prejudices against young working-class women, especially the widespread assumption that their alleged obsession with fashion ended in moral and financial ruin.

Hopkins linked employers' desire to work with "safe" women—an understandable preference if Chappell is to be believed—not only to their own sexual fears but to greed and territorialism as well. Women now shared the terrain of the business world and so necessarily had to adapt to this "manly" environment, a process that required considerable social dexterity. A woman dare not assimilate into this "man's world" too well, for she was still expected to perform good old-fashioned femininity within social and domestic environs. "These men like a woman to be frilly and fluffy at home and in the evening," Hopkins explained. On the job, however, they "cannot stand having about them women who are obviously women and not imitation men. Not real men in line for promotions and salary raises and likely to holler at being passed over; but passive, sexless creatures grateful for being underpaid and overworked and convinced that the boss and God are always right."[89] Perhaps accurate, perhaps exaggerated, but as usual, Hopkins adroitly identified ways in which women's fashion colluded conspicuously with a host of other issues.

More inclined to blame women for their own fashion predicaments, the well-known women's rights activist, Charlotte Perkins Gilman, speculated about women's hidden motives for displaying themselves fashionably and heartily disapproved of those who followed the trends of fashion. In her view, such women merely catered to male whims. Gilman essentially argued that women deceived themselves—but certainly not her—when they claimed to have their own health, comfort, or other self-interests at heart. Women simply decorated themselves for men, for not to do so meant not to receive attention from men, a sacrifice most women refused to make.[90]

William Bolitho, on the other hand, quipped that if women indeed dressed to please men, "the simplest way would no doubt be not to dress at all." He added that, even so, women did not oblige men to this extent for the same reason that fishermen securely attach bait to their hooks to prevent its falling off at the first nibble on the hook.[91] Writing in 1930, Bolitho reflected more philosophically as well on the social implications of the by then lengthening skirt styles. He reminisced about the decade of the 1920s, recalling the early postwar period and its excesses, signified by short skirts and bobbed hair, as a time of a generation's wandering, the "stupid and rough time of all after-war." Women, perhaps in reaction to the disillusion men felt, adopted pragmatism and a sense of self-sufficiency that differed markedly from the romantic "woman ideal" of the prewar era. Bolitho optimistically considered that "[t]he times have changed. Romance has come back. Woman takes back her ancient prestige."[92] Little did he know that the despair of a new generation was imminent, the effects of the stock market crash having yet to be fully realized in early 1930.

Bolitho was not alone, of course, in blaming World War I for the startling social changes apparent in the 1920s, including but not limited to women's clothing. Walter G. Muirheid, for example, matter-of-factly asserted that "[e]very big war has brought a reaction in reckless dress."[93] No less noteworthy a spokesperson for the 1920s than F. Scott Fitzgerald, responsible even for the popular designator the "Jazz Age," characterized this decade as a time when "something had to be done with all the nervous energy stored up and unexpended in the War." He too referred to "flappers" and variable skirt lengths as emblems of the times in his nostalgic postscript to the 1920s, "Echoes of the Jazz Age." But by 1931, Fitzgerald ruefully pronounced the death of the era, the enormous "jolt" of the Wall Street crash indeed having become apparent and the Jazz Age seeming "as far away as the days before the War."[94]

Clearly, the 1920s were viewed by many who experienced them as a time apart, isolated in history by enormous crevices that marked their beginning as well as their end, with displays by women denoting the very character of the age. Hopkins and Fitzgerald notwithstanding, most people seemed uneasy, even disturbed, by fashions that exposed women's bodies in ever more daring ways. Time and again social observers spoke of the perceived relationship between these more revealing women's fashions and the declining morality of the nation itself. Such weighty implications meant that every detail of a woman's appearance warranted evaluation, if not censure. From silk stockings to bobbed hair, women were tediously inspected, frequently condemned. The distinction between costume and character was negligible. Virtually any rhetorical weapon, reasonable or illogical, was deployed in the ideological war against the immorality of fashion.

Fashion and Health

Although the most vociferous of the would-be dress reformers argued moralistically, those persons who considered women's health central to the fashion debates of the 1920s were by no means reticent. The items that topped their reform agenda were shoes and underwear.[95]

Shorter skirts naturally increased the visibility of women's shoes. Thus, fashion advisors in the 1920s, unlike those of previous decades, emphasized the importance of footwear to a woman's total "look." One advice columnist, for example, told women to "keep in mind that your footwear is like the caption to a picture; it tells the beholder what is the meaning of the costume, what occasions the woman who planned it intended it to grace. If the shoes are not the key to the costume then it means that they are wrong."[96] The added fashion significance of women's shoes was obviously a boon to the shoe manufacturing industry. The growth in numbers of available shoe styles during the decade is apparent from even a cursory comparison of advertisements and photographs between the late 1910s and late 1920s.

The YWCA, however, attributed the expanding variety of shoes—sensible shoes, that is—to their vigorous "shoe campaign" against the so-called style shoe, the high-heeled, narrow-toed footwear that enhanced the fashionably slim female silhouette of the 1920s.[97] The organization discouraged these trendier shoes in two primary ways: first, they tried to persuade shoe manufacturers and distributors to create shoes that were designed on the principle of health rather than stylishness; second, they taught young women about the harmful effects of style shoes. The adviser's manual for the Girl Reserve Movement of the YWCA, for example, outlined several activities designed to encourage girls to make "correct shoe" choices, that is, to choose only shoes that provided a good "five-room apartment" for their toes (fig. 18). YWCA leaders might have girls draw pictures of feet, then, based on the drawings, discuss the characteristics of normal feet. Group leaders might also provide an exhibit of "good shoes," supplemented by purchasing information about them. One example of a poster that leaders might make included sketches that depicted the uncomfortable positioning of feet in stylish shoes, under which a caption asks: "Men do not walk on pegs—why should women?"[98]

Given that morality-based complaints surfaced so consistently in most discussions of fashions for women in the 1920s, it is perhaps not surprising that one YWCA staff member, Dr. Sara Brown, associated style shoes not only with damage to the wearer's feet but also with damage to her character. She admonished:

> The wearing of tight shoes for appearance sake is harmful in many ways. Not only the physical but the mental and spiritual side of the individual suffers. One cannot thoroughly enjoy a sermon at church on Sunday in tight shoes. Children are unable to pay the proper respect to their elders by getting up and giving them their seat when their feet are cramped.
> ... Never wear ill-fitting shoes. They inhibit gentleness. . . .[99]

Another physician, Florence A. Sherman, focused primarily on the physical harm caused by wearing shoes with high heels and narrow, pointed toes. She warned against all kinds of foot ailments, of course, but she also claimed that high heels altered one's center of gravity. Besides poor posture, Sherman explained, to compensate for the destabilizing effects of high heels, the body could also develop "a train of misplacements and congestions such as prolapus of the stomach and bowels, constipation, indigestion, misplaced uterus,

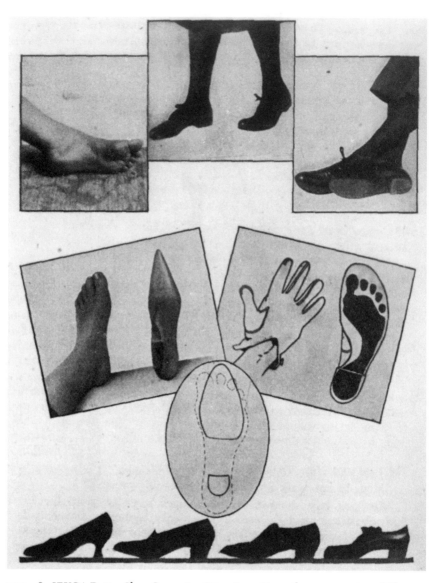

FIG. 18. YWCA Better Shoe Campaign Literature. From the 1921 version of *The Girl Reserve Movement: A Manual for Advisors* (New York: YWCA), 328. Courtesy of the Library of Congress.

menstrual pain. We might add to this list accidents, decreased working capacity, deranged nerves, lack of exercise . . . nor should we forget that the story of bad feet writes itself in wrinkles and a look of old age.[100] Perhaps it was to people like Sherman that Reese Carmichael referred when he wrote: "I have read various articles by eminent [wo]men of medicine who could prove that practically every ill of womankind comes from the wearing of high heels." He encouraged tolerance among these physicians and pointed out that women in heels had "managed to do a lot of things."[101]

Some medical doctors themselves seemed amused by their colleagues who blamed a variety of physical woes on any particular fashion evil. The *Saturday Evening Post* featured an essay by one physician who facetiously pondered the mysterious disappearance of the corset: "We doctors will miss them terribly, for they could be so neatly blamed for every sort of feminine woe, from gallstones to anaemia, from neurasthenia to consumption."[102] Another doctor, cited in the *Literary Digest*, in fact compared corsets and tight shoes and glibly predicted that: "[t]ight corsets . . . have succumbed; tight shoes will do the same."[103] More cynical fashion experts never expected that medical opinion would have any real influence on the fashion system generally or on shoe styles in particular. Paul H. Nystrom, for one, said that, in spite of the severe dangers that doctors associated with both high-heeled shoes and inadequate clothing, "[f]ashion has not given any indication of bowing or bending to these views. Apparently nothing ever comes of such criticism. People read them; they seem interested; sometimes they are convinced. In other cases they are amused. But they follow the fashion."[104]

Some fashion-related health warnings surely did elicit at least amusement if not concern. One imaginative health alert issued in 1920 stated that a London surgeon, subsequent to detailed observations of five hundred women, was convinced that "[i]nsufficient clothing about the necks and throats of women is causing an increase in goiter." The physician, Sir James Cantlie, also criticized the indecency of women's clothing styles, which he felt affected not only the health of young women but also of the older women who "follow the evil example." The report did not explain what physiological evidence led to Cantlie's conclusions, except for a vague reference to "bursts of high temperature to which the underclothed may be liable."[105]

Exposure-related health problems were more commonly linked not to low necklines of dresses but to the abbreviated underwear women began to wear by the 1920s, including the elimination of the corset (fig. 19). Katherine Taylor Cranor, a member of the Home Economics Division of Iowa State College, launched an emphatic attack against "inadequate" undergarments. She protested the way in which "Dame Fashion is tampering with the health of this and the coming generations."[106] Florence A. Sherman, the physician cited earlier, insisted that the warmth provided by underwear prevented

PLATE 145. CHANGE IN WOMEN'S APPAREL OUTFITS, 1913-1928

1913 OUTFIT				1928 OUTFIT		
	Garment	Material	Yds.		Garment	Material	Yds.
I.	Waist *	Cotton	2½	I.	Overblouse	Silk	2
II.	Vest or shirt *	"	1½	II.	Vest or shirt *	Silk or rayon	¾
III.	Corset cover *	"	1½		(Bandeau substituted)		
IV.	Drawers *	"	2	III.	Bloomers *	Silk or rayon	2
V.	Petticoat	"	3½	IV.	Skirt	" " "	2¼
VI.	Stockings *			V.	Stockings *	" " "	
VII.	Corset or brassiere	"	2				
VIII.	Underskirt	"	3				
IX.	Tailored suit	Wool	3¼				
	Total		19¼ yds.		Total		7 yds.

* Several necessary.   * Several necessary.

The great changes that have occurred in the amount of clothing worn by women is clearly demonstrated in this illustration. A complete outfit in 1913 required 30 or more yards of fabric in addition to stockings. In 1928 not more than 9 or 10 yards are required. In 1913 the dress was frequently of wool or worsted material and the other garments of cotton. In 1928 the entire outfit is usually silk or silk and rayon. Besides the reduction in yardage required to clothe the 1928 woman, the amount of laundering has also been greatly reduced.—From *Journal of Commerce*, May 31, 1928.

FIG. 19. Apparel Diagram. From Paul H. Nystrom, *Economics of Fashion*, p. 434. Courtesy of the Library of Congress.

painful menstruation. She implied as well that tuberculosis was a possible side effect that threatened the "half-clad" women and girls, who should wear more undergarments for "proper protection and decency."

Although Dr. Sherman was unclear as to what might be an appropriate quantity of undergarments, she did carefully detail the proper way to don the corset, a torturous procedure it would seem, undertaken while lying down with a small pillow under the "posterior end." Despite Sherman's claim that young girls should be taught to develop back and abdominal musculature so that "no support will be needed," she instructed readers putting on corsets to "equalize pressure by having the garter straps over the vertical, lateral, and dorsal parts of the thigh. The corset should next be laced from below upward, the lace being tied in three places; first, about the pelvic bones, second, at the level of the umbilicus; third, very loosely at the top of the corset."[107] Conflicted as Sherman's advice on the corset seems from a contemporary perspective, her views were probably moderate in her own time. She wrote, after all, when corsets had only recently become optional attire for most American women and were still actively marketed to and worn by women, many of whom still believed in their health benefits (figs. 20 and 21).[108]

The underwear controversy was taken up with great ardor, although usually with less sobriety and tedium, by those who argued that, especially in warm weather, less is more. In *Collier's,* a popular and generally lighthearted magazine, Elizabeth Macdonald Osborne enthusiastically espoused the virtues of looking cool, if not actually dressing to feel cooler.[109] More interesting from a historical perspective, however, is Osborne's attempt to classify women solely on the basis of the amount of underwear they wore.[110] Osborne described the "Standpatters," who dressed the rest of their lives as they did when they were eighteen years old and still wore every conceivable female undergarment invented, from "teddys" to petticoats. In marked contrast to the Standpatters was another group of women, unnamed but apparently known to readers of *Collier's* as the ones who mortified the saleswomen who discovered their nudity when assisting them in trying on dresses. These women, though few in number, were to be blamed for the "legendary" posting in clothing stores, "No naked ladies fitted." Perhaps these women were responsible as well for another form of crisis, reported in at least one department store: due to lack of demand, it was considering the discontinuation of its women's underwear department altogether.[111]

Osborne defined a third category of women, the Radicals, as women who wore only those garments for which they could identify a real purpose and begrudged the wearing of even these items. While they might differ from one another in deciding the exact pieces of underclothing that were useful, all Radicals eliminated the wearing of a vest underneath their outer clothing. They also willingly resorted to a "five-in-one" garment (details of which are

FIG. 20. Corset Advertisement. *Delineator* 98 (May 1921): 31.

left to the reader's imagination) if it achieved the same effects as the multiple undergarments of the Standpatters.

Osborne focused largely on the so-called Liberals, women whose underwear practices were so varied that it is impractical to summarize them here. Despite her clear intentions not to be taken too seriously, Osborne's essay does illustrate quite effectively just how significant were a woman's choices in clothing in the 1920s, right down to her choice in underwear. A story in the *Woman Citizen* addressed this point as well. A woman described as "socially prominent" entered a milliner's shop and confronted a young saleswoman with the news, "I am a woman who wears a chemise. Also, I wear a corset. And a union suit. Have you any hats that would suit such a person?"[112] That underwear itself was an identity marker for women in the 1920s, that it was used even in jest to categorize women, substantiates again that women were in no small way viewed as of a piece with the fabric of their fashions, and their fashions with the very fabric of society.

By the end of the decade, debates that focused on a woman's health as it related to her clothing had come full circle. With moralists having led in the assault on short skirts, those speaking on behalf of women's physical well-being began an equally adamant attack on what was feared to be a return to the long-skirt styles of an earlier era. Physicians surveyed about the apparent return to dress fashions that emulated the long, form-fitting styles of prewar days used phrases such as "unmitigated evil," "deplorable," and "unhealthful" to describe this latest fashion trend. The prospect of full, trailing

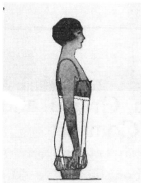

CORRECT POSTURE
—erect type

This is the ideal posture — head and body erect, shoulders square, weight supported by both feet. Normal posture not only insures better health; it also gives you a graceful, erect carriage and a smart-looking figure, which lends an air of distinction to the simplest garment. A Spencer Corset, especially designed to meet your needs, assures this posture.

WRONG POSTURE
—fatigue type

Rounded shoulders, flattened spine, and sagging abdominal wall. Organs in abdominal cavity displaced. A wrong corset makes this condition worse.

WRONG POSTURE
— swayback or lordosis type

Exaggerated curve at back of waistline. Stomach and other organs forced out of place. Often due to poorly designed corset.

FIG. 21. Health Benefits of Proper Corseting. Corset advertisement, *Woman's Home Companion* 51 (June 1924): 99.

skirts and a return to corsets suggested to them a severe reduction of physical activity among women, specifically, less female participation in "healthful athletic activities which have kept them out in the fresh air and sunshine in the years since the World War."[113] Many worried that women would adopt the proposed fashions reactively, not considering their own health and instead obediently following the edicts of the fashion industry, whose very authority had itself become a major point of contention.

Conclusions

Whether based ostensibly on concern for a woman's autonomy or for her financial, moral, or physical well-being, specific arguments against fashionable displays by women of the 1920s seemed, as often as not, to have been ultimately little more than red herrings. These issues were secondary at best to the much more vital question of what a woman's clothing said about the degree to which she belonged to her society. Moreover, the complexity of her relationship to her society increased as women struggled against still enormous odds to define this nebulous entity in terms of their own identities. The paradox involved was monumental. Although in many ways women were being encouraged, if not actually thrust, into the difficult work of self-disocvery, they were stymied in this process at a most fundamental level; even the clothes they selected were still clearly in the public domain. Women received multiple and conflicting messages about who they should be. On one hand, self-assertion and autonomy were valorized. On the other hand, women were told that they were still very much under orders to obey. Moralists, fashion and health experts, family members, and even those who otherwise staunchly defended women's equality and independence all wanted to control women's choices in clothing. The controversies that raged about women's fashions throughout the 1920s do indeed mark this era as a particularly important one in which to assess the interplay between conflicting social and ideological agendas as inscribed on the bodies of women.

In her introduction to an anthology of essays originally written for the *Nation*, Freda Kirchwey noted, "John Roach Straton and Billy Sunday point a pleasant way toward hell, while sensationalism finds in new manners of life subject for five-inch headlines, and . . . modern novelists make their modern characters stumble through pages of inner conflict to ends of darkness and desperation." Kirchwey observed as well, however, that in spite of the furor over perceived changes in morality, "a few people are at work quietly sorting out the elements of chaos and holding fragments of conduct up in the sun and air to find what they really are made of."[114] Certainly, many of the writers and speakers noted in this survey of "fashionable discourse" participated in the work to which Kirchwey referred; others only added to the pandemonium. In either case, their rhetoric unquestionably demonstrates that, within the complex and intricately woven social fabric that was the American 1920s, fashionable displays and disguises by American women—the performance of fashion—raised troubling and troublesome questions, ranging from propriety to pragmatics with many stopping points in between.

FIG. 22. Body-Conscious Bathers. Cover illustration, *Life* 88 (26 August 1926). Courtesy of the Library of Congress.

64

3
Fashionable Display and the Problem of Bathing Costumes

According to the fashion historians Richard Martin and Harold Koda, "Swimwear has served throughout the century to establish and represent standards of beauty and morality. Swim clothing serves this role supremely, not just because it can exchange dress and undress in the twinkling of a cabana or locker, but because water and the beach are the great proscenium of twentieth-century dress."[1] Certainly it is true of the 1920s that, although there was much ado about fashion generally, no particular fashion aroused more anxiety and strife than did swimwear, nor did any other fashion more concisely signify the widespread cultural dissonance about the display of the female body. Public bathing was, after all, an experience largely associated with looking at others and being looked at by them (figs. 22 and 23). Moreover, it was clearly perceived as a performative event—even requiring a "costume" for participation. Conflicts over women's swimwear during this era uniquely foreground historical assumptions about feminine modesty and virtue and about censorship as a means by which to legislate both.

The gradual acceptance of ever more abbreviated swimwear in the 1920s, concurrent with the growing popularity of "bathers' revues," underscored the performative dimension of public bathing (fig. 24). The conjuncture of these practices especially highlights the critical role of performance in framing otherwise improper display. Simply stated, it would seem that, in the 1920s, for a woman to swim in an abbreviated bathing costume was less acceptable than for her to parade in one. The distance between the beach and the boardwalk was, in this respect, miles. Body-revealing styles of swimwear, although more practical for swimming, were initially opposed by many morally minded Americans who were already concerned that contemporary fashions for women lacked basic decency. When municipal authorities discovered that, worn by local "bathing beauties," these swimsuit styles attracted tourism, however, the decency dilemma in some towns and cities was quite quickly dismissed in the interests of capitalism.

FIG. 23. Gibson "Bathing Beauties." Illustration by Charles Dana Gibson, *Cosmopolitan* 85 (August 1928): 28. Courtesy of the Library of Congress.

Swimming, the activity for which bathing costumes were ostensibly designed, had been an increasingly popular pastime since at least the latter third of the nineteenth century. Early on, it appears, many felt that swimming was quite dangerous and relied on ingenious methods to reduce its risks. Charles E. Funnell, for example, describes two unusual devices dating from 1870 that were used to prevent drowning. The "bathing car" was a large wire cage with attached floats. Bathers could occupy the cage and then immerse themselves by means of a pulley system to whatever depth they preferred.

"Life Lines for Surf Bathing" were more simply designed, consisting merely of cables attached on one end to masts on the beach and, at the other, to anchors offshore. Lines hanging down from these cables at intervals could, theoretically, allow bathers to reach from one cable to the next while in the water without fear of endangering themselves.[2]

Not only was there great apprehension about bathers' personal safety in the late nineteenth century, but many worried even more about bathers' modesty. In fact, most public bathing at that time was a sexually segregated event. Women were carefully shielded from men's view. They rode wheeled "bathing machines" discreetly into the surf instead of forthrightly walking into it, the "modesty hoods" attached to these machines keeping the submersion process hidden.[3] The paranoia over personal safety as well as the strict segregation of male and female bathers eventually passed, and by the turn of the century desegregated bathing was common, particularly at seaside resorts. Still, bathing apparel for women was only somewhat less voluminous than everyday street wear (fig. 25). Martin and Koda explain that the "long civil war of swimwear" went on for nearly three decades. In the early years of the twentieth century, women began to reveal their arms; by the 1920s the war intensified over the progressive revelation of women's legs; and by the 1930s the primary change in swimwear was that men began to go without shirts.[4]

In the 1920s no seaside resort town could claim greater popularity than Atlantic City. To attract tourists, city promoters emphasized the safeness of

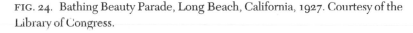

FIG. 24. Bathing Beauty Parade, Long Beach, California, 1927. Courtesy of the Library of Congress.

FIG. 25. "Gibson Girl" in Bathing Costume, 1907.

FIG. 26. 1920s Atlantic City Postcard.

its beaches. The back of the postcard shown in fig. 26 states: "Atlantic City's Bathing Beach is famous for its safety, made so naturally, and kept that way by the finest Beach Patrol organization in the world. The beach slopes gently, there is no undertow, consequently life lines are unnecessary and even children can play in the water without danger—-it is the safest beach in the world." Promoters also tried to offset the widespread perception that cities were disorderly, busy, and immoral places. Funnell notes (and fig. 26 suggests as well) that in these promotional efforts the image of the sea was juxtaposed with that of the city in such a way as to provide "a sanctifying backdrop for the inviting disorder of the city." Moreover, he contends that the "purity attributed to the sea sanctified pleasure which otherwise would have aroused guilt for breach of discipline. Discipline and pleasure could coexist."[5]

Funnell's observation is especially provocative when interpreted in light of two events. First, in 1921, Atlantic City businesses initiated the Miss America pageant, the most successful and enduring of all the "bathers' revues" of its time.[6] Second, that same summer one woman went to extraordinary lengths to resist attempts by civic authorities of Atlantic City to censor her bathing costume. Carefully contextualized, these two occurrences in and of themselves quite amply reveal the full range of sentiment about the "problem" of bathing costumes. As such, they each deserve emphasis here.

"Annette Kellermans": A Line in the Sand

As I explained in the previous chapter, many people perceived fashion trends of the 1920s as nothing less than a visual synopsis of all that was morally wrong with American women. And some felt that the sartorial freedoms women began to enjoy connoted a tide of increasing moral laxity that must not merely be objected to but decisively curbed. Consequently, certain fashions for women, formerly the objects of heated debate, now were legally prohibited as well (fig. 27). The one-piece bathing suit, which had been popularized by the champion swimmer and later star of vaudeville and motion pictures, Annette Kellerman, was legally banned in some parts of the country. Kellerman herself was arrested for indecent exposure when she first appeared in her "body stocking" style suit at Boston's Revere Beach in 1908, and responses toward her attire would not have been much different in many places throughout the United States until late in the 1920s.[7] Not only was the sleek Kellerman-style suit physically freeing compared with the bulky yards of fabric in which women had formerly "bathed," but it was specifically problematic in that it quite clearly revealed the contours of the female figure. The suit was doubly offensive to some when stockings were eliminated or were not worn according to regulations, which usually meant they were rolled below

FIG. 27. Arrest for Bathing Suit Code Violation, Chicago, 1922. UPI/Corbis-
Bettmann.

the knees. In any case, the "Annette Kellerman," or more simply, the one-
piece bathing costume, was considered the most daring kind of bathing
apparel and therefore became the focus of many censorship efforts, not to
mention sarcastic innuendo (figs. 3 and 28).

    Controversies over swimwear fashions also broadened the already gaping
division among ranks of feminists. Women's reactions to bathing suit restrictions in Atlantic City in June 1921 effectively illustrate this point. The beach
season opened that year with bitter sparring, publicized by the local press,
over the town's bathing suit ordinances. One of the first indications that a
storm was brewing was in the form of a letter written to Mayor Edward L.
Bader by Mrs. John J. White in response to a recent announcement that one-
piece bathing suits would be permissible in the Bathers' Revue planned for
late in the summer. White accusingly asked the mayor why, when these suits
had been banned, they would "now not only be permitted but invited on our
Boardwalk for thousands to look at?" Mayor Bader reassured White that he
appreciated her motives and had no "intention to allow anyone to parade
upon the Boardwalk in any costume that may be a discredit to the Pageant
Committee."[8]

White's understanding of local ordinances was accurate, to be sure. Bathing suit regulations prohibiting one-piece suits had just recently been announced by Dr. Charles Bossert, commander of the Beach Patrol.[9] Furthermore, all suits for women were to be "neither too low in front or back," and the attached skirts "must be of reasonable length—at least half way to the knees. Bare limbs will not be tolerated; full length hosiery must be worn."[10]

Bernice: AREN'T YOU COMING IN SWIMMING?
Bertha: I CAN'T. A MOTH ATE MY BATHING SUIT.
"THE LITTLE RASCAL! HE MUST HAVE BEEN ON A DIET."

FIG. 28. Bathing Suit Cartoon. *Life* 88 (9 September 1926): 25. Courtesy of the Library of Congress.

Although Mrs. White clearly wanted a strict and consistent enforcement of these rules, other Atlantic City residents, including many young women, were incensed.

Ada Taylor, a young woman described as a Presbyterian Sunday school teacher and president of the "exclusive" Ambassador Swimming Club, wrote to Bossert, protesting the city's restrictions. She complained that "bare legged bathers attracted less attention than short-skirted, silk-stockinged wheel-chair patrons" or indeed, less than "milady who rolls along the Boardwalk with legs crossed, showing her costly silk stockings at least to the knee."[11] A more tempered letter to Mayor Bader, signed by "Miss Fenwick" and "Miss Krauth," who described themselves as "sixteen and not bold girls" but ones who were decidedly in favor of one-piece suits, argued that a "good swimmer cannot possibly swim with skirts dangling around her knees."[12] A Newark physician, George W. Smith, also wrote to complain to Atlantic City's mayor. His letter, printed in the local newspaper, indicates—and quite possibly exaggerates—the magnitude of the city's quarrel. "Dear Sir—Thousands of people are getting disgusted with Atlantic City as far as beach regulations are concerned. The people who wear short bathing suits, allowing the feet and lower limbs to have the benefit of the water are all right. Anybody knows that the action of the water is more beneficial without stockings than with them."[13] In spite of pragmatic appeals like this one, many people still felt that morality, not better swimming, was the crux of this controversy. The Atlantic City Rotary Club even staged a debate on the question of whether or not one-piece costumes were "conducive to morality."[14]

Focusing especially on generational tensions between the women who participated in the fracas over the city's beach regulations, one report noted, "The constantly growing strength of advocates of more liberality in costumes has amazed the conservative element." The "conservative element" was apparently the local League of Women Voters, whose membership had instructed the organization's secretary to write city authorities "commending them for their strict censorship on the beach." This news account of a philosophical rift between Atlantic City women concluded with the following commentary:

> Politics is all-important in Atlantic City and officials are frankly surprised at the growth of the one-piece bathing suit sentiment. They are wondering just what political effect the controversy will have. The last thing the officials want to see is a definite line-up of the newly enfranchised women, with the younger women demanding more freedom on the beach, and the older, but more influential, insisting upon a continuation of the present rules. Such a division of sentiment, the leaders fear, might seriously affect the political fortunes of several of them.[15]

In spite of officials' concerns for unity among Atlantic City women, Mayor Bader and his colleague Dr. Bossert soon found in any case that their initial responses to the bathing suit problem were inadequate in the face of the sharp controversy that had ensued. By the time Bader revisited the issue, less than two weeks after he was first criticized by Mrs. White, he had become a veritable expert on styles in women's swimwear. "This one-piece suit agitation has created a wrong impression. What I meant was the form-fitting swimming suit." Bader's clarification followed upon his own attendance at the beach, where he acted as a censor for several hours, observing "the thousands of fair visitors who disported in the breakers or cavorted on the beach." Subsequent to his beachside deliberations, Bader also announced that the "Annette Kellerman," that is, the suit worn without a skirt, was "still under official ban." One-piece bathing suits with an attached skirt reaching to the knees were "perfectly proper," as they gave the "freedom of limb desired by the fair swimmers without a disgusting show of form." He added, however, that stockings were still required. Indeed, "beach cops" enforced the hosiery rule "religiously" with a curt "Roll 'em up, sister," to which "fair visitors, ignorant of the law, smilingly complied."[16]

It is perhaps worth noting that bathing costumes, which, by the early 1920s, were considered old fashioned and impractical by the likes of Ada Taylor, the Misses Fenwick and Krauth, and many other young women, did protect the pride of some women. As Lencek and Bosker state in *Making Waves*, "For many luxuriantly proportioned Victorian matrons, the emergence of a stripped-down suit was an event bordering on catastrophe . . . a humiliating ordeal."[17] In a lengthy article that advised women on current fashions in swimsuits and how best to wear them, one columnist, undoubtedly to the chagrin of certain readers, noted: "But any sort of corset is eliminated now from the bathing costume. No woman who weighs less than a hundred and eighty wears a bathing corset now. The rigid, formal, corseted silhouette of the stout figure is considered grotesque with bathing attire which much [*sic*] suggest supple natural lines."[18] Undoubtedly, such proscriptive, even insulting fashion directives irritated those who wished not to reveal the "natural" contours of their body. In any case, one is left to ponder at will the complex nature of motivations underlying the apparent rift between older and younger ranks of feminists on the matter of beach modesty.

Although debates as to what constituted proper bathing attire certainly occurred between women, this was by no means an issue left to women to decide for themselves. Not only resort towns like Atlantic City but most cities that had public bathing facilities or beaches had regulations by which to govern bathers' appearance. As with proscriptions against short skirts, however, in the early 1920s local municipalities throughout the United States varied considerably in terms of interest in and approaches to the regulation of

bathing costumes. Some communities had quite heavy-handed means of enforcing bathing dress codes, while others seemed virtually unconcerned
about female swim attire.[19] These differences are difficult to account for consistently or explain rationally. For example, while it was generally true that
resort areas in Florida and California were among the least restrictive in the
regulation of bathing costumes, it is not possible to conclude from this that
coastal regions were more lenient than inland areas. Throughout the East
Coast there were heated debates over women's swimwear, with significant
differences in dress codes for bathing from one town to another. And while
bathers in some California and Florida cities may have been relatively at their
ease in what they chose to wear on the beach, it is no doubt true that the
restrictiveness of codes varied in these states as well.[20]

Chicago was comparatively censorious about women's swimwear, a con-
servatism in keeping with the Windy City's attitude toward theater, discussed
in chapter 5. Within the first few days after the opening of the beach season
in June 1921, Chicago's deputy commissioner of public works, William Burkhardt, announced that bathing costumes would no longer be left to the con-
sciences of the women who wore them, as had been the case the previous
summer. Burkhardt felt it necessary to impose more precise regulations for
the new season since, referring to last year's bathers, "[s]ome of them apparently didn't have any such thing as a conscience." For emphasis, he added,
"If it had not been for the unsympathizing policewomen on duty the city's
beaches would have looked like a second garden of Eden. No, sir, we are not
leaving anything to conscience this year."[21]

By way of enforcing the new regulations, including a ban on one-piece
bathing suits, female bathers were required to pass the inspection of what
Ione Quinby, writing for the *Chicago Evening Post*, called "bathing beach
tailor[s], first aid to the inadequately clad mermaid."[22] According to Quinby,
whose report is heavily laced with sarcasm, Mrs. A. M. Loucks carried a black
bag with her that contained sewing paraphernalia as she presided over
Chicago's Clarendon beach. Each "mermaid" under her jurisdiction passed
before Loucks who, if necessary, used a tape measure to determine whether
the bathing costume complied with beach regulations. If the costume failed
this test, she withdrew the necessary items from her bag and "an emergency
operation was begun." Quinby's report included the following script of
Loucks's dialogue in such instances; although embellished perhaps, it does
suggest what Chicago authorities felt to be the most objectionable features of
female swimwear at the time.

> "Now that armhole, dearie, . . . don't you think it's really a bit too ample?"
> Or: "You'll pardon me, I know, but they're wearing the skirts a trifle longer
> this year, and it will take me just a second to remodel yours."

. . . "This will hold you for today," the beach tailoress would add sweetly. "When you go home, you can just run the hem thru the machine, and all will be hunky-dory."

Quinby observed that some women protested when their suits were mutilated in this way. Loucks was adamant, however, insisting that "she would have the rules complied with if she had to remodel every bathing costume on the north side."[23] Loucks's legalism might also explain why fewer women were reportedly on the beaches of Chicago than usual, even though the city was experiencing a tremendous heat wave, with early summer temperatures already reaching the mid-90s. The excessive heat had, in fact, prompted the decision to open public beaches two days earlier than usual.[24] The *Chicago Herald and Examiner* published a photograph of two bathers at the Oak Street beach, the caption for which also acknowledged beach censorship as a possible explanation for the reduced number of women at municipal beaches in spite of soaring temperatures: "The heat wave has jammed the beaches, but many girls are still making over their suits to conform to 'knickers two inches from knee and skirts to within two inches of knickers,' ordered by city."[25]

Newspapers were, of course, a heavily utilized medium by which to convey, if necessary even indirectly, views that countered those of local policy makers. It is not uncommon, for example, to find newspapers from one city that contained photographs of female bathers from other cities who wore bathing costumes unacceptable by "hometown" standards. The implicit assertion clearly was that one city's ordinances were tolerant compared with another's. A photograph placed near one of Chicago's Oak Street beach bathers showed a woman from California who modeled the latest fashion in eye shade for the beach—merely a hat with a brim—but who also wore, more noticeably, a one-piece, form-fitting bathing suit, with bare feet and bare legs revealed to at least twelve inches above her knees. The *Louisville Courier-Journal* contained an equally "persuasive" photograph of a parade of women wearing bathing costumes, under which a caption reads: "Folks lucky enough to go to Florida in the winter have many interesting diversions. One of these at Miami is the annual bathing suit *revue* pictured here. The rolled down socks and the one piece suits show what a carefree place Miami is."[26] Some attempts to influence local policy were more direct, of course. For example, to convince the Atlantic City Rotary Club of the need for relaxed standards of swimwear—part of the same Atlantic City debate noted earlier—proponents of a change in the statutes reportedly circulated pictures of parading "bathing girls" of Venice, California.[27]

Even without photographic evidence, bathing regulation news from other municipalities provided a point of comparison by which to contest local ordinances. Within days of the opening of the controversial 1921 Chicago beach season, this quip appeared in a local newspaper: "Bare legs for women are O.K. at city park bathing beaches this Summer [in Cleveland]. The new bathing suit regulations contain no provision for covering 'em."[28] Such information would not have been newsworthy were bathing dress codes not already such a point of contention in Chicago. To those who were paying attention, this story surely seemed none too subtle an argument against local codes.

No doubt, the proscriptive attitude of Chicago city authorities in the summer of 1921 did come as a surprise to Chicagoans. The 1911 city bathing suit code, still effective at the time, required simply that bathers wear "suitable" bathing dress, a term that was not defined.[29] By 1922, however, a revised manual of city ordinances did define what "suitable" was in excruciating anatomical detail, including specifications that the top of the patella rather than simply the knee was the point from which to determine the four-inch maximum gap allowed between it and the bottom of "trunks" worn under a bathing skirt. Notably, possibly reflecting a compromise of sorts, the four-inch allowance was generous compared with Burkhardt's ruling of a two-inch allowance the previous summer.[30]

In 1923, *American City* published the results of a survey of municipal codes regulating bathing suits in selected cities. The fact that such a survey was conducted may indicate a concern for code consistency among those whose job it was to govern America's cities. It is puzzling, in light of the Chicago reporter's reference to Cleveland's alleged laxity of bathing costume codes, to find Cleveland and Chicago regulations described in this article as "practically identical." Both city's codes are tactfully portrayed as "carefully considered" by the author for *American City* but are perhaps more honestly assessed by the terse survey response of P. V. Gahan of Bridgeport, Connecticut: "No regulations on suits. We find the public fairly sane on this matter, and prescribing the inches above the knee, etc., is all tommy-rot." If magnanimous toward Bridgeport residents, Gahan was nevertheless critical of foreigners, or "newly arrived bathers from the other side," whom he accused of wearing underclothes as bathing suits.[31]

Notwithstanding Gahan's criticism of non-natives, most beach censorship was directed specifically at women. William Burkhardt of Chicago was confronted about his own bias against women after he had harshly berated their "lack of conscience." Asked then to explain beach regulations governing males, he reportedly threw up his hands in despair, and at length replied, "Oh, well . . . the experience of the commission is that most of the males wear two-piece suits, consisting of shirt and trunks. However, we'll keep close tab on those animals, too."[32] This exasperated rejoinder does not seem a satisfactory response to the questioner's implication that the new Chicago beach regulations were unfairly prejudiced against women. Burkhardt's reference to men as "animals" does suggest, however, what is more explicitly stated in a report from Long Island; that is, that men were probably more likely to be censured for their behavior toward women at beaches than for dress code infractions. Long Island's police captain, Walter Barriscale, proclaimed that "beach lizards," or "bald-headed men who come to the beach to stare," would "get in trouble." By way of clarification, the report about this 1921 edict stated that "[i]t was understood that the rule would apply also to men who are not bald-headed."[33]

Atlantic City officials were apparently even more determined to keep their beaches free of this particular species of reptile. Reportedly, the ranks of beach supervisors were to be supplemented by undercover "copettes attired in nifty bathing suits," whose job it was to "nab ogling male bathers and break up love matches on the beach." "Flirts and beach 'lizards'" alike would have a "tough Summer ahead of them," one report noted, since the newly installed officers would also be on the lookout for members of their own sex whose "beach togs" did not conform to the requirements that had become such a pivotal issue in the city.[34]

These examples of beach censorship and regulation indicate not only particular concerns about decorum but also more general and historically grounded anxieties about cultural "playgrounds" as sites of sexual transgression. As I discussed earlier, in previous eras such worries were allayed at the nation's beaches in part by segregating the sexes for swimming and, later, by using "modesty hoods" to conceal women's bodies. In the 1920s the "beach censor" who patrolled the shore assumed a primary place as guardian of public morality when America went swimming. Not all municipalities, of course, assigned the title of "censor" to the person(s) whose job it was to regulate behavior at places designated for public bathing. Whether "copette," "tailoress-censor," or simply a police officer, the job endowed its possessor with considerable authority and sometimes not insignificant financial remuneration. Certainly, lifeguards also monitored swimmers, but responsibility for enforcing codes of conduct was, at least in more heavily utilized locations, clearly distinct from that of lifesaving. The *Atlantic City Daily Press*, for example, regularly ran a column devoted to "Chat by the Surf and Tent," entitled "Beach Combers." Victor Jagmetty, author of the series, reported on all sorts of beach-related news in this forum, including in at least one instance a discussion of both beach censors and lifeguards. In advance of the appointment of a "squad" of beach censors for the new season, Jagmetty noted Bossert's announcement about the duties attached to this occupation. The responsibilities of a beach censor, whose pay was anticipated to be a respectable five dollars a day, were to "keep off the beach athletes who become nuisances, watch over the deportment of the bathers, suppress profane language and control all misbehavior of any kind." The latter point presumably encompassed the "supervision of the suits worn by the bathers" stressed in a separate statement by Bossert.

The employment of these censors was apparently a novel tactic, urged on Mayor Bader by the "women's organizations of the resort, who feared that too much liberty was extended to the bathers" and that "license" was all too frequently the outcome."[35] The authority granted to beach censors, the relatively high pay, and probably other personal agendas attracted a number of applicants. In 1921, the year the position was created in Atlantic City, William Cuthbert, the director of public safety, as well as Mayor Bader, reportedly found the commotion surrounding the subject quite "interesting." Rumors that Bader had been "overwhelmed with applications" for the openings were common.[36]

Meanwhile, seventy-year-old Commodore William Tanguy, described as a man who "limps about with a cane," applied for the position of beach censor in the nearby town of Somers Point, New Jersey. He felt qualified to be censor in that he could still "see right well without the aid of glasses." Tanguy—whose name, surprisingly, elicited no ironical asides from reporters—understood that Somers Point had no funds to pay him, so he offered his services for free, contending that "the people seem to want a censor right bad, so why not please 'em." Tanguy further made it known that "I have my own ideas about what should be allowed on the beaches here, and I'll say I'm not in favor of restricting the girls too much in their swimming togs." Perhaps due to "beach lizard" suspicions against Tanguy or perhaps simply respect for women, a local minister, Rev. T. D. Stultz, spoke out against the censorship of Somers Point women: "It has been my experience [in] close to fifty years in the ministry that [the women] are quite capable of handling such situations as this without any other assistance."[37] Ultimately, Somers Point authorities were inclined to agree with Stultz, a point to which I will return momentarily.

Although women and men enjoyed the nation's public swimming sites together by the 1920s, men's swimsuit codes, even if similar to those imposed on women, were not usually stressed and so received considerable attention when they were.[38] For example, in Zion City, a small town near Lake Michigan in the northernmost part of Illinois, a ruling that men's bathing suits must be long enough to cover their knees and that a "skirt flapping over the thighs must be worn" was reported by major newspapers in both Chicago and New York.[39] Apparently, the Zion City mayor and aldermen met to discuss women's dress codes but got sidetracked by an argument over styles in men's bathing suits. The mayor, who held the most conservative view among the group, contended that a person—regardless of gender—should dress as decently on the beach as in town. Several aldermen, however, protested that to require a man to wear "trousers," so designated because they extended below the knee, as well as a "skirt flapping at least halfway down his encumbered thigh," was ridiculous. "Might as well jump in the lake with your winter clothes on," argued one alderman. "As it is now, a law-abiding Zionist bound for the beach might add a sack of gum drops and look like a polar explorer. . . . It's a great mode for sedentary citizens with knobby knees and lean shanks. They are as safe from uncomplimentary comparison with the beach Hermes as if they wore overcoats. But for swimming, the Zion style is little better than a suit of armor." The meeting ended with the objectionable regulations for men's bathing suits still intact in spite of the heated debate against them. The matter of women's clothing remained unsettled as a result of the prolonged discussion.[40]

This amusing anecdote was probably viewed only as such even at the time. Reports about the incident clearly belied the smirks of the journalists who wrote them. Except that the contestants in this argument were men, however, the complaints about excessive and impractical swimwear were familiar. Women had been saying such things for years. When men found themselves censored in similar ways, however, their situation was felt to be absurd, both to themselves and to others.

The Profitable Decency Dilemma

Commodore Tanguy's willingness to serve his community as beach censor came amid what the *New York Times* described obliquely as "the situation at Somers Point." The *Times* report briefly summarized this situation as follows. Robert Crissey, the mayor of Somers Point, a small resort town only ten miles from Atlantic City, had announced that women would be permitted to wear one-piece bathing suits with no stockings. He also extended a "country-wide invitation to bathing girls to disport themselves" on the beaches of Somers Point. When the invitation was "accepted by a hundred-fold," the mayor reportedly strolled down the beach, examining the costumes of some five hundred young women, after which he announced his intention to buy his wife an "Annette Kellerman."[41]

Atlantic City news sources described events at Somers Point in considerable detail. One of the first such reports announced Mayor Crissey's reaction to the letter to Bossert in which Ada Taylor criticized Atlantic City's regulations. Expressing his agreement with Taylor's views, Crissey said, "I cordially invite Miss Taylor and all other bathers who feel that the one-piece suits are more satisfactory . . . to inspect our beach at Somers Point."[42] Shortly thereafter, according to reports, "scores of shapely maids" who were "peeved at the edict of the Atlantic City censors" made their way to the neighboring town's beach. The flood of "scantily attired damsels" tied up traffic, and many cars were parked along a highway that afforded a "fine view of the 'passing show' and the beach beyond." The young women who visited Somers Point at the mayor's invitation were a bit unprepared, however, for the more "primitive" conditions there. Described in one account as a "combination seashore and 'swimmin' hole' effect," the beach of Somers Point was less than three blocks long, and boasted no facilities.[43] The process of changing from street clothes to "water togs" was thus left to improvisation, and some bathers merely hid behind the nearby plum bushes while they dressed. The president of the Somers Point Board of Trade, John J. Arnold, announced within the week that he would have bathhouses built to accommodate the flood of visitors. By this time there was also talk about building a public park and small boardwalk at the beach.[44]

The groundswell of publicity and the presence of many scantily clad young women did not go unnoticed by those who had more conservative views on the matter of swimsuits than Somers Point's mayor had. Mrs. Mary North Chenoweth, president of the Women's Republican League of Somers Point, said: "I am not puritanical in my ideas as to bathing attire, but I think the regulations in Atlantic City permit wide enough latitude in the mode of dress for any member of my sex. The matter will be taken up officially at our meeting tomorrow night." The report in which Chenoweth was quoted also noted, however, that even if the women were to vote in favor of assigning a beach censor, the mayor had "put one over on the fair voters," having already stated that the city did not have funds for such a position.[45] Mayor Crissey may have been less calculating than this reporter suspected. Asked why he had issued his invitation to women in one-piece suits, he said that he had read in the newspaper that California towns approved these suits and so thought he would too. As to whether he considered the suits immoral he replied, "I don't know, I never saw one." Perhaps to avoid sounding overly glib, he added: "I'm told there [are] six or seven kinds of one-piece suits. We'll allow the kind that are modest. Any sensible man can tell whether or not a suit is modest, can't he?"[46] Many people were unconvinced on this point. Indeed, Crissey's actions elicited negative responses from other municipalities along the eastern seaboard. The controversy had reputedly been "a source of considerable annoyance in and about Boston," and it was expected that several welfare and antivice groups would forward "vigorous protests" to Mayor Crissey.[47]

Whether unflattering or positive, the publicity over Somers Point's relaxed dress codes undoubtedly profited the town considerably—at Atlantic City's expense—by attracting tourists who wished to experience such permissiveness for themselves and/or to observe the women who also enjoyed it. Moreover, by late June the Somers Point Chamber of Commerce prepared for an anticipated "rush of spectators," eager to watch and perhaps participate in the filming of several photoplays featuring "one piece bathing beauties." The Philadelphia-based Selznick Film Company was scheduled to arrive 6 July to begin production of not only their own commercial films but also promotional films for the city of Somers Point. As one report astutely noted, "This city is at last reaping the fruits of Mayor Robert Crissey's recent declaration . . . that fair mermaids with one piece bathing suits and bare legs will be tolerated on the beach this summer."[48]

Although the sparring between Somers Point and Atlantic City may seem curious in retrospect, Crissey was certainly not the only mayor who promoted his own town's interests by advertising its relaxed dress codes for female bathers. The mayor of St. Petersburg, Florida, Frank Fortune Pulver, for example, was pictured in a Chicago newspaper, seated on the beach, closely encircled by six young women in one-piece bathing suits, one of whom rests her chin on his shoulder. The caption beneath this photograph reads in part: "This mayor is strong for the one-piece bathing suit. . . . Kinda snuggly picture, isn't it?" Another Chicago newspaper also noted that Pulver had been asked by the local Purity League of St. Petersburg to "protect defenseless married men" by restricting "sea vamps" but that he had not complied with the request. Pulver appeared in the photograph accompanying this report as well. In this instance, six young women, each of whom wears a form-fitting one-piece suit and no stockings, look pleasantly toward the mayor, who stands in the far left corner of the picture looking back at them.[49] Such photography may have been an effective way to sell newspapers as well as an effective means to promote tourism. In any case, the widespread dissemination of these kinds of images undoubtedly had a homogenizing effect on national standards of modesty for women.

It is, of course, also likely that there were discrepancies between municipal codes as they appeared in printed legal documents and the manner and consistency with which they were actually enforced. For example, while Somers Point's mayor welcomed the nation's women to his town's relatively permissive beaches, women on the beaches of the neighboring town of Atlantic City, despite more stringent dress codes, reportedly went about in less than regulation attire, and some even went barefoot. Atlantic City "beach guards" admitted that it was often "difficult to tell where the suit stopped and the law began."[50]

Predictably, people generally found ingenious and sometimes impudent ways to circumvent unpopular clothing regulations. In Hawaii, for example, a clergyman senator, Stephen Desha of Hilo Island, unhappy with local bathers' indiscretions in public places, enacted a law that no one over fourteen years of age could appear in a swimsuit unless "covered suitably by an outer garment reaching at least to the knees." It was later announced that bathers had begun to throw bath towels and mackinaw coats around their waists, thereby keeping their knees covered. These means, one report wryly noted, "did not fully accomplish the object of the law."[51] In the early 1920s such accounts originated from all parts of the United States. It is significant that these stories were considered newsworthy even when, as in this case, they came from what was then merely a remote U.S. territory. It is also telling that, by the end of the decade, bathing costume standards were no longer of such interest. In fact, photographs indicate that, by 1930, bathing costumes that were once permitted primarily in western resort areas were worn regularly even in formerly censorious regions of the country.[52]

The declining concern over modesty in swimwear undoubtedly resulted from multiple factors. As I have already suggested, mass media surely influenced national standards of decency by drawing attention to the variety of ways these issues were handled throughout the country, thus creating a reference point by which to gauge and modify the idiosyncrasies of local norms. This principle may well have worked in reverse also, as when moviemakers were attracted to Somers Point because of the opportunity to film women in one-piece bathing suits. In either case, the mass production of photographic images, both in print and in movies, popularized fashions that might otherwise not have been as quickly introduced or accepted in certain regions.[53]

Over time, the effect of such publicity was inevitably to promote greater uniformity of modesty norms and consequently to increase tolerance for styles that, although initially thought to be offensive, were eventually accepted as a matter of course. It was in the early 1920s, however, that the erosion of Victorian-era standards of conduct for women was most conspicuous. Less voluminous styles in bathing costumes represented, for the average woman at least, the farthest possible remove from a tenacious value system that both literally and figuratively would cloak her body and check her movements. As such, these styles were most vehemently opposed by those who would have retained such a value system. Abbreviated bathing costumes were so clearly justifiable from a purely pragmatic standpoint though that proponents of practical swimwear were just as prone to be vociferous. Thus, attempts to control morality by enforcing strict bathing dress codes and attempts to exert autonomy by resisting such codes were often equally emphatic.

Performed Resistance: The Arrest of Louise Rosine

The sometimes extreme opposition between forces for and against the rights of a woman to define "suitable" bathing attire for herself are nowhere more vividly illustrated than in an incident leading to the arrest of Louise Rosine, a resident of Los Angeles who visited Atlantic City in the late summer of 1921. Rosine's rejection of what she felt were unreasonable dress codes and the circumstances surrounding her blatant defiance of them provide a vivid glimpse of the clash between opposing ideologies of "appropriate" femininity that coexisted in American culture in the early 1920s. Her story exemplifies as well the way in which history itself is a multifaceted culture appropriately encountered by ethnographic means.

Rosine's ordeal began when she refused to roll up her stockings to cover her knees when ordered to do so by a police officer.[54] News reports of the incident describe this recalcitrant woman in detail, compared with many women noted in stories about noncompliance with bathing suit regulations throughout the early 1920s. Readers learned not only her name and where she was from, but also that Rosine was a novelist, thirty-nine years of age. Several accounts of her arrest, at least four of which were in New York newspapers, quoted and paraphrased her opinions at length.[55] While such attention to her views may seem an attempt to represent her side of the story fairly, the feeling one gets when reading any of the reports of Rosine's arrest and eventual imprisonment is that of being audience to a freak show. If accurately reported, Rosine's actions were indeed unorthodox, yet her reduced status as outsider or "other" was clearly stressed by journalists. Furthermore, her arresting officer and even the warden of the prison where she was detained were portrayed as abused victims of her unruly behavior, in spite of their clearly marked status as empowered authorities in the situation.

Except for minor variations, the following report is representative of those published by New York newspapers.

> Miss Louise Rosine . . . most emphatically declared to-day it was "none of the city's business whether she 'rolled her stockings up or down,'" and is now in the City Jail in a state of mutiny and uncovered knees. She has avowed she will fight her arrest in the courts, even if it must go to the United States Supreme Court.
>
> Miss Rosine appeared on the Virginia Avenue beach this morning with her stockings rolled below her knees. Beach Policeman Edward Shaw informed her courteously that it was against the regulations here.
>
> "I most certainly will not roll 'em up," she retorted. "The city has no right to tell me how I shall wear my stockings. It is none of its business. I will go to jail first."
>
> The policeman then said he would have to take her there. As he took her by the arm she is alleged to have swung a right to the officer's eye, nearly flooring him. He recovered and blew his whistle. Life guards responded and Miss Rosine was taken to the jail in the wagon.
>
> The officer, his glasses broken and his dignity ruffled, has preferred a charge of assault and battery in addition to disorderly conduct against Miss Rosine.
>
> Advised by the police matron to roll up her stockings, the novelist still refused, and, according to the latest reports, is occupying a cell in the glory of uncovered knees. She has, further, refused to try to get bail.[56]

In contrast to New York news coverage which, as shown here, focused on the violent encounter between Rosine and Officer Edward Shaw, the *Atlantic City Daily Press* report about the incident emphasized events following her incarceration in the city's jail, as well as even more personal and, by today's standards, inappropriate commentary about Rosine herself.

Beneath the title of the local report on the arrest, a subheading proclaimed: "Arrested for Clawing Beachcop When She Refused to 'Roll 'Em Up,' Pacific Coast Visitor Takes Off Bathing Suit in Cell and 'September Morns.'" Obviously poking fun, the reporter next announced that Rosine weighed over two hundred pounds. Not content to leave this point alone, however, the reporter also stated that Rosine weighed "as much as Jack Dempsey and looks as powerful." This intentionally unflattering portrayal was repeated again in the lengthy account when, in describing her scuffle with Officer Shaw, the author noted:

> First was a righthand wallop that landed with Dempseyan precision on Shaw's nose. Then Miss Rosine crossed with her left a bit higher, smashing the policeman's glasses and ruining his coat of tan with painful lacerations. They clinched.
>
> No referee volunteered to break them and Miss Rosine, using her weight, Shaw estimated it at "210 or more," gave a snappy exhibition of in-fighting, sadly mussing up the policeman's features. Exhausted from the rain of blows, she freed Shaw, who charges she then fastened her teeth in hi[s] wrist.

A crowd of "fully 1000 persons" reportedly watched this bout, which ended when two lifeguards assisted Shaw in carrying Rosine to the beach tent where she was detained until the arrival of the patrol wagon.

Because it comprises the first one-third of the report, the story of Rosine's behavior subsequent to her incarceration takes precedence in this account. According to the "blushing warden," Wes Brubaker, Rosine, once in jail, disrobed entirely and announced her intention to remain undressed until she was freed. Although hunger strikes had been attempted under his authority, the warden was unprepared to deal with this form of rebellion. He finally called upon the assistance of two female inmates whom he instructed to pin blankets around Rosine's cell to shield her from view.

Rosine's original infractions against city bathing costume regulations are characterized only briefly in this report, specifically, that she had come "tripping out on the sands at Virginia ave. in a near one-piece suit that flirted precariously close to the legal limits. Her hosiery barely topped her ankles." The author added that the city's codes for beach apparel were "very specific," requiring full-length hosiery to be worn by "sea nymphs." Except for the presence of so many visitors in the city at this time, these details about

Atlantic City dress codes hardly needed reiteration given the flap early in the summer when they were first announced.

Rosine's opposition to Atlantic City regulations for bathing costumes and all that ensued as a result of her "mutiny," although probably exceptional and certainly extreme, are no less representative of the operative standards by which her own worth and that of her female contemporaries was determined.[57] A provocative analogue to the essential premises of this study, the incident projects a startling image of the nature of personal autonomy and resistance among women within American culture in the early 1920s. Rosine's "performed resistance," ethnograpically encountered, enhances our understanding of the complex power negotiations between an individual and her society. Clearly, gender, age, occupation, and geographic origin were perceived to be and undoubtedly were significant in this struggle. Although these aspects of Rosine's identity apparently qualified as newsworthy, their relevance to her arrest is never articulated within the narrative accounts. Why were these personal details mentioned? Did Rosine herself emphasize them? For example, was it important to her or to her captors (or both) that she was a novelist? What were the connotations of this term when applied to a woman? How was the fact that Rosine was from Los Angeles significant? Did that mark her as "just a tourist"? Would a "hometown girl" have been treated in the same manner? Does the fact that Rosine was thirty-nine years old make her behavior less acceptable? How might her marital status, denoted by the frequent use of "Miss," figure into this scenario?

These kinds of questions may in part be explicated by means of parallel and corroborative investigation, some of which I have already presented. For example, to document the broader context of fashion and its censorship in America at this time is to effectively frame the cultural landscape within which Rosine finds herself abused as well as abuser. To understand that certain regions of the country were more censorious than others regarding women's fashions is to know that Rosine, as a visitor to Atlantic City, may well have felt justified in her noncompliance with local and, to her way of thinking, provincial codes of conduct. Indeed, another Los Angeles visitor to Atlantic City during the great debacle earlier in the summer had been quoted in a news column as saying that in the former city "there is no decree against one-piece robes or Annette Kellermans. And they let the mermaids on the Pacific coast bathe without socks if they care to."[58]

Even a cursory examination of women's fashion in the 1920s reveals, moreover, that a youthful and slim appearance was considered ideal. The fashion industry itself was quite unambiguous as to which women looked best in the newest styles, and it communicated this information largely through the women it selected as models. But there were clearly many other means by which permission was granted or denied to women who wished to dress fashionably. As I discussed in chapter 2 and as I will reiterate in chapter 4, reformers commonly belittled some women in the apparent attempt to shame them into dressing "appropriately."

Certainly, Rosine was perceived to be obese, but undoubtedly she was also considered too old to be dressed as she was according to standards of beauty that had by this time come into vogue. Age was clearly a factor in these bathing costume controversies, not only in terms of differing feminist philosophies but also in terms of aesthetics and propriety. One Kentucky senator, for example, speaking in support of a bill he had proposed to regulate women's swimwear and thus "protect the eyes of the old men and the morals of the young men," claimed that it was "an awfully pitiful sight to see an old, grayhaired woman with her skirts above her knees."[59] Rosine's "unacceptable" body presence, coupled with her willingness to expose that presence, was itself an act of nonconformity. Although an attractive, unmarried flapper of twenty might sun herself on the sands of a resort area without drawing suspicion, an overweight, thirty-nine-year-old single woman who proclaimed herself a novelist and vacationed far from home, apparently without a companion, was surely trying to create a stir. After all, even flappers, at some point in their youth, were expected to settle down as devoted wives and mothers.[60] In these ways, Rosine not only defied the beach codes of Atlantic City but much more pervasive cultural expectations about femininity as well.

Contemporaneous reports from Atlantic City and elsewhere provide a sense of both the physical and emotional climate of the city such that Rosine's extraordinary revolt in late summer 1921, although no less surprising, appears more rationally motivated. Knowledge of the controversy over bathing codes early in the season certainly complicates our reaction to news accounts of Rosine's experiences in Atlantic City. And it is only fair to point out that September 1921 was, by all accounts, the end of a long, very hot summer. Not only parts of the United States but regions of Asia and Europe as well had endured extended and extreme heat and drought.[61] The day Rosine was arrested, the *New York Herald* reported that temperatures had reached record highs the previous day and that no relief was expected before the next evening. Seven people had been "prostrated" as a result of the intense heat, and one woman from Port Chester died.[62] Also in the *Herald*, a local weather summary for 3 September, the day of Rosine's arrest, showed that humidity was at 80 percent by eight o'clock that morning, and by noon the temperature had already reached 88 degrees, still 3 degrees shy of the day's high.

Perhaps no one perceived any irony in the fact that these weather statistics appeared directly above the story of Rosine's arrest for having her stockings rolled below her knees.[63] Indeed, neither New York nor Atlantic City accounts of the arrest in any way acknowledged the possibility that Rosine rolled down her stockings quite simply because, like everyone else on the

East Coast, she was hot—unless a reference to Rosine's incarceration as the authorities' attempt to "let her cool off" counts as such.[64]

In addition to the likelihood that extreme heat and humidity motivated and probably exacerbated Rosine's response to Officer Shaw, she must also have observed the growing fanfare and bustling activity preceding the city's imminent Bathers' Revue and thus was unprepared for her own rude reception at the beach. The front page of the 3 September *Atlantic City Daily Press* contained extensive coverage of the preparations underway for this "great Carnival affair."[65] Columnists noted the welcome presence of many tourists as well as the extra effort needed to accommodate them in the city's already heavily booked hotels. An entry blank for the upcoming Bathers' Revue was also printed in the local newspaper. Reports stressed the fact that all entrants were required to wear bathing costumes, as well as the need for full participation in this civic celebration. Announcements described several categories within the Bathers' Revue, including divisions for organizations, children, men, and of course, "beauties." The overall Grand Prize would be awarded to the young woman selected as "America's Most Beautiful Bathing Girl" from among the beauty contest winners from other cities who would come to Atlantic City to compete for this title. None other than Annette Kellerman donated the prize, a silver cup. And no doubt to the consternation of Mrs. John White, the second-place winner would receive an Annette Kellerman swimsuit.[66]

Although local newspapers played an essential role in publicizing these upcoming events, encouraging Atlantic City guests and residents alike to participate in the Bathers' Revue, the *Atlantic City Daily Press*, perhaps inadvertently, likely discouraged many women from joining the ranks of "beauties" who competed for the Grand Prize. Beneath a photograph of Josephine Charles, sister of the woman who had been chosen to represent Atlantic City in the upcoming pageant, a caption reads: "Although Miss Charles is very pretty, she did not stand a chance among the many entries." Clearly a climate of evaluation was already well established, and women were the primary objects of study, whether "pretty" like Charles or "Dempseyan" like Rosine.

Rosine's enactment of resistance, properly configured, seems outrageous, yes, but not without a certain logic. We may easily imagine the anger she felt. As a tourist, Rosine should have received not censure but the same welcome so generously extended to others who, at the city's invitation, had come to celebrate. As a woman, Rosine must have been doubly offended that, although others were in fact being encouraged to join in the bathing beauty portion of the revue, the requisite qualifications were highly selective and plainly excluded women like herself.

Just as Rosine's defiance and punishment in early September 1921 were not isolated events detached from contextual and precursory influences, the

newly created Atlantic City bathing beauty contest itself was also both product and process of ongoing cultural transformations. As I suggested earlier,
Atlantic City depended on, even vied for income from tourism, especially
during the summer months. The "situation" at Somers Point shows to what
lengths competitors went to attract tourists to their own towns. After the negative publicity it received early in the summer, coupled with Mayor Crissey's
unorthodox tactics, Atlantic City undoubtedly needed the financial boost that
a bathers' revue would provide. Furthermore, what better way to respond
to the bitter complaints that the city was unduly strict in regulating bathing
costumes than a beauty contest whose winners received Annette Kellerman
swimsuits as prizes? These circumstantial considerations must be identified
in a worthy analysis of the inception of the Miss America pageant in 1921.
Along with such immediate contextual factors, it is also necessary to investigate earlier moments in the development of this national ritual. In other
words, in addition to particular moments of cultural transformation, as the
1921 pageant and events surrounding it indeed represent, we must explore
what is, in essence, the history of the history. All such information contributes
to a sensory, embodied, and, one hopes, truthful accounting of the performed
events of history.

It is, of course, widely accepted that the revolution in industry in the
nineteenth century provided many people with more time to pursue leisure
activities. Furthermore, as A. R. Riverol notes, the industrial revolution ush-
ered in an "age of leisure" and "industries associated with leisure sprang
up, including carnivals, fairs, circuses, musical theatre, Wild West Shows,
amusement parks, and sea side resorts." Women were heavily exploited by
the various amusement industries. Although paid for her contributions, it is
not difficult to recognize that a woman's employment as entertainment at this
time was, quite simply, her commodification. Entrepreneurs like P. T. Barnum and "Wild Bill" Cody found that "freaks, animals, and Indians" could
attract a paying audience, but so too could women. "The time for beauty as a
legitimate, socially approved, financial commodity had arrived, transforming
women from the prize to the priced."[67] Carnivals and freak shows notwithstanding, producers of even more "respectable" theatrical venues found that
the display of women, particularly in scanty attire, was lucrative business.
This point is, in fact, a central feature of my analysis in subsequent chapters.

Within this curious and dissonant sociocultural milieu, which found its
members simultaneously applauding and prohibiting a woman's right to display her body publicly, emerged a new social phenomenon, the American
beauty pageant. Lois W. Banner traces the historical development of this
venue from approximately the beginning of the nineteenth century and acknowledges multiple precursors to the culminating 1921 Atlantic City contest.[68] Riverol, while citing Banner's conclusions extensively in his history of

the Miss America pageant, narrowly defines prerequisite events and thereby shortens the developmental phase substantially, compared with Banner's record. He contends that pageants "as we know them today could not have existed anytime in our history outside the last hundred or so years. Before then, social conditions made the respectable, institutional, flagrant, and profitable exposition of scantily clad girls before a paying audience inconceivable."[69] Whereas Banner includes many types of contests in which winners were selected or elected as pageant antecedents, Riverol includes only those events that "base the selection of winners on the decision of judges who must operate under formal rules and criteria as well as on the basis of informal traditions and standards."[70] In either case, the American beauty pageant certainly owes its existence in part to such events as nineteenth-century May Day celebrations, widely varying festivals in which there were "competitions for the gauge of beauty," as well as Twelfth Night parties and tournaments that included rituals related to the selections of a "queen" and, not infrequently, a "king" as well.[71]

P. T. Barnum is generally credited with initiating, in 1854, the first American beauty contest. Presuming that the display of physical beauty on stage had become an accepted practice in American society, given the success of many theatrical ventures that did so, Barnum invited entries to his contest and promised lavish prizes to the winner. However, when it became clear— due to the questionable reputations of the entrants—that the contest was morally suspect, Barnum changed its format and judged contestants on the basis of daguerreotype submissions rather than in-person appearances. The contest, so altered, then became widely popular. Indeed, many businesses copied Barnum's format in promotional efforts well into the early twentieth century.[72] Eventually, of course, the actual physical presence of beauty contestants became commonplace at dime museum, fair, and carnival beauty contests. Still, the use of judges to evaluate the physical merits of young women remained somewhat taboo until modeling became a socially sanctioned career for women in the early part of the twentieth century.[73]

In his history of the Miss America Pageant, Frank Deford names the "Miss United States" competition, held in 1880 at the resort town of Rehoboth Beach, Delaware, as the event most closely approximating the 1921 Atlantic City pageant. Although the Delaware contest was not repeated, it nonetheless included most of the now standard components: unmarried contestants who were physically attractive, prizes, and judges, among whom, incidentally, was one Thomas Alva Edison. Another now predictable feature was the 1880 contest winner's response to her good fortune. When announced as the first "Miss United States," Myrtle Meriwether "almost fainted from shock and trembled like an aspen when she was led forward."[74]

While this first American beauty pageant clearly foreshadowed the later and immensely more successful Miss America pageant, the 1880 contest lacked one important feature that might have ensured it a more prominent place in the history of beauty pageants in the United States, that is, a bathing suit competition. As I noted earlier, public bathing in 1880 was an awkward prospect at best, but by 1921 both beauty contests and swimming were popular pastimes. Staged performances of physical beauty, especially revues, had become widely accepted in the theater, due largely to Florenz Ziegfeld Jr.'s annual *Follies* productions. A by-product of all of these trends, the American beauty pageant now easily assumed a niche within the entertainment industry. Credit goes to H. Conrad Eckholm, owner of the Monticello Hotel in Atlantic City, who "hit on the scheme of displaying female bodies outside the confines of the vaudeville revue. He devised an idea for a beauty pageant with the bathing suit competition as its centerpiece."[75] Eckholm convinced the Atlantic City Business Men's League of the potentially profitable nature of such an event, and plans for a full-scale civic celebration of young American female beauty began.[76]

When judges declared sixteen-year-old Margaret Gorman of Washington, D.C., "the most beautiful bathing girl in America," no one seemed to mind that she was wearing her stockings rolled below her knees, nor did anyone seem to care that, just five days earlier, another woman had been taken away in a patrol wagon for wearing her own stockings in such a manner. Pictures of Gorman, bare knees in plain view, were even published on the front pages of Atlantic City newspapers (fig. 29).[77] Moreover, another newspaper photo presented several young women who "starred" in the Bathers' Revue, and in the center of the group was one Ada Taylor, "champion of the one-piece suit."[78] In the pivotal summer of 1921, the question of beach modesty in Atlantic City thus appeared to be settled on the side of less restrictiveness in bathing attire, in spite of vigorous protests by the likes of Mrs. John J. White.

Perhaps it is more accurate to say that the question of modesty was simply no longer being asked, at least not publicly. One observer did note, however: "The Bathers' Revue was remarkable for the uncensored costumes. One-piece suits were the rule rather than the exception. Nude limbs were in evidence everywhere—and not a guardian of the law molested the fair sea nymphs who pranced about the sands. Every type of beauty was on exhibition, shown to its best advantage in the cut of sea togs permitted. It was a vision of beauty unrivalled in any beach carnival the coast has seen before." While onlookers watched from the boardwalk, the "mile-long line of mermaids" paraded from the Garden Pier to the Steel Pier, the latter of which, notably, was located on the Virginia Avenue beach where Rosine was arrested.[79]

Clearly, censorious codes of personal modesty that quite literally limited a woman's freedom were relaxed on the occasion of this first Miss America

FIG. 29. 1921 Miss America Wearing Stockings Below Her Knees. Margaret Gorman, Winner, Second From Left. AP/Wide World Photos.

pageant, not for reasons of practicality nor as a response to broader ethical concerns for human autonomy. Instead, these proscriptions were apparently reduced in deference to the financial interests of hotel owners in Atlantic City who wished to lengthen the summer beach season.[80] Couched in the rhetoric of civic and national pride, this pageant appeared at first glance to be an affirmation of American women and secondarily a concession to their preferences in bathing costumes. This perspective is difficult to maintain, however, if one is mindful that, meanwhile, Louise Rosine kept her strange and lonely vigil in the city's "hoosegow," as the party went on without her.

Subversive Stories I: Mae West

As the Miss America pageant gained notoriety, it was more frequently criticized by those who suspected that there was in fact a dark side to its influence. Few of her contemporaries were as quick to recognize or call attention to the paradoxes of 1920s American culture, especially as manifest in its attitudes toward women, than Mae West. Her unpublished play, *The Wicked Age*, or *The Contest* (1927), indeed quite pointedly deprecates the beauty pageant phenomenon of the 1920s.[81] In this work, West depicts pageants as merely a strategy to promote commercial enterprise. Further, she criticizes women who participate in such pageants by portraying them in an unflattering way.

West's play opens with an argument over a beauty contest proposed for Bridgeton, New Jersey, the town where most of the play is set. Warren Hathaway, one of several businessmen considering the proposal contends: "This town has come to a situation in its life— where it cannot stand still— it needs boosting." Robert Carson, an opponent of the pageant, responds: "No one would want to see this little town grow more than I— But not at the expense of our women—." One of the primary pageant promoters, who is not from Bridgeton but whose job it is to "sell" the beauty contest idea to towns that want to grow, counters Carson by saying that he has taken the "wrong attitude" and that for fifteen years "we have been putting towns on the map in the same way—."[82] The committee schedules the pageant over Robert Carson's protests, and his own daughter, a prototypical flapper named Babe, wins the beauty contest. The rebellious Babe next sets her sights on Atlantic City, hoping to become the "most beautiful girl in the world" with a bit of help from the influential Alec Ferguson, who will "fix" things for her at the Miss America pageant.[83]

Whether Babe Carson ever reigns as Miss America is immaterial to this play, and in fact the play ends before any such thing happens. West seems primarily concerned in this work with the broader implications of the exploitation of females in the entertainment industry. Her critique of beauty pageants is of course not subtle; she pointedly uses this play to accuse beauty pageants specifically but also the entire American entertainment system of commodifying the female body. Through the character of Ferguson, West contends:

> The basis of any industry that needs immediate attention of the public for success today is based on the exploitation of the female form—I can prove my case. Let us take any business that depends on the public for support. Take the theatre, which plays get over, and make money for their producers, those that try to uplift the public and teach it bigger and better ways of living— Don't make me laugh— Those plays go over that exhibit the woman's body in some way or another. . . . [L]ook at the musical comedies—with their beautiful curtains of living beauties—their tableaux, their beautiful scenes—everything is an excuse for a horde of almost naked women to parade up and down the stage, to give the out of town buyers a kick—[84]

If *The Wicked Age* accurately reflects West's personal views, she plainly felt that beauty contests were part of a parasitic system by which men profited at the expense of women. Further, she seems keenly aware of the personal and social effects of this exploitation. Robert Carson, for example, who believes that the "fall of every great nation in the past has been preceded by the immodesty of its womanhood," questions Jack Stratford, a member of the Bridgeton committee who favors the idea of a beauty contest: "How would you like your sister to be on exhibition before a mob of morons—while they passed all sorts of vulgar remarks about her and at her—put on exhibition like prize cattle while they judged her fine points—"[85] Stratford weakly counters that "times have changed" and that "we are living in a fast age." Carson retorts, "Wicked Age."[86]

West seemingly uses the character of Lottie Gilmore, a former actress and model who in her old age supports herself by selling lingerie, to critique a system that places a premium on a woman's appearance over nearly every other consideration. Lottie's pitiful circumstances show the consequences of such a system over time. The elderly woman warns Babe that "when you start to lose your youth and beauty no one wants to win[e] and dine you then—there is always someone there to take your place, younger, more beautiful, so the thing is to guard it, treasure it, hold on to it as long as you can . . . when you've once been the toast of the town, when you once have the world at your feet and you lose it—that's the time it hurts." After Lottie leaves Babe's room, Babe imagines herself an old woman and abruptly discards the cocaine she keeps nearby.[87]

Given the feminist themes of *The Wicked Age*, it may seem incongruous that West was herself criticized, even imprisoned, for her allegedly indecent performance earlier in 1927, the same year this exposition on the devastating sexism of the entertainment system was first produced. I believe, however, that this play suggests that West's own participation in a system that so exploited women's bodies was, first of all, a conscious one and, second, not a little self-exploitation. Her career in fact was surely nothing less than a shrewd ploy to appropriate her own body to garner for herself the financial rewards men usually procured from women's performances. In this sense, West fits naturally within the ranks of those many resourceful women in the 1920s who, while not able or perhaps even willing to completely eradicate systemic injustices against themselves, nonetheless managed to transform such injustices for their own ends.

Subversive Stories II: "Mrs. Brown"

The popular men's sporting magazine, *Outing*, offered a lengthy, detailed, highly textured narrative that may or may not represent an actual experience but nonetheless provides valuable insight into female performances of the ritual of public bathing in the 1920s. As a personal narrative, it also exemplifies the value of this kind of primary resource within an ethnographic exploration of performed history. Such stories provide an insider's perspective, often directly explaining motives for personal acts of resistance, conformity, and perhaps more interesting, exposing the methods by which performers transpose proscribed ritualistic behaviors for their own purposes. The author's self-deprecating humor in describing her attempts to learn to swim reflects her intense awareness of bodily display as a prime feature of this activity. She notes, for example: "In an abrupt resolve to do the thing right, I had donned a one-piece suit. I am not a large woman, not fat; that is, not as fat as many others whom I could name, but a one-piece suit stretched over one hundred and eighty-five fairish pounds, feels as conspicuous as a red lantern. I know."[88] Similarly,

> Have you ever stood daringly submerged to your waist in the surf, grasping the lifeline and clinging to it desperately as each succeeding wave threatened to upset you, and have one of those beautiful sea-nymphs with naturally curly hair looking sleek as a seal in a one-piece suit come splashing by, laughing over her shoulder at a bronzed young giant who follows? A bronzed young giant follows a sea-nymph, always.[89]

This plaintive admission indeed offers the reader insight as to the motives beneath the surface action of the plot illuminated in the remainder of the essay.

"Mrs. Brown" (or "Rufus Brown's wife") and her four young children are at a seaside resort while her husband is away on business in Chicago. As Mrs. Brown later confesses, "It is a modest wish, perhaps, but I have always wanted to go to Chicago. And I have always wanted to take a trip anywhere with Rufus, but he has never dreamed of asking me before. My sphere is so obviously the domestic one."[90] Perhaps her limited sphere also helps to explain Mrs. Brown's heightened sensitivity to the public nature of the ordeals that follow. Deciding to try to overcome her sense of humiliation on the beach, Mrs. Brown asks a handsome young lifeguard employed at the resort to give her swimming lessons. He agrees to help her, and her first appointment is set for ten o'clock in the morning or, as Mrs. Brown describes it, "the hour at which everyone who is anyone in Sunshine Beach, gathers in the natatorium for recreation and amusement. Particularly amusement."[91] A keen sense of herself as performer pervades this experience and, after a number of embarrassing failures, Mrs. Brown finally learns to swim. She even attempts the "f-stout woman's jack-knife," so named by Billy the lifeguard. Her actual success with this dive is unclear as the narrative is filtered, not by Mrs. Brown's own view of the experience but by her perception of the reaction of her audience.

While legally enacted censorship is missing from this account, other forms of social control are indicated in Mrs. Brown's confession that "[t]he impression of that dive that has remained longest with me is, what extraordinarily disagreeable laughs summer resort idlers have" and, still referring to her jackknife dive, "Well, I kept at that thing for two weeks and I must have improved a lot because I heard a man say to another man that it was worth the price of admission to see me."[92] Even her children would join in the gaping throng, as it were, adding to what seems an extreme and all-pervasive level of public scrutiny of a woman who, undaunted, dares to challenge norms of appropriate display for heavy, middle-aged wives and mothers. Assigned by Billy the task of going home to "practice," that is to "[l]ie on your stomach on the piano stool in front of the parlor mirror and go like a frog," Mrs. Brown forgoes her homework. "But I did not 'practice.' I have small children. Have you a mental picture of a keenly interested group pushing each other away from the parlor door key hole?"[93]

Ultimately, despite her relative audacity, Mrs. Brown comfortably resumes her family-centered priorities, the ones that presumably would have most reassured the audience she addressed in a generally male-oriented sporting magazine. Realizing that she has been spotted spending time with the handsome lifeguard by one of her husband's friends, Mrs. Brown contrives a plan to have Billy send her husband an anonymous telegram with the message: "Better come home. Wife carrying on intrigue with handsome life-guard. Beach scandal." When Rufus Brown returns home suddenly, much agitated by the news he has received, she chides him for believing such gossip. Later, when the furor subsides, Mr. Brown himself proposes his wife's next performance. "Get some spiffy clothes in town to-morrow, and bring along that one-piece thing you tell about. There's a swell natatorium in Chicago. I'll bet you can make them open their eyes!" Even the youthful Billy, a key player throughout, is brought in for a final appearance in which he responds precisely on cue. After paying him for his trouble on her behalf, Mrs. Brown admits:

> "It's worth more than that to me, Billy. I've excited a husband who for years has taken his wife as he has taken his meals—for granted. And that's not all—I've lost ten pounds." I pivoted on one toe; six weeks ago this couldn't have been done. "How do I look in this blue serge, eh?"
>
> "Slim, Mrs. Brown, slim."[94]

This narrative, thinly veiled as humor and probably contrived, only partially manages to conceal a troubling configuration of performer, audience(s), and cultural context. The self-censorship depicted in this account, comprised of the performer's sense of embarrassment, inadequacy, ridicule, and impropriety speaks profoundly of the body as a powerful site of cultural control.

Remarkably, the disparaged body of Mrs. Brown was her primary cultural collateral. She contended for and appropriated to her advantage the very power that others appeared to have over her body, whether that power took the form of superior knowledge, such as that of the lifeguard/teacher; the possessive relationships of husband and children; or the power of an audience to ridicule. Hers was an act of resistance to the cultural hegemony that would have defined for her appropriate modes and norms of performance. Granted, Mrs. Brown was duplicitous in retrieving even a portion of her power, but this aspect of her resistance serves to accentuate both the power she does not possess and her determination to possess it. Publicizing such a stratagem via a men's magazine would have been extraordinary in itself were it not for the way in which this narrative ultimately reinforced the very norms Mrs. Brown seemed initially to be contesting and the ones that it was to her readers' advantage to retain. But like a burlesque that mocks both performer and performed, challenging as well as enabling the values it parodies, Mrs. Brown's performances were also coyly and expertly managed, with precision accuracy as to how far was far enough.[95]

Conclusions

The radical changes in fashion—including the changes in women's swimwear —allowing women freer movement and increased body display were part of a transformation that, thought it began somewhat earlier, by 1920 had registered resoundingly in the public consciousness. Many assumed, and still do, that these less restrictive clothing styles for women went hand-in-hand with less restrictive moral and behavioral codes.[96] The sport historian Donald J. Mrozek suggests, however, that the 1920s were by no means an era of "new morality," as is commonly believed. He especially differs with those who suppose(d) that increased public display by women proved that sexual mores were changing. He states that "although opportunities for public display broadened, significant constraints on the manner of display remained. This emphasis on *how* one engaged in public activities became a hallmark."[97]

Furthermore, while 1920s fashions for women suggested an active, even athletic lifestyle, this "look" was just that, as posing took precedence over accomplishment. Mrozek also notes: "Though stylistically different from some of the more static images of women in the nineteenth century, this new vivacity and dynamism extended the restrictive tradition of decoration rather than that of public achievement."[98] In short, surface emblems of increased autonomy for women in the 1920s are misleading. As "decorations" their lives were still quite contained, although clearly some women were quite ingenious and even brave in attempting to stretch their confines.

In my examination of the performance of fashion, I too challenge the notion, based as often as not on flapper folklore, that the American 1920s represent a high-water mark in female autonomy. Rather than suggest that increased opportunity for body display via fashion truly represented a woman's greater autonomy or even a significant shift in American attitudes toward morality, I contend that the female body and, consequently, the fashions a woman wore were crucial sites for the contestation and negotiation of authority. This alternative emphasis, essentially a body-as-site rather than body-as-symbol focus, may well clarify to the extent that it complicates our perception of what it meant to be female in the 1920s.

FIG. 30. Gloria Swanson, Popular Actress, from *The Walgreen Health and Beauty Magazine*, n.d., n.p.

The Right to Bare

Containing and Encoding American Women in the Popular Theater

> Some of the so-called best people in the profession are
> using the "shimmy shake" in song, dance and pantomime.
> Barefoot dancing with naked limbs being shown through
> transparent nets, abbreviated skirts, with flesh colored
> tights emphasizing the form and contour of the body
> by effective colored lights, are all a part of the nefarious
> business which escapes the ban under the guise of "art."
>
> —Anonymous vice investigator, 1920

The decade following World War I was at once the most tempestuous and the most productive in the history of the American theater.[1] The theater experienced the same schizophrenia that characterized the social milieu in which it thrived; the serious dramatic efforts of Susan Glaspell and Eugene O'Neill played concurrently with the frolicsome farces of Avery Hopwood and the mesmerizing revues of Florenz Ziegfeld. During this period of American history that was so clearly marked by profound sociocultural dissonance, mores by which society governed itself were held up under the stage lights and critically examined, disputed, often mocked, and sometimes affirmed. The American theater was, as usual, extremely vulnerable to the attack of reformers who felt it their solemn duty to regulate public taste and to safeguard morality. In fact, when reviewing the voluminous discourse about the American theater of the 1920s written by those who were present to observe it, it is often difficult to determine where aesthetic criticisms leave off and accusations of immorality begin.[2]

Although his campaign against what he felt were the offenses of the theater began well before the 1920s, the evangelist Billy Sunday spoke for many who would come after him when he said:

> If you want obscenity you will find it in the theater. . . . The capacity for amusing people along decent lines seems to have gone by. That may sound foolish, but you let somebody go out on the road with a Shakespearean play and that somebody will go into bankruptcy while the musical show and the burlesque show and the leg show are playing to full houses across the street and the people are drinking in from them gutterish ideas and filthy lines and obscene songs.[3]

In 1926, a writer for the *Literary Digest* declared that, indeed, stage reform was the "problem which, next to Prohibition, probably causes more wrangling in press and pulpit than any other in which moral interests are involved."[4] Given the tenor of the times and especially the variety of shows produced whose main attraction was women in provocative attire, attempts to reform the theater were probably inevitable.

Many public forums were host to debates about the immorality of the American theater generally and American women especially. Rev. John Roach Straton, for example, was as apt to conduct his tirades in theater trade magazines as in the pulpit of his own church. The general tone of diatribes against women who did not conform to the narrow criteria for conduct that such moralists preferred is effectively illustrated by a sermon Straton preached to his congregation on 26 June 1921. Having already condemned the shorter skirts women had begun to wear in recent years in the poem with which I opened chapter 2, Straton then pontificated: "Yes, I believe that there is a good time coming when maidenly modesty, instead of brazen sex assertiveness, will prevail, and we live in hope of the harmony of that better day when the principles of purity and womanly sweetness and grace will be triumphant."[5] The ideology implicit in Straton's remarks is clear, its Victorian logic readily discernible. Women establish the moral climate of society. The defining aspect of a woman's character is her attitude toward sexuality. Her aloofness toward her own or anyone else's sexuality serves as a hallmark of her good character.[6] Furthermore or by extension, this attitude is typified by her aversion to self-display. Reformers like Straton maintained such reasoning staunchly as they worked to rid American society, as well as its theaters, of the evil influence of the Sexual Woman.[7]

On the other hand, those who dubbed Straton and others of his ilk as prudes were equally inclined to announce their expectations of women, especially those women who earned a living in America's theaters. Censorship of the theater in the United States during the 1920s has been noted frequently;

certainly, the Wales Padlock Law, enacted in 1927, is generally recognized as a milestone in the history of American censorship.[8] Fewer scholars, however, have explored the decade with a view toward understanding the circumscribed nature of theatrical performances by women or the precise means by which women's performances were, in fact, contained.[9] The outcries of moralists were so strident that it is tempting to presume that they effectively commanded the attention if not the actions of their generation.

We may well suppose that the forcefulness of these reformers' demands bolstered their efforts to control the American theater and, in turn, the women who substantially comprised it. However, I contend that while moral prejudices and preferences were the most obvious traits of discourse that advocated censorship of the American theater and the women who worked within it, as with the censorship of fashion, there were less obtrusive ideological assumptions embedded within such discourse. These assumptions proved over time to be equally, if not more, influential in containing the performances, careers, and ultimately the lives of American women. In this chapter I attend especially to the enshrinement and circumscription of women in performances that were primarily visual in appeal, in an effort to identify the ways in which the iconicity of the female body was thereby amplified in American culture. I will focus on responses to women's performances in "leg shows" of the 1920s—by which I mean primarily burlesque and revues —as these vehicles most consistently and conspicuously appropriated the female image.

The aesthetic theorist Francette Pacteau describes the image of woman as cultural "hieroglyph": even the abstract notion of "woman" evokes a body image, clearly implicating a "corporeality" that "suffuses the woman's relationship to the environment of signs."[10] Similarly, the art historian Anne Hollander contends: "On the reverse of any picture of a naked woman . . . is printed her image as sexual power, an image that seems always to show through."[11] Indeed, a sidelong glance at the mud flaps of a semi truck is proof enough of how the mere silhouette of the female body translates into a sexual message. How, in fact, have we come to the point where the female form is such an instantaneously recognizable emblem for sex? Although I have outlined the historical influence of 1920s fashion in this regard, I believe some answers to this question are also to be found in an analysis of the ideological terrain between the censure and sanction of female display in popular entertainments of the past.

Within most performance venues of the 1920s, including but not limited to burlesque and revues, the female body was appropriated extensively as a sexual signifier (frontispiece and fig. 31). Erotic meanings were disguised, albeit ineffectively, by other agendas—the promotion of consumerism, patriotism, and even civic pride. The encoding of the female body in sexually

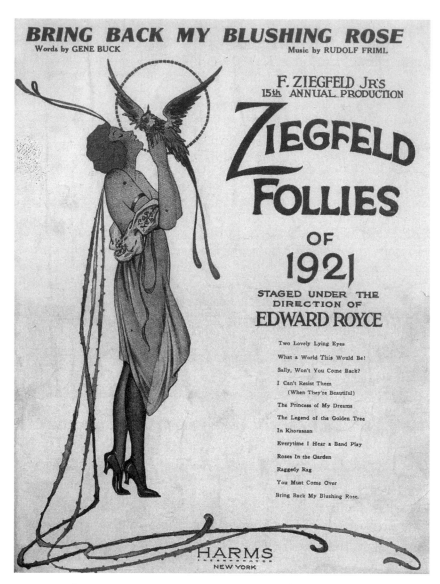

FIG. 31. *Follies* Sheet Music, 1921.

explicit ways was thus made more palatable, at least to some. The farther the remove between the connotations of her body and the actual experiences or aims of her life, however, the more detrimental her body iconicity became to a woman. Thus, when a woman's body came to stand almost exclusively for her sexual potential, as it certainly did in some of the most popular entertainments of this decade, her personal worth was also, more often than not, summarized on the basis of her physical allure. When she ceased to appeal to her audience as an object of sexual pleasure, she usually ceased to have a career.

Clearly, there were those as well to whom the care with which a woman cloaked rather than displayed her sexuality was a crucial measure of her worth. Ultimately though, this perspective also attributed little significance to unique aspects of a woman's identity or purpose. To those more concerned with concealing or at least muting a woman's sexuality, acceptable display was governed by the nebulous and, as my discussion of fashion indicated, highly contested concept of "modesty." Displays of the female body were most easily justified within a performance framework. The popularity of leg shows and bathers' revues alike suggests just that, especially given that performers in each of these venues frequently transgressed the usual standards of feminine propriety. Simply stated, entertaining women were allowed to display their bodies in ways that were otherwise considered immodest. And when she performed for the pleasure of others, a woman was granted permission to break the same rules that limited her own pleasure in other circumstances; in fact, she was usually well compensated for her willingness to break such rules. In the effort to gain body autonomy and economic autonomy as well, then, the theater was a place where at least some women enjoyed a comparatively large measure of independence.

Faye E. Dudden has discussed the paradoxical nature of performance, particularly its capacity to function both as a means of personal empowerment and as a strategy by which one may exploit another for personal gratification. Specifically, Dudden stresses that the "theatrical enterprise . . . contains two divergent possibilities for women: transformation and objectification. Theater may enable women to rehearse the most radical projects of self-creation or may reduce them to bodies and present them as objects. Theater may do either of these, or both, or neither."[12] Indeed, although performance afforded some women greater autonomy in the 1920s, the relative novelty of a woman's displayed body was interpreted by others as proof of a sexual agenda. In terms of her exposed body, perceptual distinctions between female presence and performance were negligible, confounding a woman's embodied experience of life and vividly inscribing the iconicity of the female body in the cultural consciousness.

The Beauty Clause

Although immorality was the most predictable charge levied against controversial theatrical displays by women in the 1920s, there were several other
premises on which performances by women were censured. One of the most
binding proscriptions against women was that a pleasing physical appearance, exclusively defined, was the essential prerequisite for a successful career in the theater. This is not to say that attractive and successful female
performers lacked talent. Talent, however, was rarely, if ever, enough; good
looks were indispensable.[13]

Even among those who advocated that theater reform must include the
censorship of female nudity, many were reluctant to banish *all* such nudity
but rather the nudity of *some* women. The dancer Ted Shawn, for instance,
asserted:

> The only thing that it is shameful to expose is ugliness. To look at a nude woman
> whose breasts are flabby and discolored, whose body is gross and fat—pro-
> duces only nausea and disgust. To see the naked body of one who is healthy,
> strong, symmetrical and of noble proportion is to experience a sense of divine
> revelation, and one is moved to something akin to exaltation.[14]

Shawn's opinion, while expressed more graphically than some, was by no
means atypical. In the not so convincing guise of humor, another writer noted
the theatrical trend toward a "constantly more daring display of feminine
nakedness." Contesting the usual justification for such exhibitions, that is, the
aesthetic appeal of the human—but specifically female—form, the author
retorted:

> The truth is that they are simply ludicrous, due to the fact that the "human
> form divine" has done considerable backsliding in the past few hundred years.
> Knees and elbows, and waist lines and other things, are not what they used to
> be. The cavorting of a 200 lb. twentieth century Venus in the altogether is not
> exactly a spectacle to delight the gods.[15]

Body shame has long been one of the most powerful yet insidious forms
of censorship. From the Creation story of Genesis to present-day fashion
magazines, women learn that their bodies are not good or at least not good
enough. Modesty is, after all, a highly contingent virtue and needs most to
be practiced by the unworthy. Methods of censorship by ridicule, directed
against those with "undesirable" bodies who do not otherwise take the hint
and keep covered, is articulated clearly in the essays excerpted here. Although

presumably directed toward female performers, these comments surely elicited at least a moment of self-evaluation among other women as well: Are my breasts flabby? What does he mean by discolored? Is there a *correct* breast color? How are elbows supposed to look? And so on.

Undoubtedly, neither of the writers quoted here would have counted themselves censors. Nevertheless, they shared with the Stratons of their day the same desire to banish from the stage all but what squared with their own sensibilities. One assumes that women whose forms appealed to their personal tastes would have been welcome to "cavort" across a stage in the "altogether." Indeed, in spite of the cries of moralists, nudity was common theatrical fare even by the early 1920s, especially in revues, with more to come soon in burlesque. However, the women who performed in revues were, as a rule, carefully selected on the basis of exacting standards of appearance. Theater producers were highly influential in establishing the tenets of beauty by which American women were judged. No one was more influential in this regard than Florenz Ziegfeld Jr.

In the late 1910s and early 1920s, Ziegfeld wrote several articles for popular magazines in which he described in excruciating detail the qualities he looked for in selecting women for his revues. In those essays, Ziegfeld usually assumed an advisory tone, giving beauty and career tips to women, a demeanor he also assumed in product endorsements (fig. 32). His opinions on the subject of female beauty were not merely the stuff of which advice columns or advertisements were made, however; they were considered "news" as well. James Whittaker, in a report that appeared in the *Chicago Tribune,* announced: "Extra! A Ziegfeld Follies Girl Need Not Be a Raving Beauty." According to this account, Ziegfeld had admitted that women he picked for his choruses did not always meet his beauty criteria but were subjected to the "wizardry" of lighting and other technical effects, including costuming.[16]

Although clearly tongue-in-cheek, Whittaker's report suggests the degree to which Ziegfeld was assumed to define standards of female beauty in America. Noting Ziegfeld's reputation as a connoisseur of beauty who, "in the course of any year, sees and appraises the beauty of the most beautiful girls of America, for the same reasons that Mr. Heinz views and chooses America's most nearly perfect pickles," Whittaker bemoaned the loss of his illusion that, if nowhere else, at least in the *Follies* chorus one could find true feminine beauty. Adopting a sarcastic attitude typical of such discussions, Whittaker described alleged "imperfections" of the women Ziegfeld evaluated when choosing his choruses: "He will make the best of the bad matter that is the state of physical grace of American female charm. Enormous numbers of the applicants . . . are total lemons." And although his "yearly beauty problem" might be quite daunting, given that the new "crop of fair flesh will have the

FIG. 32. Ziegfeld Product Endorsement. This advertisement (apparently the back cover of a magazine) was torn off the original publication and thus contained no source information. The date 1928 was written in pencil in the lower right-hand corner.

usual average of angular ankles and misplaced muscles," Ziegfeld knew that at least he had the assistance of a "deceitful crew of stage beauty doctors."

The theater critic Richard Dana Skinner confirmed Ziegfeld's status as the definitive authority on American beauty:

> No one really thought he was glorifying American girls. In fact, he was actually putting most of them to shame by selecting only such astonishing beauties that they did little more than remind us of the shortcomings of those we ran across during the daily humdrum. A Ziegfeld show girl was about as unlike the daily flapper as a prize cow is unlike the obscure heavy duty animal who keeps the milk trains going.[17]

Skinner's and Whittaker's unfortunate husbandry analogies appropriately characterize Ziegfeld's participation in and promotion of the objectification of women in American culture in the 1920s. Ziegfeld's own words clearly reinforced the notion that women were, first and foremost, bodies to be assessed on the basis of visual appeal. Ziegfeld's influence in this regard, on his own and successive generations, was profound. Not only did he determine who and what was beautiful, popularizing if not creating certain standards by which beauty is still largely judged in American culture, he also emphasized beauty itself as an essential feature of female worth.[18] Ziegfeld promoted himself as the nation's final authority on female beauty, adamantly proclaiming the superiority of his tastes in this matter. Referring to his competitors who produced revues, for instance, Ziegfeld claimed that "[t]hese chaps are under the impression that any one can stage a revue, so called, by going to the Atlantic City beauty contest and hiring a mob of bathing girls. The Atlantic City beauty show is a joke. Mob selections are always a failure when one is in quest of beautiful girls."[19]

Although magnanimous in praising women he considered beautiful and generous in remunerating the women he employed in his revues, Ziegfeld actually trivialized a woman's human worth by unduly emphasizing the importance of her physical characteristics. Adding insult to injury, Ziegfeld declared that, as crucial as beauty was to female identity and worth, it was in fact unattainable for most women. According to Ziegfeld, "[f]ive per cent of all American women are beautiful. Five of every hundred conform to the established canons of perfection in loveliness. Fifty per cent are pretty, pleasing or personable. . . . Over the remaining forty-five per cent we will draw the veil of kindly silence. I want to live long."[20]

Ziegfeld's attitude toward women resonates clearly in the following comments as well:

> In trying out girls for our companies, the first thing we do is to weed out those who are not pretty in face and form.

A lot of girls make the mistake of trying to imitate the vampire type. Most of them are not vampires by nature, any more than a kitten is a hyena. . . . My advice to them is to forget it! The vampire is not a popular household pet.[21]

Time was when big women were admired on the stage. They were so tall and broad that skirts were imperative. One sees them on the boards no more.

Grey eyes cannot be beautiful. They are too hard, too intellectual. They are the eyes of the typical college girl.

And, perhaps most disheartening: "Beauty and brains are not often found together."[22]

That Ziegfeld and others were fond of pronouncing such epithets is not difficult to understand. This calculating, impersonal, animal-husbandry attitude toward another human being is, for all its unpleasantness, an effective way to assert presumed personal superiority. Seen in this light, Ziegfeld, who purported to "glorify the American girl" by exposing and decorating her body, bore an uncanny resemblance to moralists like Straton who would have used opposite means for similar ends.

Clashing Contingencies: An Analysis of Leg Shows

Aesthetically based censorship, usually misogynistic in spirit, was clearly a means by which to shame and thereby censor undesirable female performers; by the same token, this kind of censorship fostered a reward system that encouraged "desirable" female performers to participate in alluring displays. Either way, such evaluations presumed the critic's right to set the standards by which a woman was judged to be beautiful enough to be on display. Such criticism was also used to praise or pan certain theatrical productions and even entire theatrical genres, especially burlesque. While critics usually avowed that their underlying concern was that the theater maintain high artistic standards, it is not difficult to detect their primary preoccupation with the display of female bodies—displays common to most of the decade's popular entertainment forms.

Again, in terms of its intent to assert authority, this type of censorship was much the same as that which claimed a basis in morality. As theater critic for the *Boston Evening Transcript*, for example, a young J. Brooks Atkinson decided to tour what he referred to as the "minor theatres of Boston," that is, its burlesque houses. His review of this excursion was exceptional in that burlesque shows of this era were infrequently critiqued in big-city dailies. In his detailed and disdainful essay, Atkinson repeatedly complained about the unattractiveness of the women in the shows he visited; and, except for the lengthiness of his discussion, his appraisal of burlesque was fairly standard for that time. In addition to his disappointment with the appearance of the female performers, he was scornful of the audience and disgusted with the general ambience of the theatrical experience.[23]

Not all critics considered burlesque the affront to their artistic sensibilities that Atkinson did. Carl Van Vechten expressed his fondness for this venue in an essay for the liberal magazine *American Mercury*. He observed: "The ladies in these entertainments may be overplump, a trifle se[re] and yellow, but they suggest sex, in a sense that the ladies in our over-refined musical comedies do not."[24] Clearly, Van Vechten realized the symbolic function of women's bodies in burlesque, particularly their sexual encoding. Indeed, he not so subtly implied here that he preferred the candor with which burlesque appropriated women's bodies. He was, moreover, as quick to judge these women on the basis of their physical appearance as was Ziegfeld, Atkinson, or for that matter, John Roach Straton.

R. L. Lurie described burlesque as an unsavory, unkempt, low-class amusement, buttressing criticisms of the genre by likewise snubbing the female performers, as well as the audience who attended their show. In an essay for the *New Republic*, Lurie recalled highlights of a recent burlesque show, conveying to readers a vivid image of the nature of performances by women in what was by then increasingly viewed as an ignoble theatrical form. Lurie noted: "The curtain rolls up and twenty chorus girls prance uncertainly about the stage singing, 'We are the chicks from gay Paree!'" A "rosy cheeked milk-man" disgustedly declares, "God, what a mess of prunes!" and receives sympathetic grins from the men seated around him. During the "bathing scene"—a popular theatrical pretext for the display of women's bodies—the "ingenue appears in a kimona [*sic*] and complains of the naughty, naughty men at the beaches, while the chorus clad in one-piece bathing suits pose daintily. After repeated urging, the reluctant ingenue opens the kimona to display her own lavish figure to the audible delight of the whistling gallery." Lurie observed that meanwhile the musicians took little notice of any of the women who performed and instead stared intently at their musical scores, "sated with the repeated displays of legs and thighs and breasts."[25]

A common complaint against both revues and burlesque shows had to do with a kind of weariness or feeling of tedium that arose from being inundated with the very image that created the shows' appeal—parading, scantily clothed or nude women. In a review of the 1926 edition of *Artists and Models*, Leon Whipple, for instance, objected that "Broadway as usual achieves so little with its audacious freedoms. We grant these managers the free use of the human body, all our armory of light and stage effects, every ancient and modern device—and they produce a bore!"[26] Leg shows were often criticized in this way. And although for moral as well as aesthetic reasons some complained bitterly about the nudity common to these entertainments, others seemed capable of, at best, ambivalence toward such productions.

Mixed reactions toward the commercialized display of women's bodies were inevitable within a culture that simultaneously valorized capitalism, patriotism, female virtue, and physical beauty. Leg shows both celebrated and challenged these ideals. To the degree that the celebratory offset the challenging, leg shows succeeded. Producers of revues, especially Florenz Ziegfeld, prospered largely because they deftly managed the paradoxes inherent to their shows. By extravagantly and patriotically framing performances by beautiful women—performances that otherwise seemed less than virtuous—Ziegfeld transformed his shows into a respectable national ritual, producing new yearly installments for over two decades. It is probably no wonder that he was defensive about the Miss America pageant; its producers had obviously borrowed Ziegfeld's techniques for commercial success and had thus become to some extent his competitors.

By 1930, John Bakeless declared, burlesque was no longer a mere "leg show." Instead, he called it "anatomical drama" and noted, among other things, burlesque's transition to a performance venue devoted to the "display of all the law allows." Acknowledging, on this basis, the resultant sameness of all burlesque shows, Bakeless characterized burlesque as a venue that regularly included the "strip tease," a dance performed on runways where the female chorus "prance[d] merrily forth . . . their high heels exactly on a level with the audience's eyes."[27] Although the striptease was unique to burlesque, Joseph Kaye noted that the revue in fact appropriated many other burlesque techniques and thereby accelerated the demise of burlesque. That women appeared nude in revues was the final straw in a progression of one-upmanship between the two entertainment forms.[28]

Notably, burlesque, the venue so condescendingly viewed by critics and even patrons, was at the time one of the most accessible points of entry into the theatrical profession for women. While few women would be chosen for elite revue choruses and even fewer cast in significant roles in the "legitimate" theater, burlesque as well as vaudeville offered work in the entertainment industry to talented women who might not otherwise attract the attention of Broadway's beauty scouts.[29] Thus, though stigmatized by such employment, especially by her participation in burlesque, a woman who was serious about pursuing a career in the theater and who could not gain entry into the profession as quickly as an extraordinarily beautiful woman had little choice but to perform in these shows. Even avenues such as these were closed, however, to women who did not meet the less exacting but still appearance-based terms of employment. And while Atkinson and other theater critics often assumed arch tones when discussing burlesque, if they mentioned burlesque at all, they were generally enthusiastic about revues like those produced by Florenz Ziegfeld, Earl Carroll, and the Shuberts—men who were nothing so much as choosy about the female bodies on which they were willing to put money—and sometimes little else. Still, the realization that revues in fact offered more female nudity than did burlesque and did so with more finesse only partially explains why the former so appealed to audiences of the 1920s.

In his critique of the *Earl Carroll Vanities* and the *Greenwich Village Follies*, the noted critic Joseph Wood Krutch identified another reason that revues fascinated American theatergoers. He claimed that these shows essentially were "to a democracy what troupes of dancing girls were to kings."[30] Krutch's analogy perhaps unintentionally but nevertheless quite starkly denotes the complex interplay of political, socioeconomic, and gender issues inherent in the public display of women's bodies. Moreover, his words aptly depict anonymous, uniformly fashioned women, displayed en masse, automatons performing rituals of the body to the delight of powerful others. As Krutch noted a few months later in his discussion of a Shubert revue that had recently opened, "I suspect, indeed, that these spectacles possess in a mild way something of the same charm which the audience in a Roman amphitheater perceived when it watched . . . Christians driven in to the lions; for it gives one a pleasant, almost Oriental, sense of magnificence to see so much endured for one's mere entertainment."[31]

In response to the 1928 edition of *Artists and Models*, Rolphe Humphries admitted to the same feelings of superiority that Krutch had expressed; like Krutch, he also was especially impressed by the strenuousness of the performance, defining its success in part by the effort the chorus exerted on his behalf. Specifically, Humphries noted that "the harder a dancer keeps working, the better the dance must be." Humphries clearly viewed the audience's relationship to the performers as analogous to a consumer's relationship to a product purchased. He characterized his enjoyment of the production as a natural response to "high art," that "culminates, for the mood of this house, in two achievements . . . an elaborate and extravagant surplus of persons and material, a visible assumption of expenditure."[32]

Indeed, the allure of the revue from the perspective of consumerism was noted by several critics. Its appeal was often explained in terms of an appreciation for modern technology, however, underscoring the way in which revues objectified and commodified women's bodies. Louise Bogan, for example, noted the "so-admired clockwork creature: twenty girls in line, twenty left legs that swing automatically out, twenty right legs that swing across, as accurate as crank-shafts seen in slow motion—engagingly mechanical flesh and blood."[33] Gilbert Seldes claimed that the revue was attractive to watch because it simulated the wonders of the machine age.[34] He attributed the perfection of the revue form to Florenz Ziegfeld and took exception to the phrase "glorifying the American girl" that was commonly associated with Ziegfeld's revues, claiming instead that "[w]hat Mr. Ziegfeld glorifies is the American habit of doing things slickly and smoothly and as well as possible: a habit largely extended to motor cars."[35]

The suggestion that revues appealed to a modernist aesthetic and that the women in these revues were little more than the proverbial spokes in a wheel is amply illustrated by the responses it elicited. Moreover, these critiques easily accommodated nationalistic biases and often helped to frame racist commentary as well. Ann Douglas recently observed that "[i]t is one thing to be in search of the 'primitive,' as white artists of the 1920s were; another thing to be told, as the black New Yorkers were, that you are the primitive, the savage 'id' of Freud's new psychoanalytic discourse, trailing clouds of barbaric, prehistoric, preliterate 'folk' culture wherever you go."[36] In his review of two African American revues, Francis Fergusson contended that

> [t]he Negroes, in fact, as animals, are freer than we are; and a mutual recognition of this fact has made the success of many a hula-hula dance, many a jazz band. Both *Blackbirds* and *Brown Buddies* exploit this element. Their tom-tom rhythms and their undressed dances put to shame the business-like capering of the naked whites.[37]

Fergusson's implication that African American revues could be viewed as sincere expressions of racial pride was complicated, however, by his own experience during *Blackbirds*, when he "had the weary feeling that they meant it to be simply what a white public wanted."[38]

The reality of African American marginalization within the entertainment industry was lost on many, but not all, white observers at the time. Edmund Wilson, for one, offered this backstage glimpse of a *Follies* production: "They [the women of the chorus] crowd the wings. Behind them, the negro wardrobe woman waits, patient and with a shade of sullenness—knowing herself handsome in another kind, she bides blinking at all that white beauty—those open-eyed confident white girls in their paradise of bright dress."[39] Meanwhile, in Harlem, whites owned most of the bigger clubs and saw to it that their shows also appealed to a Eurocentric aesthetic but one that propagated white assumptions about blacks belonging to a "natural race." Thus, in black revues, women were usually light-skinned to appeal to white beauty standards, yet they projected an exoticism that was read by whites as animalistic and therefore sensual.[40] Whites were, for their part, quite self-conscious and even blatant about some attempts to appropriate the "primitive" for themselves (see fig. 9).

Chorus Girls: Legends in Their Own Time

> I am longing to get something I can branch out in and be an actress, to act
> really, not bob my curls about and wear pretty frocks and crinkle up my
> nose and be cute, but touch some deeper chord in the hearts of my audi-
> ences, for I feel they like me and somehow I feel that I have something
> better to give them than I do now. If I can only find an outlet to these
> ambitions I may do something yet.
>
> —Billie Burke, 1910[41]

As discourse about women's performances in popular entertainment venues
of the 1920s indicates, the authorization but also the prohibition of such
performances facilitated a troubling complex of assumptions about human
worth. Sexual, aesthetic, socioeconomic, and racial prejudices were nowhere
more pronounced than in discussions of America's preferences in entertainment. Women were enabled as well as contained by their participation in
"show business." And discourse *about* female performers themselves, especially the women of the chorus, was another powerful means of circumscrib-
ing behavior, identity, and theatrical careers.

Theatrical choruses constituted the largest single category of regular employment for women in the entertainment industry in the 1920s. Female
choruses were indispensable to several theatrical genres, including musical
comedies, revues, vaudeville, burlesque, and movies. Notwithstanding their
inevitable presence in the theater and in the press, the individual women of
the chorus were and remain, in many respects, invisible.[42] Barring exceptional cases, they were routinely codified as a group rather than noted as individuals. The monolithic identity of chorus girls seemed itself a curious by-
product of the unanimity suggested by their collective performances (fig. 33).
These women who were everywhere on display in the American theater from
the late nineteenth through the early twentieth century were the subject of
voluminous conjecture and caricature in the popular press.

The folklore that accumulated about chorus girls not only distorted their
real identities but also contained them within an undesirable image. They
were considered "gold diggers," "vamps," unintelligent, and generally of weak
moral fiber. That the bare-legged and often bare-breasted women of the
chorus were so prominently situated, both on the American stage and in the
popular imagination, points to their particular status as cultural icons and the
ways in which that status restricted their existence.[43] One writer openly acknowledged the dehumanization of these women, asserting that "the chorus
girl is essentially not a person but a tradition—a rollicking, laughing, careless

FIG. 33. Chorus of *Blossom Time*, a Shubert Musical, 1928.

child of a day and a night.[44] More compassionately, Leon Whipple asked, "What about the girls who offer their beauty for the show? What happens to them when the little moment of fleshly pride is done?"[45] Unfortunately, such concerns were seldom expressed in discussions about the real women whose livelihood was provided by membership in that much maligned and often categorically dismissed collective known as the theatrical chorus.

Tracy C. Davis has contended that "in some respects, theatrical women are better off than their counterparts outside the theater, but social judgments and ostracism typically negate the advantages."[46] This was certainly the case with chorus girls. On one hand, chorus work paid fairly well. The average pay a woman of the chorus received in 1924 was $35 or $40 a week. Members of the *Follies* and other shows in which women were required to be "unusually beautiful" might get $75 to $100 per week.[47] A woman's beauty was viewed by the entertainment industry as a commodity to which a price could be affixed. Nonetheless, even the lower range of chorus wages was enviable, considering that the average female office worker in New York as late as 1929 was paid only $27.57 per week.[48]

On the other hand, despite comparably good pay, it was difficult for the women of the chorus to achieve respect as theater professionals, much less maintain respectable personal reputations. Betty Van Deventer openly acknowledged that the "chorus girl makes a good spot in a newspaper feature story because the public likes to regard her as a thing of beauty and wickedness."[49] Van Deventer's own discussion of the lifestyle of chorus girls reveals how advocates of these women were as likely to reify their infamy as their opponents were. Van Deventer not only refutes but also reinforces certain negative assumptions about the women of the chorus in treating her topic. As to the popular perception that chorus girls were gold diggers, for example, Van Deventer rather flippantly dismisses this accusation by stating that many women who were not chorus girls could be called this as well. Moreover, she relates anecdotes about specific gold-digging ploys used by some chorus girls, fueling popular but unflattering images that many people were only too ready to assume applied to all women of the theatrical chorus.

Marian Spitzer similarly challenged the common assumption that chorus girls lacked intelligence. Like Van Deventer's gold-digger defense, Spitzer's rejoinder was of dubious merit: "The tradition that chorus girls are stupid was probably originated by a homely woman as a form of self-defense."[50] Well-meaning sympathizers like Spitzer and Van Deventer invariably defended chorus girls in ways that further ostracized the women of the chorus, setting them up as rather a different species of woman altogether.

Spitzer's comments do nonetheless contain an important truth about women of theatrical choruses of the post–World War I era: though much maligned, these women were also much envied. They were examined in painstaking detail from the seats of the theaters where they performed. Everyone knew that regardless of any extraordinary talent such women might possess, their membership in the chorus was, at a most essential level, based on their appearance. For this they received the admiration of their audiences and relatively good wages besides. Still, with few exceptions, the careers of chorus girls lasted only as long as they were in fact "girlish," or young usually no more than twenty-two years old.[51]

Some discussions of chorus girls focused on their exceptional qualities; in other words, the ways in which such women did not, in actuality, resemble their identity as it resided in the popular imagination. These defenses too usually amounted to little more than backhanded compliments. Some writers emphatically declared—as though the discovery had startled them—that chorus girls were both intelligent and virtuous.[52] That they were, contrary to popular opinion, "wholesome" was often substantiated by references to their ability to maintain relationships traditionally considered crucial to women— the fact that they were loyal daughters trying to provide for ailing parents, for example, or that they were the kind of women who would make good wives.[53]

Occasionally, instead of generalized portrayals of chorus girls as a group, individual women were featured. Many of these discussions were uncomplimentary, due to a fixation on misdeeds of certain women.[54] Others, conversely, idolized a woman if she had achieved outstanding success—by becoming a principal performer in the *Follies*, for example.[55] The inconsistency of these portrayals is itself representative of the fact that, although chorus girls were often ridiculed, they were members of a profession about which

many women fantasized and to which a few eagerly aspired. In bold contrast
to the legendary hardened, worldly-wise gold digger, the sweet hometown
girl who went off to the Big City to join the ranks of the chorus also figured
prominently in chorus girl folklore. The *Atlanta Constitution* offered a variation of this oft-told tale. A Broadway producer came to town and found himself short by one chorus girl. He decided to audition women from Atlanta
who might be interested in filling the missing spot, noting that he had been in
the city several times and had "marked the style and vivacity of Atlanta's girl
supply." Although it is not clear from this report how many women actually
auditioned or who was eventually chosen, the sense of hometown pride is apparent: "the whole bunch appeared to be perfect . . . and some little Atlantans
will be full fledged actorines."[56]

Within the theater itself, chorus girl lore was no less imaginative than in
the mass media.[57] One of the most comprehensive sources of such lore—a
virtual index of the themes and variations noted above—is a play by Avery
Hopwood predictably entitled *The Gold Diggers*.[58] This play has in common
with Hopwood's *Ladies' Night in a Turkish Bath*, discussed in chapter 5, the
fact that it explores as well as exploits stereotypical images of women that
were popular in the 1920s. In *Ladies' Night*, Hopwood and his coauthor,
Charlton Andrews, create female characters who are recognizable physical
"types"; *Gold Diggers*, however, psychologically and behaviorally typecasts
women, specifically, the women of theatrical choruses.

In the opening scene of *Gold Diggers* we meet the jaded and opportu-
nistic Mabel, a longtime chorus girl and classic gold digger, who openly acknowledges that her idea of matrimony is "the kind that ends in alimony."[59]
In stark relief to Mabel is Violet, the naive chorus girl "with a heart of gold"
who is in love with Wally, a young man whose uncle and guardian, Steve, has
announced that he will withhold a sizable inheritance if Wally marries her.
Because of her profession, Steve assumes that Violet is a "vampire" who really
only wants Wally's money. Steve has no basis for judging Violet's character or
intentions, however, as he has never met her. This miscalculation leaves him
vulnerable to a plot hatched by Violet's friends that concludes with not only
Wally engaged to a chorus girl—Violet, of course—but with Steve set to
marry one as well. Consistent with chorus girl mythology, the woman with
whom Steve falls in love, a friend of Violet's named Jerry, left her small hometown for New York when she was only sixteen. She since achieved great success as a chorus girl, and her "rags to riches" story, briefly recounted in the
play, is as much about the fulfillment of the American Dream as it is about the
fulfillment of dreams of stardom shared by many young girls of the 1920s.
Her accomplishments have not spoiled her though; Jerry is as wholesome as,
even if more savvy than, Violet.

Also thrown into the mix of characters in *Gold Diggers* is the "has been" chorus girl, Cissie Gray, who at forty-five years of age sells soap for a living now that she is no longer beautiful. This character is remarkably similar to Lottie Gilmore, the woman in Mae West's play, *The Wicked Age*, who, no longer young or beautiful enough to support herself as a model or actress, sells lingerie. The chorus girls buy soap from Cissie out of pity, but when she leaves their presence, Jerry summarizes the lesson they learn from Cissie Gray's experience: "But we won't be young forever, and we won't be good looking forever, and—well, the question is—how to make the best of our youth and good looks while we've got them."[60] To some extent then, Cissie Gray helps her younger counterparts rationalize their own gold digging and explains to the audience the motivation for the gold-digging strategies of some women.

Through the character of Violet as well as the character of Jerry, Hopwood identifies and confounds popular chorus girl mythology of the 1920s. His play so overtly manipulates this social lore that it essentially demystifies the image of chorus girl even while it reinforces widely held prejudices against the women of the chorus. What is more, Hopwood deprecates the men who exploit the women of this play, in part by making the former seem little more than helpless prey to the feminine beauty and charm of the latter. The male characters are unfavorably presented in another way as well, however. This play, for all its caricatures, exaggerates nothing so well as the shallow sensibilities of those men who, again in the words of the worldly-wise Jerry, "will do a good deal for us now—but, oh, girls—lose your figures or your complexions —get a few lines in your faces get tired out and faded looking, and a little passé—and the fellows that are ready to give you pearls and sables now—well they'd turn the other way when they saw you coming!"[61]

Thus, in *Gold Diggers* and in *Ladies' Night*—for reasons which I will explore more fully in the next chapter—Hopwood critiques or at least admits the unflattering and unrealistic images of his female contemporaries in ways that seem thematically to play both ends against the middle, as it were. In this he differs only slightly from those who passed off criticisms of chorus girls with mere defenses rather than denials of their alleged misconduct. But unlike chorus girl defenders such as Spitzer and Van Deventer, Hopwood seems aware that if indeed the stories told about chorus girls were true, even in part, they reflected a pervasive pattern of social exchange in which women were significantly disadvantaged. Still, the female characters who comprise *Gold Diggers* hardly failed to live up to audience expectations of chorus girls, given the way the play mirrored popular media representations of them. *Gold Diggers* was, in fact, one of Hopwood's most successful plays, running in New York for more than a year.

In any case, as these several examples suggest, the chorus girl folklore of the postwar decade foregrounds the ways in which "good looks" were both a blessing and curse to female theater professionals. The quantity and quality of discourse about chorines also underscored American curiosity as to the lifestyles and morality of the women who comprised so large a percentage of the entertainment industry. As cultural legends both envied and repudiated, these women were torturous reminders of America's cultural and moral schizophrenia. The chorus was a vehicle by which to "glorify the American girl," usually by emphasizing her sexual allure, and yet no profession except for prostitution so stigmatized women. To interrogate this paradox is to reveal much about the history of women's curious entrapment between the empowering potential of performance and its equally powerful potential to immure. From gold digger to Ziegfeld Girl, the women of 1920s theatrical choruses deserve to hold a more prominent place in the story of the American theater.

Decoding the Debates

Although the display of the female body had become practically routine in many popular entertainments by the early 1920s, the practice nonetheless generated considerable dissonance and contention within and outside the theatrical community. In 1923, for example, an essay appropriately entitled "A Naked Challenge" appeared in the *Nation*, attacking the capriciousness of a system that both rewarded and punished staged female nudity. The unidentified essayist quoted a New York theater critic's description of the latest Shubert revue.

> The audience realized, with appropriate gasps, a few moments after the curtain had risen, that the girls of the ensemble were entirely unclothed from the waist up . . . they saw one young woman wearing nothing except a slender piece of chiffon draped rather carelessly about her hips, and twenty-five other young women with nothing on about the waist except a still more slender bit of chiffon.[62]

In the *Nation* essayist's opinion, the acceptance of such blatant displays of nudity clearly represented a double standard of morality. Noting that "so responsible a press critic as Heywood Broun" felt the show to be "permissible," the author expressed indignation at the incongruity that such a show could succeed unchallenged in light of recent events. The New York Society for the Suppression of Vice had, for example, been making itself "particularly obnoxious by proceeding against various publishers of works of art and literature." A production of Sholom Asch's *God of Vengeance* also had been censored despite what, in terms of conventional ethics, the *Nation* writer felt merited the "hearty approval not only of the vice suppressors but of every Sunday-school

teacher and of every John Roach Straton." Furthermore, the Shuberts themselves had spoken against such "salacious" plays in an interview with the *New
York World* following the conviction of the manager and actors of Asch's play.
The Shuberts had piously professed: "Anything that tends to lower the standard of public morals *should never be produced.*" Practically seething by this
point, the essayist for the *Nation* exclaimed: "Yet these sanctimonious moral-
izers are now coining untold dollars out of the openly displayed nudity of
twenty-six women. From the scribes and the Pharisees, good Lord, deliver us!"

In 1926, *Theatre Magazine* reported that a controversy was underway
between "our two arbiters of American theatre," Florenz Ziegfeld and Lee
Shubert. The subject of their debate was not new; indeed it was by now
commonplace. But the irony of Ziegfeld and Shubert's row escaped no one;
having made fortunes on the display of nude female bodies, these theater
tycoons now argued the moral fine points of such exhibits. According to the
report, for example, Ziegfeld acknowledged his own contribution to the
trend toward more nudity on stage but claimed that he no longer approved
of the commercialization of "fleshly charms." His shows had revealed nude
women in what was to him the artistically defensible manner of the tableau.
These presentations were innocent enough, but "other managers," Ziegfeld
felt, had taken the liberty to extremes and now had nude women moving
around in all sorts of dance numbers and processions.[63] Ziegfeld was apparently still in this self-righteous mood when, the next year, after the Wales
Stage Regulation Bill was enacted, he reportedly sent word to New York District Attorney Banton: "Note that you have convinced producers and actors
filthy plays will not be tolerated in New York. Now clean up the revues and
night clubs. Clean shows up for good, not just for the night that police are in
evidence. Let's have a clean slate for the theatre, now that you have found an
effective way."[64]

In an interview published in *World's Work*, Ziegfeld's comments on the
depravity with which he felt revues were now associated were more expansive: "But nowadays, the orgies of nakedness that some producers stage make
one ashamed of ever having had anything to do with revues. It is simply disgusting, worse than one can find in the lowest 'dives' of Europe. Incompetent
amateurs and utter 'low-brows' who bolster up their ignorance of stagecraft
by these displays."[65] Apparently, Ziegfeld's concerns, like those of so many
others who protested the manner in which women were featured on stage,
were only partially represented by claims of moral indignation. As in his criticisms of the Miss America pageant, Ziegfeld seemed anxious to prove his
professional preeminence. For his part, Shubert, far from contrite, gave no
indication that the women in his own shows would be wearing any additional
apparel, whether in tableaux or dance numbers. In response to Ziegfeld's

new plan to "purify" instead of "glorify" the American girl, Shubert reportedly commented that "nudity is on the stage to stay."[66]

Using the debate between Ziegfeld and Shubert to express personal scruples about female nudity in revues as well, the editor of *Theatre Magazine*, Arthur Hornblow, added:

> The attitude of the authorities towards these naked spectacles is one of indifference and tolerance—a position that, on the face of it, is somewhat inconsistent. If a woman walked naked down Fifth Avenue or even exposed her bare breasts on a bathing beach, she would be arrested. Yet on the public stage, exposed to the ribald, lascivious gaze of thousands, young and old, she is allowed to display her charms with impunity![67]

The Ziegfeld/Shubert dispute and Hornblow's commentary on it offer a synoptic view of the constant bickering about displays by and of women that so characterized the popular theater of the 1920s. As I have shown, the presentation of the female body was the subject of an exceptionally wide-ranging cultural discourse at that time. The commandeering of women's bodies was promoted by means of increasingly sophisticated mass media. Fashion, in tandem with the media, played an enormous role as well in exposing women's bodies by removing layers and inches and yards of unnecessary and even unhealthy clothing. Everyone seemed to notice what women were and were not wearing, and most had an opinion to express on the subject. The American theater, however, was a context in which the controversy over female self-presentation and self-stylization became especially charged. Despite much publicized disapproval of stage nudity, the post–World War I decade saw the heyday of revues like the Ziegfeld *Follies* and its many imitators, shows that were known primarily for female choruses who wore revealing costumes. The oft-cited goal of "glorifying the American girl" helped sanction the commercialization of youthful but mostly white, female nudity. The women of the chorus were themselves the object of censure and represented a brand of femininity both admired and suspect.

Perhaps more telling than the particular values expressed in debates about female display is the tenor of the arguments themselves. The sense of superiority, ownership, and callousness running through this body discourse was by no means unique to the 1920s. Its bluntness and crassness, however, graphically expose the latent and sinister ideologies of our own body talk. And though we may—or may not—speak of women's bodies with greater sensitivity than our forebears did, our carefully phrased words at best only minimally mask the larger cultural reality of the female body as icon. To probe the ideologies underlying discourse related to the staging of female nudity and other forms of sexual display, with sensitivity to the complex cultural terrain of the 1920s, is to locate the origins of many present-day criteria by which a woman's worth is evaluated within mass media and entertainment venues and subsequently within her own social circles.

5 The Transgressions of Ladies' Night

From the late 1910s through the mid-1920s, Avery Hopwood achieved phenomenal success in the American theater as a comic playwright. He was especially famous for his sex farces. In the fall of 1920, four plays authored or coauthored by Hopwood ran simultaneously in New York theaters.[1] *Ladies' Night in a Turkish Bath,* one of those plays, ran for an enviable 375 performances. Hopwood reportedly earned $89,000 in royalties for this play alone.[2] A. H. Woods, who produced the show, took it to Chicago where it opened on 20 March 1922 (fig. 34). But the play was not a success in the Windy City; it lasted barely six weeks, during which time it was also censored.

These diverse reactions to *Ladies' Night* invite our attention to the intriguing paradoxes inherent in this play. On the surface merely a frivolous sex romp, in the course of its three acts this play in fact trivialized some of America's deepest anxieties about changing sexual mores, especially such changes as they were inscribed on the bodies of women. From its thematic and visual focus on women's fashion, particularly bathing costumes, to the way in which this play essentially commandeered women's bodies for the financial benefit of the men who wrote and produced it, *Ladies' Night* uniquely exemplifies and reinforces primary conclusions I have forwarded in previous chapters. When we examine this play, we realize that, at the very least, Hopwood and his coauthor, Charlton Andrews, exploited the female body as conspicuously as did Florenz Ziegfeld in his *Follies* revues.[3] When we look more closely, however, we also understand that the authors of *Ladies' Night* further compounded what was already a convoluted process of female commodification and objectification in American culture of the 1920s.

In one sense, *Ladies' Night* merely appropriated the already familiar, albeit complicated, sexual iconicity of women. But in its portrayal of exaggerated male sexual desire for women and the use of women's bodies to accomplish what I contend is, in the end, a subversive parody of heterosexuality, *Ladies' Night* richly illustrates that performance may be transgressive on

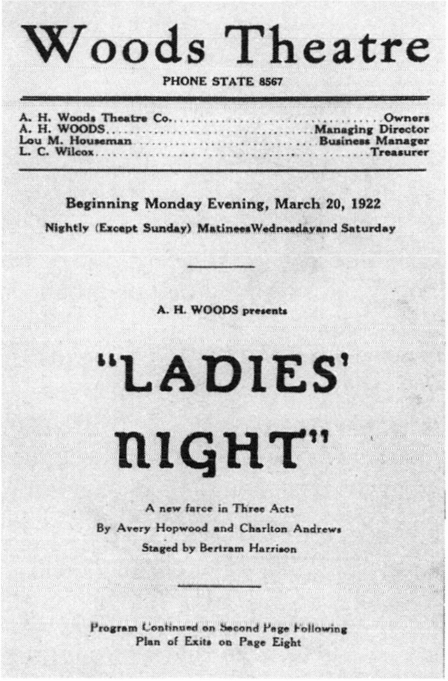

Woods Theatre

PHONE STATE 8567

A. H. Woods Theatre Co..Owners
A. H. WOODS.....................................Managing Director
Lou M. Houseman.................................Business Manager
L. C. Wilcox...Treasurer

Beginning Monday Evening, March 20, 1922

Nightly (Except Sunday) Matinees Wednesday and Saturday

A. H. WOODS presents

"LADIES' NIGHT"

A new farce in Three Acts
By Avery Hopwood and Charlton Andrews
Staged by Bertram Harrison

Program Continued on Second Page Following
Plan of Exits on Page Eight

FIG. 34. Playbill for *Ladies' Night*, Chicago, 1922. Department of Special Collections, the University of Chicago Library. Playbills and Programs, ser. 2, box 32, folder 14. Used by permission.

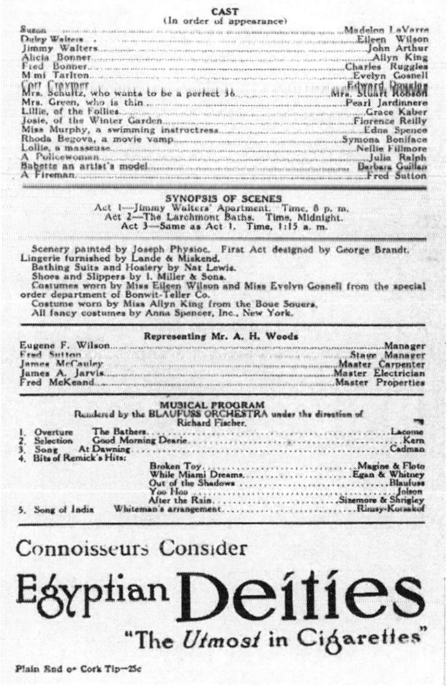

CAST
(In order of appearance)

Suton ....Madelon LaVarre
Daisy Walters ....Eileen Wilson
Jimmy Walters...John Arthur
Alicia Bonner...Allyn King
Fred Bonner.......................................Charles Ruggles
Mimi Tarleon.....................................Evelyn Gosnell
Curt Cremmer.....................................
Mrs. Schultz, who wants to be a perfect 36......................Pearl Jardinnere
Mrs. Green, who is thin...
Lillie, of the Follies...Grace Kaber
Josie, of the Winter Garden....................................Florence Reilly
Miss Murphy, a swimming instructress..........................Edna Spence
Rhoda Begova, a movie vamp...........................Symona Boniface
Lollie, a masseuse...Nellie Fillmore
A Policewoman...Julia Ralph
Babette an artist's model....................................Barbara Gurlan
A Fireman..Fred Sutton

SYNOPSIS OF SCENES
Act 1—Jimmy Walters' Apartment. Time, 8 p. m.
Act 2—The Larchmont Baths. Time, Midnight.
Act 3—Same as Act 1. Time, 1:15 a. m.

Scenery painted by Joseph Physioc. First Act designed by George Brandt.
Lingerie furnished by Lande & Miskend.
Bathing Suits and Hosiery by Nat Lewis.
Shoes and Slippers by I. Miller & Sons.
Costumes worn by Miss Eileen Wilson and Miss Evelyn Gosnell from the special order department of Bonwit-Teller Co.
Costume worn by Miss Allyn King from the Boue Souers.
All fancy costumes by Anna Spencer, Inc., New York.

Representing Mr. A. H. Woods

Eugene F. Wilson...Manager
Fred Sutton..Stage Manager
James McCauley...Master Carpenter
James A. Jarvis...Master Electrician
Fred McKeand..Master Properties

MUSICAL PROGRAM
Rendered by the BLAUFUSS ORCHESTRA under the direction of
Richard Fischer.

1. Overture   The Bathers...................................Lacome
2. Selection   Good Morning Dearie.............................Kern
3. Song   At Dawning.......................................Cadman
4. Bits of Remick's Hits:
        Broken Toy....................................Magine & Floto
        While Miami Dreams........................Egan & Whitney
        Out of the Shadows..............................Blaufuss
        Yoo Hoo...Jolson
        After the Rain.........................Sizemore & Shrigley
5. Song of India   Whiteman's arrangement................Rimsy-Korsakof

Connoisseurs Consider

Egyptian Deities

"The *Utmost* in Cigarettes"

Plain End or Cork Tip—25c

123

multiple levels simultaneously. Furthermore, this play compels us to consider the labyrinthine ways in which culturally subordinate groups may vie for social power at each other's expense. Indeed, we must ethnographically explore the blending and layering of sexual and social agendas in *Ladies' Night* in order to determine the particular ways in which it was transgressive.

In spite of commercial popularity in New York and in addition to commercial failure in Chicago, critical reaction to *Ladies' Night* in both cities was generally dismissive. The play was deemed unworthy of its authors, although their royalty checks provided Hopwood and Andrews with sufficient proof to the contrary.[4] Alexander Woollcott, who attended the opening of the play in New York, called it an example of the theatrical efforts of those playwrights and managers who seem "bent on seeing how far they can go without being arrested."[5] Bernard Sobel, less affronted than Woollcott, nevertheless agreed that the play pushed the limits of decency. "Where other lingerie plays stop, 'Ladies' Night' begins. It disappoints no one who wishes to be shocked, for it presents all the old thrills and a few more—bare legs, the shimmy, jokes with double meanings, vampires, bath-room scenes, underwear and infidelity."[6] Chicago reviewers also varied considerably in the degree to which they seemed personally offended by the risqué elements of the production, but most concurred that the salacious intent of the play was more than proved by its incessant recourse to the exhibition of female bodies, both literally and thematically.

The text of *Ladies' Night*, including specifications for costuming and movement, certainly confirms these critics' assessments. All things considered, however, we may reasonably assume that the bodies of female performers were not necessarily more flagrantly exposed in *Ladies' Night* than in many other theatrical entertainments of the 1920s. But what the play lacked in visual explicitness it compensated for in dialogue *about* explicit display and sexuality. The combination of physical as well as verbal "undress" renders the text of *Ladies' Night* and other extant historical evidence related to its production and censorship particularly useful as a measure of the kinds and qualities of female display that were considered most transgressive in the 1920s.

The censorship of *Ladies' Night* and the lukewarm response it received in Chicago also remind us that the commercial theatrical fare of New York City often misrepresented the tastes and mores of the nation. Sheppard Butler, a Chicago critic who expressed his disdain for the show when it opened at the Woods Theatre, smugly editorialized six weeks later about the early departure of *Ladies' Night*, bluntly calling it a "flop." He facetiously apologized to his readers in that he had erroneously predicted that *Ladies' Night* should do well in Chicago since, after all, "most of the dime museums are closed."[7] Butler claimed that the play had been "designed frankly for 'hick' consumption" and that even in New York, it had probably played to out-of-town visitors who came in droves to "sit, as they thought, at the feet of Satan." Butler dourly concluded:

> So, having rounded out a brilliant career in the dramatic metropolis, Mr. Hop-wood's idyll went forth, flushed with success, for further conquest. And lo, in Chicago it flops. Where are the celebrants, with their expense accounts and their flair for the seeking out of forbidden joys? Where are the trustful natives, tremulous with the joy of seeing an original New York cast? Here was a 'hick' show; we, they say, are a 'hick' town. Why didn't we get together? How come that 'Ladies' Night' must depart while 'Anna Christie' remains and thrives? Did some one make a mistake, or is it possible that our taste in the theater is better than we thought?[8]

As these remarks so forcefully suggest, New York theatrical exports were not always welcome in other major cities of the nation.[9] Butler obviously resented New York's reputation as the arbiter of theatrical tastes, and he seems equally perturbed that Chicago was considered less culturally sophisticated than New York. Not coincidentally, controversy over *The Demi-Virgin*, another Hopwood sex farce produced by Woods, was in full swing at this time, generating widespread discussion about theater censorship in light of what some felt was New York's ethical obligation to the nation as the leader of the theater industry.[10] Theater patrons in Chicago were hardly unaware of this row—the newspapers were full of it—a point that must be factored into any assessment of the Windy City's reaction to *Ladies' Night*. Although the *Demi-Virgin* fiasco did not singularly cause *Ladies' Night* to fail in Chicago, it is likely that the latter play was an unwelcome reminder of a perceived "breach of faith" by the New York theater system. In any case, that *Ladies' Night* did not prosper in Chicago as it had in New York is one of several clues that point to the play's complex relationship to specific—even geographically specific—questions of sexual hegemony, female exploitation, and censorship.

Briefly summarized, the central character in *Ladies' Night*, Jimmy Walters, is so sexually aroused at the sight of women in the new, revealing fashions of the early 1920s that he avoids most social contact. His hermit lifestyle inconveniences his wife, Dulcy, and several of the couple's friends. The play opens on an evening in New York City with the Walterses at home preparing to go out to dinner with two other couples. Their friends arrive, and as they wait for Jimmy and Dulcy to finish dressing, they speculate as to whether Jimmy will actually join the party this time or again decline to go at the last minute as he is in the habit of doing. True to form, Jimmy reneges, and Dulcy, at her wit's end, also decides not to accompany the others to dinner. Instead she announces that she will follow the advice of her doctor, who has told her that her frazzled nerves—a result of her life of isolation—would benefit by the use of "Turkish baths."[11]

The Walterses' friends decide to intervene on the couple's behalf. The women, Mimi and Alicia, will accompany Dulcy to the Larchmont Bath, where it is "ladies' night," which means that no men will be allowed to come in, and they can conveniently initiate her to the luxuries of the bathhouse. Unbeknownst to Mimi and Alicia, their partners, Cort and Fred, propose to Jimmy that the three men attend a masquerade ball, or "pagan revel," so that he will grow accustomed to seeing women's scantily clothed bodies and will no longer be incapacitated by the sight. All proceeds according to plan until police raid the masquerade ball, and Jimmy, Fred, and Cort must flee or be arrested by the invading officers. As luck and dramatic contrivance would have it, the ballroom from which the three men escape is only two doors away from the Larchmont Bath. They sneak into the bath through a window to avoid capture. Thereafter, the play is mainly about ridiculous attempts by these men to hide and, failing that, to disguise their identity from the women at the Turkish bath, especially their wives. The men are eventually discovered and lamely defend their presence at "ladies' night" to their dubious partners. Still, the play ends happily, true to genre, and Jimmy is "cured" of his disabling fear of the sight of women's bodies.

Jimmy's phobia is, of course, the glue that barely holds the plot of *Ladies' Night* together. As he lurks here and there in the bath, trying to avoid detection, he struggles to deal with the sight of minimally clothed women. These women are, in most cases, designated in the script solely on the basis of prominent physical features; for example, Fat Woman, Thin Woman, the Blonde, the Brunette, and so on.[12] A close textual analysis of *Ladies' Night*, especially act 2, set in the Larchmont Bath, suggests that its authors deliberately staged women's bodies in ways that enhanced the visual and comic appeal of the play while disguising its gay subtext—the latter a point to which I return momentarily. The male cross-dressing in this act humorously underscores these multiple agendas as well.

Fat Woman and Thin Woman represent undesirable femininity. The authors draw audience attention to the "imperfections" of their physiques when, for example, the two bemoan their husbands' complaints about the extremes of their figures and pose grotesquely and unhappily before a mirror. Fat Woman's large size is most fully emphasized when she submits to the tortures of the electric "obesity machine," which makes a loud whacking sound as it manipulates her body. Fat, thin, or otherwise, however, Hopwood and Andrews designed numerous situations in which to present the bodies of the female characters of the play in ways clearly intended to be titillating. According to stage directions, most of the women, when not costumed in swimsuits, drape towels or sheets loosely around their bodies. The removal of these items is a frequent "bit," usually performed in silhouette when the women step behind a shower curtain or a hazy steam room door. At such moments, the script instructs the actors to agitate shower curtains or perform other business that attracts audience attention to their presumed nudity.

At one point in act 2, the Swimming Teacher, described as "a handsome young woman, with a splendid figure, which is very adequately revealed by her extremely abbreviated Annette Kellerman," enters and talks to the Movie Vamp. The latter announces that her director wishes her to take off five pounds but that he is unable to decide where. This sparks a brief side exchange, in undertones, between the Blonde and the Brunette, the former observing that she had never before seen the Vamp wear so much clothing. She sarcastically adds "Gee—what the United States don't know about her anatomy!" Dialogue between the Swimming Teacher and the Vamp then resumes as they discuss the Vamp's new movie entitled, predictably, "The Naked Woman."[13]

In addition to these kinds of obvious references to women's bodies, the authors of *Ladies' Night* also incorporate many other devices by which actors and designers must have made this play a highly sensory as well as sensual experience for viewers. Staging notes call for offstage sounds of splashing from the direction of the swimming pool. The vapor of the steam room drifts out to the stage, in reference to which one woman remarks that its effect is to make one's body "so lithe, and supple."[14] Several of the women "shimmy" to the strains of music from the ball down the street at Kensington Hall. The Fat Woman dabs at wet spots on the sheet she donned after her shower. She also consumes a good deal of food onstage. These kinds of sensual and even private behaviors abound in the play and are perhaps what led the Chicago critic Ashton Stevens to describe the experience of *Ladies' Night* as "frankly, a peep show, with the audience playing the principal Peeping Tom."[15]

The loudly whacking obesity machine also must have intensified the play's sensual immediacy for the audience. The brute physicality of this device is in fact one of two aggressive means of body manipulation utilized within *Ladies' Night*. The other is Lollie, a "fat good natured negress" and powerful masseuse. Watching the obesity machine as it strikes Fat Woman's body, Lollie remarks: "I wish I had do loan ob dat machine fo' my chillen!" When Fat Woman asks how many children she has, Lollie confesses that she is ashamed to admit just how many she has since "[w]hen it comes to married life, I sho' am impulsive!"[16] Lollie then leads Fat Woman to the massage couch where the latter pleads with her not to "beat her to death" this time. Impervious to her pleas, Lollie handles Fat Woman "as if she were a featherweight" and pummels and pinches her unmercifully.[17]

This curious scene pairs two women whose cultural marginalization is clearly imprinted on their bodies. Fat Woman, repeatedly portrayed as subservient to her appetite, and Lollie, whose character constitutes a racist portrayal of her susceptibility to sexual impulses, are transgressors and must be

punished. Their flippant dialogue, humorous at first glance, takes on a troubling aspect when one sees how cleverly the words of these transgressive
women are literally punctuated by the sounds of slapping flesh and "squeals
of protest." The Brunette jokingly narrates, "Ouch! —Mamma! I won't never
do it again!" after Lollie puts Fat Woman in the reducing machine.[18] Neither
Lollie nor Fat Woman seems particularly gendered, nor even fully human.
In one instance, Alicia calls Lollie a "cave-woman."[19] Her unnatural strength,
like a man's, and her sexual drive, which has resulted in children too numerous to mention, are animalistic. After repeatedly succumbing to physical
cravings as well, Fat Woman is likewise powerless to control her own destiny
or even the actions of someone for whose services she presumably paid. In
such ways this brief scenario graphically links women's disobedient or unrestrained bodies with punishment and pain.

The comedic staging of women's bodies—in essence making women the
butt of jokes—is a well-established trend in *Ladies' Night* by the time we
meet Lottie and Fat Woman in Act 2. In the very first moments of the play,
for example, Suzon, a "pretty French maid," answers the door of the Walters
home and discovers Bob Stanhope, who introduces himself as a newspaper
reporter. When Suzon invites him to enter, Stanhope admits that he is not
acquainted with the Walterses but states that he "can't imagine being invited
anywhere by [Suzon], and refusing!" According to the script, the actor who
portrays Stanhope then gazes admiringly at Suzon. He adds, superfluously,
that he is a "judge of feminine beauty" and substantiates this claim by noting
his prior employment as a chorus boy in the *Follies*.[20] Flirtatious banter thus
monopolizes the opening of the play and continues thereafter to comprise a
substantial portion of its dialogue.

Sometimes sexual innuendo is quite overt. In her initial conversation with
Bob Stanhope, for example, Suzon describes her boss, Jimmy Walters, as
preoccupied with his inventions. When Stanhope asks what kinds of things
Walters invents, a giggling Suzon, in her characteristically awkward English,
replies that he once invented a "peekle [pickle] protector," used to "protect
the shirt front, when the peekle, he squirt!"[21] This jest becomes even more
significant, of course, when we learn of Walters's obsessive efforts to avoid
contact with women so as to keep his passions in check. This early dialogue
between Stanhope and Suzon accomplishes two dramatic objectives central
to the themes of this play: it establishes a tone of jocularity, particularly about
sex, and it introduces the play's compulsive focus on the bodies of women.
The visual objectification of a woman by a man, any man in fact, is presented
as natural, even as a given. Suzon, for instance, seems hardly to notice, let
alone take offense at a stranger's forward attentions. And when Stanhope
implies that she may be the reason for Jimmy Walters's reputation as a "stay-
at-home," Suzon protests, but not because of the adulterous theme of his

allusion. Instead, she states that Walters does not like women, noting as proof that he never looks at her.[22]

After Jimmy steals into the Larchmont Bath, his woeful attempts to cope with the sight of women's exposed bodies underscores the varying states of undress in which the women appear. When Jimmy ventures out momentarily from his hiding place behind the shower curtain, for example, he sees the Blonde backing into the room from the swimming pool. She wears "only a very large Turkish towel, wrapped around her body, but leaving her legs, her arms and shoulders and most of her bust bare. Jimmy gasps and then once more disappears behind the shower-bath curtain."[23] Jimmy's scripted nonverbal response thus draws as much attention to the woman's physique as the business of agitating shower curtains and the wearing of loosely draped towels.

Clearly, these stage directions to the Blonde, as well as similar actor instructions throughout the play, prescribe appearances with calculating detail, carefully designating the liberal degree to which the bodies of women are exposed. This specificity suggests a sexual agenda that both Hopwood and A. H. Woods denied. The latter characterized the sex farces he produced not as salacious, of course, but as "zippy" or "spicey" and a worthy antidote to the gloomy days of Prohibition. In light of the recent war and relentless efforts of reformers to take away life's joys, Woods felt that he should be considered a "public benefactor" for trying to "drag people up out of the depths of despond."[24] Similarly, Hopwood stated: "People love a touch of the *risqué* just as they love a cocktail before dinner—if they can get it in these curious times."[25] He emphatically denied accusations that he intended *Ladies' Night* to be lewd and said he felt that the comic aspect of the play defused its potential to carry even a "trace of sexual feeling" so that "one is never conscious of the presence of Aphrodite."

Hopwood noted that new, revealing fashions for women signaled the passing of the Victorian era and claimed to be exploring this issue in *Ladies' Night*. He argued that the play was little more than a satire of the perennial war between "Mrs. Grundy and Dame Fashion."[26] In light of the heated fashion controversy that was underway, some viewers were surely offended that *Ladies' Night* travestied what was to them a very serious matter. Not only does the play feature scantily attired women, it also mocks those who prefer the ostensibly more chaste styles of an earlier era. Be that as it may, however, *Ladies' Night* undermined far more than the fashion debates.

Getting the Joke: An Analysis of Ladies' Night

We have good reason to question Hopwood's seeming oblivion to the sexual implications of this play. Careful scrutiny of the text and performance dynamics of *Ladies' Night* reveals the play's veiled as well as explicit sexuality and particularly how the bodies of women symbolize such sexuality. Evidence that became available subsequent to Hopwood's untimely death in 1928 also raises the interesting question of how his own homosexuality may have influenced the themes of and audience reaction to this play.[27] Indeed, I contend that, on several levels, *Ladies' Night* may be most satisfactorily interpreted and its audiences' reactions assessed in light of Hopwood's sexual orientation.

Jimmy Walters prefers, or at least feels "safest" sexually in the company of other men—or "boys" as they are frequently called by themselves and others.[28] He avoids women, not apparently out of sexual desire for men but because he can barely contain his sexual desire for women. His passion ignites, in Pavlovian fashion, at the merest glimpse of exposed female anatomy. Walters's magnified heterosexuality, in fact, obscures the affront his character presents to socially sanctioned sexual pairings. He burlesques heterosexual male sexual attraction to females and thus trivializes "normal" sexual relations. Nonetheless, a heterosexual imperative carefully contains this parody, however irreverent or grotesque.

As George Chauncey notes in his extensive historical analysis of gay male culture in New York, gay men responded to their marginalization in society by "playing on the artificiality of social roles and mocking the conventions of gender" through "camp." This term encompasses a wide range of behaviors by which gay men subversively responded to a social order that "represented itself as natural and preordained," including "natural" family and kinship structures.[29] To be sure, *Ladies' Night* expressly portrays "normal" male sex drives as a threat to family relationships. Dulcy, for example, given her husband's compulsions, glumly compares her marital life with that of her friends. She complains that "all my friends' husbands go out with them—and when I go, I have to go out alone—or else tag along with some other woman's man!"[30] Marriage in the world of *Ladies' Night* is a fragile thing. Male infidelity is ever near the surface in the action and dialogue of the play. In this way, the play mocks the hegemony of heterosexuality. In another instance, Babette, a woman Jimmy meets at the ball, exclaims: "I might have known it! It's always the married guys that are out painting the town red!"[31] Babette's words clearly denote the precarious foundation on which the conventional family structure rests. Her emphasis on the promiscuity of heterosexual men may also be seen as an attempt to transpose accusations, to "reverse the charges," as it were, that homosexual men behaved immorally.

Chauncey contends as well that "[g]ay men . . . used gay subcultural codes to place themselves and to see themselves in the dominant culture, to read the culture against the grain in a way that made them more visible than they were supposed to be, and to turn 'straight' spaces into gay spaces."[32] This in mind, we note with particular interest the early moments of the play subsequent to the arrival of the Walterses' friends. Mimi and Alicia and their respective partners, Cort and Fred, exchange lighthearted banter while waiting for Jimmy and Dulcy to appear. On one level, their dialogue appears perfectly uncomplicated—just ordinary chitchat between good friends. On another level, however, the words seem to alert gay males that this play may also be experienced "against the grain." As the couples speculate about whether Jimmy will join them, the women express exasperation at the prospect that he may again sabotage their plans. The following conversation ensues:

MIMI: What in the world's the matter with the—the—
FRED: The poor fish!
MIMI: Thanks! That's just the word!
CORT: The poor fish has inventionitis!
ALICIA: But must he be inventing twenty four hours a day?
FRED: And then, Jimmy doesn't *like* parties! He always *was* shy, when it came to women!
CORT: Yes—you see, he had no sisters.
MIMI: *You* never had any sisters—and it doesn't seem to have cramped *your* style!
FRED: Jimmy doesn't seem to be so bad in the *afternoon*—I mean, at tea-fights, with women—but in the evening—well, there must be something about seeing women décolleté—that upsets him. He's such a quiet, bashful chap![33]

Chauncey states that "gay men developed a rich language of their own, which reflected the complex character and purposes of gay culture generally." He quotes Donald Vining, who used the following example to explain how gay men used double entendre to code their conversations. "I adore seafood [sailors]. Gorge myself whenever the fleet's in. But I can't abide fish [women]."[34] It is possible, especially given the attention-getting way in which the word is supplied in this scene, that "fish" is also a gender marker, an invitation to read alternative meanings into Jimmy's character.

When Fred describes Jimmy as shy with women, Cort explains that Jimmy has no "sisters." Again, in the vernacular of gay male culture, "sister" denoted a particular kinship relationship between gay men.[35] A "tea-fight," furthermore, alludes not only to gatherings between society women in polite cafés but also to "tearooms," slang for "toilet-rooms" or restrooms where gay men could meet and have homosexual encounters.[36] Notably, the authors textually configure each of these terms so as to be highlighted when spoken. Mimi stammers until Fred supplies the word *fish*; Cort emphasizes the word *sisters* with the otherwise superfluous phrase "Yes—you see." It is as though he were letting someone in on a secret. Pauses, as well as the hedge "I mean," frame the line about "tea-fights." Moreover, that the three terms appear in the exposition of the play and before we ever meet Jimmy suggests that they are crucial to understanding his character and the play as a whole. That they are essentially clustered together in a few lines of dialogue also increases their conspicuousness and thus signals their employment as gay argot.

Another scene in this play indicates that his creator(s) meant for those who knew the lingo to "read" the character of Jimmy Walters as a coded joke on heterosexuals. When Jimmy agrees to go to the ball with Fred and Cort, Fred tells him to be sure to shave—even though he will be wearing a mask. When Jimmy insists that he shaved that morning, Fred tells him to do so again anyway.[37] Chauncey explains the care with which some gay men "engendered" their appearance to approximate the "ideal gender types" of gay culture. The removal of facial hair and the application of makeup were common techniques. Also, gay men appropriated "stereotypical" voice inflections and manners and modes of speech that enabled them to signal their sexual identities to others.[38] Indeed, the script explicitly states that Jimmy is "soft-voiced" and "mild-mannered."[39] Through these designators, Hopwood and Andrews again seem to hint that Jimmy's character may be interpreted in more than one way.

In James C. Scott's anthropological analysis of the multifaceted nature of human resistance, he describes the various means by which discourse empowers both socially dominant and socially subordinate groups. In addition to discourse that overtly flatters dominant groups and, conversely, that which, hidden from social superiors, sharply criticizes them, there is a third realm of discourse that "lies strategically between the two." Scott emphasizes the importance of this third realm of discourse, stating that to ignore it "reduces us to an understanding of historical subordination that rests either on those rare moments of open rebellion or on the hidden transcript itself, which is not just evasive but often altogether inaccessible." Scott argues that an examination of resistant discourse of this third variety reveals a "politics of disguise and anonymity that takes place in public view but is designed to have a double meaning or to shield the identity of the actors." Furthermore, Scott contends that a "partly sanitized, ambiguous, and coded version of the hidden transcript is always present in the public discourse of subordinate groups." Scott's words may reasonably apply to *Ladies' Night* if, as I propose, we interpret the play as a coded, public text excerpted from a much larger underground narrative of homosexual resistance to heterosexual hegemony. Apropos of this discussion as well, Scott admonishes: "Interpreting these texts which, after all, are designed to be evasive is not a straightforward matter."[40]

Is *Ladies' Night* in fact a public and, paradoxically, hidden transcript of Hopwood's private resistance to those who would impose their sexual standards on him? It is, of course, impossible to say for sure whether Hopwood wittingly lampooned the sexual mores of a dominant culture—mores to which he himself would never fully subscribe. Still, *Ladies' Night* clearly does travesty heterosexuality. But that is not the only way in which the play may be viewed as camp.

Another significant indicator of the potentially subversive nature of this play is that it occurs primarily in a bathhouse. Again, the work of George Chauncey illuminates this issue. He describes the importance of the bath-house to gay male culture in the early part of the century in this way:

> Most amenable to the interests of gay men were the private Russian and Turk-ish baths that dotted Manhattan. As the middle class's preoccupation with the body intensified . . . such baths became highly respectable and fashionable resorts by offering a wide range of services. By the 1920s there were fifty-seven of them in Manhattan, some located in the basements of hotels, others in their own, often lavishly decorated buildings. It is likely that sexual encounters oc-curred occasionally at most private bathhouses."[41]

Chauncey further explains that the bathhouse became a "fixture in gay life and culture," part of a "gay folklore." These baths tended to attract an afflu-ent clientele, and some baths became among the first commercial and "exclu-sively gay" spaces in New York.[42]

One source Chauncey cites also suggests that bathhouse steam rooms were reserved for more explicit sexual encounters.[43] That the Larchmont Bath was one of the primary locations for the action of *Ladies' Night* surely represented something quite different to gay members of an audience for this play than it did to "straight" viewers. That it was intended to do so seems especially likely in that Dulcy tells Jimmy that she will be thinking of him "even in the steam room," and Jimmy, "touched," says to Fred: "Did you hear that? Even in the steam room!"[44] Dulcy later learns of Jimmy's exploits in part from Babette, who claims that he had grabbed her in the "shimmy." Dulcy then cries, hysterically: "Oh—you dreadful man! I suppose that's what you were doing in the steam room, too—grabbing women's shimmies!" Much agitated, Jimmy responds: "Oh, Dulcy, those women in the steam room didn't have any shimmies to be grabbed."[45] Such jests seem extraneous unless inter-preted in light of the significance of the bathhouse and especially the steam room within urban gay culture in the 1920s.

Masquerade balls were also a prominent fixture in gay male culture. Jack F. Sharrar states that Hopwood and Carl Van Vechten, a well-known New York author and theater critic now thought to have been gay or bisexual,[46] used to borrow costumes from the Victoria Theatre in New York. They would then attend the "season's fancy dress parties tricked out as 'the fairest ones of all.'"[47] Chauncey describes the enormous popularity of such parties and notes: "Inversions of race, class, and gender status were central to the conceit."[48] That the action of this play includes a masquerade ball, as well as a Turkish bath, both prominent and clearly marked "gay spaces" within New York's homosexual culture in the 1920s, seems to point decisively to a reading of *Ladies' Night* that responds to the play's subversive implications.

Jimmy attends the revel at Kensington Hall dressed as a Spanish toreador. Fred and Cort dress in "fantastic costumes," including Spanish shawls and stockings.[49] Each man alters his disguise to some degree, however, when he enters the bathhouse on this night when only women are allowed. He must, of course, conceal not only gender and ethnicity but avoid recognition entirely. It is not hard to imagine that the ludicrous costumes the men wore and especially the fact that they were compelled to disguise themselves as women at the bath were great fun to watch. Here again, though, the humor of the play is at least in part at the expense of women. Jimmy, Fred, and Cort's campy femininity—and ethnicity as well—seems of a piece with the indiscriminate visual typecasting of women throughout this play.

In spite of the necessarily circuitous process of interpreting *Ladies' Night* as camp or, in Scott's terminology, as part of a larger subversive "hidden transcript," I would argue that such a reading illuminates the work. This view of the play poignantly underscores its censorship and complicates our view of the female body as icon as well. Through the interpretive framework developed here, *Ladies' Night* emerges as yet another fascinating instance of the multilayered, often inscrutable forms of resistance enacted by those who are otherwise repressed by and within the mores of a dominant culture. Given Hopwood's cultural marginalization as a homosexual, even if such marginalization were known only to himself, the ways in which he appropriates, exploits, and parodies heterosexuality in general and women in particular in *Ladies' Night* may well be read as subversive. And in the sense that *Ladies' Night* represents the critical discourse of a nondominant social group, it is not surprising to find that this discourse also strikes out at other social minorities. By extension, as we have seen, it is not uncommon that members of subordinate social groups compete even between themselves for what limited influence they have. Certainly in debates over everything from corsets to careers in entertainment, women, for example, were often the first to vilify each other to forward personal agendas.

In addition to what I suggest is his coding of the plays he authored or coauthored—a point to which I also alluded in my discussion of his play *The Gold Diggers*—Hopwood's own denials that he purposefully scripted sexually illicit subject matter seem duplicitous as well. Ordinarily sophisticated and articulate when describing his artistic process, on the subject of sexuality in his plays, Hopwood seems merely coy:

I have tried not to offend. I must confess that occasionally I have been shocked by one of my own lines. . . . I listen to my audience. If it laughs wholeheartedly and wholesomely at a line, I let it stand. But if the laugh comes furtively, or only from the men, I cut it. . . . I remember [a] case, in which a magistrate took exception to certain lines in a play of mine. I could not see what he found objectionable in them. He told me. . . . I was half amused, half horrified. He was, I suppose, a man of unreproachable character, but he had the mind of the reformer—which . . . often is a moral garbage can. And when he told me that he had gone over the play with his wife and his daughter, and they had all of them found the same meanings in those innocent lines, I thought, "My God what a family!"[50]

Genuine or feigned, Hopwood's self-avowed naïveté bespeaks a carefully crafted but incongruous strategy of resistance to moral and sexual hegemony. Hopwood implies here that he willingly submits to the spontaneous judgments of his audience and that he is particularly sensitive to the responses of the women who frequent his plays. He disdains, however, the authority of those who, in this case, quite literally represent a patriarchal establishment and who, in the name of traditional codes of righteousness, calculatingly dissect the content of his plays in hopes of securing evidence for their dismissal. Hopwood privileges women by listening even to their silence, but when significant male others filter to him the responses of women, he summarily ignores these messages. His reactions in this seem not exploitive or competitive but to some extent collusive with those who are, like himself, disenfranchised within the dominant social order.

On at least one occasion, Hopwood commented expansively on the social strictures that subdued women's responses to his work.

It is a peculiar thing, though, about men and women, in an audience. I have noticed, in plays of my own, that in the evening women will often not laugh at a line which was laughed at very heartily by a matinee audience, composed almost exclusively of women. The reason, of course, for the evening restraint, is that the woman fears to laugh at a *risqué* line, before her male escort, lest she destroy some of his illusions about her. It is rather a pity that women are thus forced to control themselves, for I think that, generally speaking, they enjoy *risqué* plays more than the men do. You see, the average male lives a—shall we say, less sheltered life—than the average female. He does all the things that most of the women only think about. That is why, of course, he often reads into a play meanings which are not there, but which are supplied by his own spotted consciousness.[51]

Hopwood's professed inability to detect the sexual innuendo within his plays otherwise situates him ambiguously within the ranks of his own gender, but his implied knowledge of the sordid experiences of the "average male," such that he is reluctant even to name such experiences, clearly belies the artlessness he claimed. To be sure, Hopwood empathizes with women who, although quick to appreciate the unwholesome, are constrained by societal (i.e., male) expectations and respond openly only when not in the company of men. The text of *Ladies' Night* may even be read in part as a delightfully twisted attempt to allow women to embody and enjoy a bawdy sensuality to which they were generally not privy. The fact that a female delivers the line about the "peekle protector" is an exemplary moment, although Hopwood would undoubtedly deny its double entendre. On the other hand, that Suzon does not seem to recognize the implications of her words represents Hopwood's own subscription to a sexism that delighted in the childish innocence of women.

The incongruity of Hopwood's counterhegemonic strategy as reflected in his attitude toward women surfaces in other ways as well. For example, Hopwood and Andrews's use of the female body as a comedic device does not, as Hopwood would argue, remove the element of sexuality from the play. Instead, comedy in this instance is merely an alternative means by which to appropriate the female form for commercial profit. In this way, Hopwood and Andrews do not differ significantly from Ziegfeld, who presented the bared female body with all the reverence due a national emblem—which to him she was, provided she met his exclusive criteria. By likewise carefully styling women's bodily presentation but in such ways as to make them the brunt of unseemly jokes, the authors of *Ladies' Night* assumed an authority over the female image no less tyrannical than Ziegfeld's.

Neither a loosely draped Turkish bath towel nor a carefully placed length of chiffon is ever intended, in the theater at least, to function merely as clothing. The instability of these kinds of costumes accentuates rather than mutes gender characteristics, thereby enhancing sexual allure. A performer may seem to try to prevent seamless and/or scant articles from "slipping" too far or otherwise fully "betraying" her sexuality to an audience. The fact is, though, that these precautions themselves are often meant to attract sexual interest. For example, in act 2 of *Ladies' Night*, the Blonde encounters the disguised Jimmy and nonchalantly chats with him. Suddenly she declares, "Oh, Lord! I never can make these sheets behave! I've got it all crooked!" Parenthetical stage directions note: "Her back to the footlights, and facing Jimmy, she spreads sheet out straight behind her, to readjust it." Naturally, Jimmy is "stunned by the vision."[52] For the performers of *Ladies' Night*, costuming was clearly contrived to display their bodies rather than to conceal them.

Most leg shows in the 1920s indeed created sexual appeal by accentuating a costume's *potential* to reveal the performer's embodied sexuality. In this way such shows also deferred some measure of criticism by stopping short of full nudity. "Tentative" attire speaks not only to the accessibility of its wearer's embodied sensuality, but the manner in which such clothing is worn may enhance this message. As I noted in the previous chapter, burlesque lost what remained of its commercial popularity in the late 1920s when it resorted to actual, not simulated, nudity. Revues, which had already crossed this line, still managed to create the illusion of formality and restraint so that most audience members, men and women alike, were not offended by the occasional display of bare breasts or buttocks. The aggressive availability suggested by the burlesque striptease, however, was too extreme for many of its patrons.[53] *Ladies' Night*, whose techniques for the display of women's bodies could by no means be classified as decorous, was relegated, like the burlesque shows of its time, to a kind of theatrical limbo reserved for those entertainments that were attended perhaps by many but praised by few.

The performer's own choices with regard to her self-presentation significantly affect her relationship to her audience and thus the nature of their response to her. Again, a scene from *Ladies' Night* is exemplary. Based on parenthetical staging notes, we can imagine the actions of the actor who portrays the Brunette. Early in act 2 she enters a shower, discards the sheet she has been wearing, turns on the water, "squeals," and finally, after much agitation of curtains, dries herself while she occasionally peeks out from behind the shower curtain.[54] Her performance thus initiates a subtextual, albeit rudimentary, even subliminal, dialogue between actor and audience. A nonverbal exchange like this one, composed of the intricate layering of costume, gesture, physical presence, and physical absence or removal, need not relate to the central action of the play. But as a means by which to increase both performer as well as viewer awareness of the embodied and gendered nature of their shared experience, these kinds of exchanges are essential.

Although these particular actions are assigned within the script of *Ladies' Night*, the performer must still consciously decide in each performance how much of, what portions of, and for how long her body will be viewed. Moreover, her decision will likely be affected to some degree by the particular audience she faces. Her performance before a matinee audience—which, according to Hopwood, was composed mostly of women—might well differ from her performance before a mixed or mostly male audience.[55] Audience response itself may affect her willingness to display herself. Her own prerogatives and the actions prescribed by the script or other production authorities mark her desirability as well as the extent to which she presumably wishes to be the object of desire. In this way, through the nonverbal dialogue she creates, the performer shares complicity with the authors and producers of the play with regard to the presentation of her body and the meaning attributed to such a presentation.

In her historical study of American actresses, Faye E. Dudden also addresses the topic of performer agency. Her comments effectively supplement my own contention throughout this book that women's performances in the 1920s, though circumscribed, were nonetheless potentially empowering. Moreover, Dudden alludes to a point I explicitly articulate, that is, that women performed not only on the stages of America's theaters, but throughout their daily lives.

> Since a female actor works through the possibility of self-transformation, her work is intrinsically akin to the actions of modern women who have learned to play new roles and thus have changed modern America. This essential promise —that because a role is a role, we may yet enact a different one—continues to throw surprising spice into the otherwise predictable commercial stews the entertainment industry cooks up.[56]

Dudden thus acknowledges, as do I, that by their unique appropriation of even heavily proscribed behaviors, American women altered their society and, over time, the nation itself.

Throughout the history of the American theater in particular, women have enthusiastically participated in the creative process, both as artists and as "consumers." Despite the tendency of the theatrical industry to exploit human resources—and certainly the resources of women—the theater itself nevertheless affords a transcendent space in which both privileged and marginalized groups may, as Dudden suggests, "live . . . within disguise or lose themselves temporarily in playfulness."[57] In this way, a play such as *Ladies' Night*, at first glance a trivial sex farce, created a world that women watched and enjoyed and perhaps felt empowered within. Likewise, if I am not mistaken, the play also made a "straight" place gay, with homosexual men the viewers who were most "in on the joke." Indeed, *Ladies' Night* encouraged gays to laugh at the expense of heterosexuals who, if aware that the joke was on them, would have tried even harder than some did try to deny them the opportunity.

Although he did not emphasize performer agency to the extent that I do, A. H. Woods nevertheless acknowledged the impact a particular performer might have on the perceived sexual content of a play. Within the context of a discussion of *Ladies' Night* he noted:

> Certain actors and actresses can lend delicacy to a part which would seem vulgar and common handled by less capable artists. I am particularly careful in making up the casts of these plays. A young, flippant, little actress can succeed in making the character which she portrays in the play seem merely saucy, while another, older, more sophisticated woman might make the character appear absolutely loose and immoral.[58]

Curiously analogous to Hopwood's tendency to employ childish innocence to offset or deny lewdness, Woods also factors in youth as an important way to maintain the illusion of at least a modicum of propriety in potentially objectionable plays. Youth mattered a great deal as well to producers like Ziegfeld, who felt that the oldest "chorus girl" he knew, a thirty-six-year-old woman, was "unique in her record."[59] Ziegfeld noted in morbid detail the "inexorable" signs of approaching middle age, clearly indicating his familiarity with the process of detecting such signs in his own choruses.[60] Although he was surely unwilling to allow an "aging" woman into the ranks of his elite chorus because of his own aesthetic prejudices, he just as surely recognized youthfulness as important to preserving the "wholesomeness" of his productions.

Youth as an ideal of feminine beauty was well established in American culture by the 1920s and has been a pervasive ideal since then.[61] Producers like Woods and Ziegfeld frankly admitted the importance of feminine youthfulness within their own productions even while they avoided truly difficult questions about why, how, and to what ends they appropriated the youthful female form. Many women, temporarily young and contingently beautiful, nevertheless wholeheartedly embraced the shallow values that enabled their bodily appropriation, the same values that in fact empowered their commodifiers. This flimsy faith, as it were, yielded disastrous consequences in some instances.

Allyn King, the actor who portrayed Alicia Bonner in both the New York and Chicago productions of *Ladies' Night*, began her professional career in Ziegfeld's *Midnight Frolic* in 1915 at the age of fifteen or sixteen and became a principal with the *Follies* shortly thereafter (fig. 35).[62] In the tenth-anniversary production of the *Follies* in 1916, King portrayed the "Follies' Girl of 1916" for the opening number of the production. The women in this portion of the revue paraded in chronological order, one woman for each year of the *Follies'* history. King's last-place position as the representative for 1916 no doubt served as a kind of finale, suggesting an exceptional measure of performer beauty and prestige. One reviewer for the Boston edition of this production noted the "pleasant memories" brought to mind by this sequential display of "the girls who have figured prominently since 1906." He referred to King specifically when he commented that she "[i]n dress and undress . . . appealed strongly to the front row."[63]

Lilyan Tashman, a colleague of King's during their tenure in the Ziegfeld chorus, appreciated this young woman for quite different reasons. Tashman framed her comments about King as a defense of "girls that have been looked on for decades as trailing their colors in the dust," no doubt referring to the cultural stigma against chorus girls. Tashman told the story of a man who had nightly attended the Ziegfeld *Frolic* for weeks. Everyone could tell that he came to admire King, whom Tashman described as one of Ziegfeld's "rarities,"

FIG. 35. Allyn King in *Ladies' Night*, Eltinge Theatre, New York, 1920. Culver Pictures.

a woman with "a long fringe of eyelashes, like an awning over a complexion, that resembled a handful of gardenia leaves." One night the man attended the performance accompanied by a "fragile" woman Tashman identified as his wife. Tashman's unflattering description of this woman focuses largely on her unmistakable air of social snobbery. The chorus paraded around the edge of the dance floor. As they neared the table where the couple sat, the man said to his wife, while staring at King, "Look, it is the third one. Isn't she exquisite?" When King approached, the woman stood and threw a glass of champagne in King's face. According to Tashman, King "never batted an eyelid, but, gazing straight before her, with the wine dripping over her make-up, continued her march. Nor did she discuss the unfortunate incident in the dressing room." King's silence about the episode displayed to Tashman "even finer taste than her restraint."[64]

This incident was a telling moment in the life of a young woman whose experiences so starkly foreground the precarious, even ominous nature of a stardom founded on superficial assessments of human worth. Her admirer's fixation on King, his obsession with her physical beauty, and his ritualized voyeurism all speak to the mesmerizing, hypnotic effect Ziegfeld's carefully orchestrated sequence of parading female bodies had on audiences. That one who perceived in this spectacle of feminine beauty a personal threat deserving of such fury, and conversely, her husband's imperviousness to such a possibility, poignantly show how admiration and disdain mutually comprised the public perception of chorus girls. This brief glimpse of King's character as revealed in her response to the rage of a woman who viewed her as a rival says, of course, much more about King's human worth than her status as a Ziegfeld chorus girl. We also may thereby appreciate more fully the tragedy of her loss.

King performed in Ziegfeld productions until 1920. By the time she portrayed Alicia Bonner, she had earned a reputation for her work as a musical comedy actor as well. *Theatre Magazine* noted that her performance in the 1920 New York premiere of *Ladies' Night* was her first appearance in a nonmusical production.[65] Sadly, by this time as well, King was not only "past her prime" professionally, at the age of twenty, but had also already spent over half of her short life. She appeared in movies for a time, but by 1927 she was allegedly "forced to retire" due to weight gain.[66] In *The Ziegfeld Touch*, a book whose title seems pitifully ironic in this case, Richard and Paulette Ziegfeld summarize the last few years of King's life:

> After going on a self-imposed diet, King collapsed in her apartment. She suffered a nervous breakdown and spent two years in a sanitarium. After her release, King gained weight again. She became so depressed that her family would not let her go out alone. In 1930, when her aunt (with whom King lived)

left her New York apartment briefly, King jumped from a fifth-floor window
into the courtyard below.

King remained conscious after her fall and was expected to recover from the
injuries she sustained, which included fractures to her skull, arm, and leg.
Her condition worsened suddenly, however, and she died the next day. She
was only thirty years old.[67]

It is entirely possible, even likely, that other factors besides weight-related
depression prompted King to commit suicide. Based on the information
available to us, though, her weight gain was understandably very problematic
for her. That Ziegfeld's organization selected and groomed her when she was
still essentially a child must have had an enormous impact on King's subsequent life choices. Even to appear in the *Follies* chorus, not to mention to
become a principal in a *Follies* revue, was only a dream for most chorus girls.
As I discussed previously, although there were some aspects of their profession that disadvantaged the women of the chorus, especially in terms of their
personal reputations, the chorus was also one of the few careers available to
women that offered the prospect of financial independence, even wealth.
None of the members of elite choruses like Ziegfeld's could expect to remain
employed for long though, no matter how popular they were. The natural
process of aging was and still is the nemesis of female success in entertainment. But for King to have at one time met Ziegfeld's exacting standards and
then to "fall from grace" after she had committed her resources, including
her youth and beauty, to her profession was understandably devastating. This
is not to deny King's own autonomy. Based on other accounts by women who
were "discovered" by Ziegfeld, King was probably as eager as they were to
join his ranks of elite beauties.[68] King's employers, however, estimated her
value largely on the basis of her physical beauty, as did her audiences. Ultimately, it would seem, so did she.

Although King's story is unique and does not necessarily represent the experiences of other women, it nevertheless effectively elucidates the unhappy
consequences of evaluating a woman's worth by her ability to meet and maintain certain arbitrary and sometimes unrealistic physical criteria. Women like
King were cultural icons. They represented the ideal in American femininity,
especially given Ziegfeld's personal influence and the capacity of the media
by this time to disseminate their images. But that such women were so
quickly withdrawn from public view when they no longer fit this exacting
image—in some cases regardless of any talent they may have possessed—
spoke persuasively to society at large about the qualified nature of a woman's
right to be seen and heard.

When King performed in *Ladies' Night* at the Woods Theatre in Chicago,
the fifteenth annual production of the Ziegfeld *Follies* also played just two

doors away at the Colonial Theatre. Amy Leslie, a Chicago theater critic, noted this irony when she expressed special admiration for King's performance in *Ladies' Night*:

> Then there is the sculptural Allyn King, whose profile and exquisite coloring make her something like a Venus de Milo wading about in mud without galoshes.
>
> Nothing feminine even next door, where [Will] Rogers and his galaxy of beauty hold court, can hold a dim taper to Allyn. She thrills when she stands glowing in her trim bath sheet, she torments when she smiles beautifully, she awes when she turns her perfect profile sharp against the grim walls and she tricks the audience into a soothing calm by her loveliness.[69]

Notably, Leslie's comments also present King as merely a pleasurable object to gaze upon, particularly in her references to King as "sculptural" and "like a Venus de Milo." For all her specificity about King's appearance, even to the point that she seems sexually attracted to King, Leslie does not refer at all to King's acting ability. This perhaps raises questions about whether King was indeed talented or whether talent was considered unimportant in one so beautiful; more likely, it suggests once again that for a woman, talent was less important than physical beauty.

Leslie was apparently the only newspaper critic in Chicago—the rest of whom were male—who did not pan *Ladies' Night*. As noted earlier, Hopwood acknowledged the popularity of this play among women. Ashton Stevens also commented on the preponderance of women in the afternoon performance of *Ladies' Night* that he attended. "The scream of appreciation was shrill, and I missed the hoarse laughter of the avid sailor in our port. . . . But the ladies laughed long and loud for 'Ladies' Night,' seeing in it, I should have said, nothing at all sexual and much that was as ridiculous as a Mack Sennett bathing picture."[70] Although we cannot conclusively determine why women so enjoyed *Ladies' Night*, we may reasonably suppose that they did appreciate the way in which the play lampoons heterosexual males' sexual vulnerability to them. That the men of *Ladies' Night* make such fools of themselves, in large part because of their desire for as well as fear of women, undoubtedly amused and gratified the women who came to watch this play. After all, men were disproportionately advantaged in so many other ways in American culture. *Ladies' Night* reminded women that they still possessed means by which to wield power over men. This aspect of the popularity of *Ladies' Night* seems a natural counterpart to an analysis of the play that responds to the potential influence of Hopwood's homosexuality on its underlying themes. Indeed, from this perspective as well, Hopwood appears empathic toward women who, like homosexual men, endured many sexually related social prohibitions—despite the fact that *Ladies' Night* also contributed to the objectification of women in its own way.

Notwithstanding reasonable popular success and perhaps outstanding success with women, most theater critics scorned *Ladies' Night*. In Chicago the production was ultimately censored as well. Clearly, attempts by Woods, Hopwood, or anyone else to disguise the transgressions of *Ladies' Night* were not convincing. The censure of this production, critical as well as legal, surely represented a wide spectrum of individual responses, including, as Hopwood himself suggested, preferences for Victorian ideals of feminine conduct and display. Certainly the offenses of *Ladies' Night* relate in part to the kind and quality of subtextual dialogue which, as I discussed earlier, sexualized the relationship between performer(s) and audience. This "conversation," as it were, was too candid in *Ladies' Night*. The blatant and patently contrived sexual teasing within the exchange, sometimes only minimally connected to the plot and setting of the play, presumed an unwarranted familiarity between actors and audience. Such familiarity was especially uncomfortable to some in that it too closely resembled the unwelcome advances of a social and perhaps sexual (i.e., female) inferior.

Several such demographically related biases surface in a *Chicago Tribune* editorial that proclaimed the play to be "offensive in the same way that grimy finger nails, smutty linen, and dirty necks are offensive." The editorialist asserted that "[p]ity rather than condemnation should be the portion of those attracted by the salacious suggestion of the play's title. . . . The fact that the audience registered amusement is not only evidence of poor taste, and low intelligence but proof positive that in such offerings the theater is demoralizing its patrons."[71] To be sure, not everyone felt this way about *Ladies' Night*, or it would not have succeeded at all. But these comments do advance an image of the audience members who were perhaps most offended by the antics of the play and thus unwilling to participate in any exchange, subtextual or otherwise, with its cast.

The show of innocence that accompanied the preposterous machinations of *Ladies' Night* doubly infuriated some viewers. The theater critic Charles Collins, of the *Chicago Evening Post*, expressed this point candidly. He noted that the play produced a "high degree of suggestiveness without becoming indecent," but he observed as well that the hypocrisy of the play was "sublimely impertinent" and that "every leering or knowing allusion is accompanied by its alibi of perfect purity." He compared *Ladies' Night* to *The Demi-Virgin* and informed readers that the latter had initiated talk in New York of a stage censor whose job it would be to "quell such blatancies." Collins doubted that *Ladies' Night* would ever face such censorship. He observed wryly: "But if a censorship is established, 'Ladies' Night' is in no danger of being retroactively expurgated or squelched, for it manufactures its own alibis, and like the cuttlefish merrily avoids capture in a cloud of its own ink. The cleverest thing about such plays is their skill in getting by."[72] As Collins so frankly admits, *Ladies' Night* seemed to some viewers to be merely one piece in a progressive pattern of depravity in the theater, with each new installment proving more daring than the last.

It is not difficult to decipher Collins's evident irritation if, as I propose, one views *Ladies' Night* as a public, yet hidden transcript of resistance to cultural hegemony. James C. Scott, who interprets a variety of manifestations of "folk culture" in precisely this way, seems to describe *Ladies' Night* when he explains that resistant discourse often comprises jokes, codes, and euphemisms and appears on the surface to be "nothing but innocent stories." Scott also notes that at a deeper level this kind of discourse is a highly politicized vehicle by which to celebrate the "cunning wiles and vengeful spirit of the weak as they triumph over the strong."[73] From this perspective as well, women's delight at the power of their sex to "unhinge" Jimmy Walters may also be characterized as celebratory.

Whatever else it may have accomplished, the duplicity and pretension of *Ladies' Night* did sabotage some viewers' enjoyment of the play. Probably those who felt discomfited by the play were not completely sure why they felt so. If, indeed, Hopwood's sly, coded mockery of heterosexuality constitutes the subversiveness of the play, such subversion is difficult to locate, much less articulate. Still, Collins and others like him, unconvinced by any protestations of innocence by the authors of the play or its producer or even by the blinking naïveté of its actors, felt sure that, somehow, *Ladies' Night* represented far more than met the eye, in spite of the fact that there was too much of even that.

The Legal Censorship of Ladies' Night

Hopwood's claim that *Ladies' Night* satirically illuminated the clash between Victorian and modern mores, although incomplete, is useful. Individuals who preferred Victorian-style feminine modesty undoubtedly felt that this play assaulted their moral sensibilities. Such persons resembled in this way the central character of *Ladies' Night*, a man who claimed to wish for the female fashions and decorum of an earlier time. As Hopwood noted, "Well, what is my hero but a man of the Victorian type, who has to be brought up to date by a series of . . . shocks?"[74] Perhaps this description of Walters applies equally well to the man who initiated the censorship of *Ladies' Night* in Chicago, Arthur Burrage Farwell.

By the time *Ladies' Night* played to Chicago audiences, Farwell was well known for his indefatigable efforts to rid the Windy City of all manner of corruption. Born in Massachusetts in 1852, he subsequently moved to Illinois with his parents and siblings. When he died in 1936, Farwell was a major figure of social reform due to his dogged public opposition to corrupt political practices and prostitution and his unflagging support of Prohibition enforcement.[75] He held offices in several early-twentieth-century, Chicago-based reform agencies.[76] In addition to fighting illegal activity, Farwell tried to shape ambiguous moral and aesthetic codes for Chicago's artistic and cultural institutions as well.[77]

A letter Farwell wrote in 1920 to Chicago chief of police John Garrity perhaps best summarizes Farwell's views on artistic and especially theatrical censorship. Here is an excerpt from that letter:

> From my long experience in public matters in this city, I consider one of the most important duties of the city government is a rigid censorship, not only of moving pictures, but of burlesque and vaudeville shows, and many of the so-called higher class theatres. I believe that where the churches of all denominations today are helping to save one boy or one girl, that three are slipping, and there is nothing that is helping to make them slip more than the vile shows in vaudeville and burlesque and some of the so-called higher class theaters. . . .[78]

Farwell frequently conveyed his opinions on a variety of topics in correspondence with influential persons. He worked hard to impress upon others his view that theater was a powerful and usually negative medium of influence. His record of animosity toward the theater began well before he attempted to suppress *Ladies' Night*. In 1910, for example, Farwell complained about the Chicago Opera Company's production of *Salome*, in which Mary Garden starred. Farwell did not attend this production himself because, as he was a "normal man," he did not trust himself to see Garden's performance. He apparently did trust Roy T. Steward, the police chief of Chicago at that time, who attended the show at Farwell's request. Steward described Garden's performance as "disgusting," saying that she "wallowed around like a cat in a bed of catnip." Garden allegedly responded archly to this criticism: "I always bow down to the ignorant and try to make them understand, but I ignore the illiterate." Apparently, Farwell and Steward's combined opposition to *Salome* was, in the end, more effective than Garden's tart retort, however, as the show was closed after three sold-out performances.[79]

Farwell's record of artistic censorship and especially his attack on *Aphrodite* in 1920 help to contextualize his response to *Ladies' Night* in early 1922. Farwell pressed for the censorship of *Aphrodite* because, as with *Salome*, of its reported indecency and especially because of the sexually provocative performances of the women in this production. Farwell attached a copy of his second letter that month to John J. Garrity to his report for the October 1920 meeting of the Chicago Law and Order League, a reform organization over which Farwell presided for many years. Farwell wrote to Garrity to complain about Morris Gest's production of *Aphrodite* (and "similar exhibitions"),

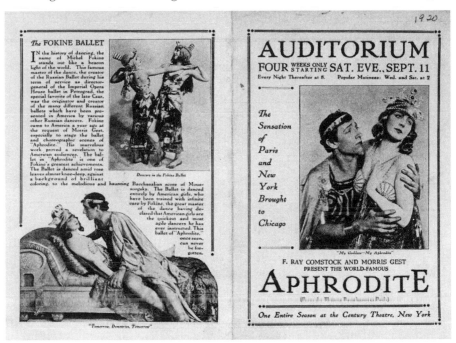

FIG. 36. Playbill for *Aphrodite*, Chicago, 1920. Department of Special Collections, the University of Chicago Library. Playbills and Programs, ser. 2, box 2, folder 2. Used by permission.

which then played at the Auditorium Theatre in downtown Chicago (see fig. 36). Farwell first acknowledged his own attendance at the play. He even admitted that he sat on the "first floor, not far from the stage." Curiously, he stated as well that he heard only one fourth of what was said. This was perhaps a concession to his advancing years. His eyes did not fail him even if his ears may have, for Farwell described in graphic detail his visual objections to the play. His lengthy letter included the following remarks:

> I think in every dance the women were bare-foot and their legs were bare, very little clothing on the upper part of the body; women lying on their stomachs on the stage, men and women lying near each other. . . . I should say the large proportion of the audience were men.
>
> The scene on the sofa between a man and a woman was extremely suggestive. . . . Perhaps the worst was the feast of the Bacchus. A figure of an ostrich was brought in, and out of the ostrich came a woman with feathers around the breasts and feathers around the hips—naked every other way. She danced on

the stage. Here we come, Chief, to almost a nude woman on exhibition in the
Auditorium Theatre. . . .

Chief, if you had a daughter . . . I think you would do everything in your
power to keep her not only from going to such a place, but above all keep her
from being one of the dancers in that wild revel of semi-nudity. . . .

I appeal to you to investigate this place, personally; and not only this place,
but some of the other so-called exhibitions in Chicago where it seems the principal attraction is the sex idea; and if this kind of a play is allowed on Michigan
Avenue, what about West Madison Street and other streets in Chicago?

. . . we believe that Chicago to have allowed and to allow today such exhibition as Aphrodite, and such exhibitions as are shown in some of the so-called
vaudeville houses in other parts of the city, instead of being a father and mother
to children, a big brother to men and boys, a help to its people, is doing the very
reverse.[80]

Many aspects of this letter warrant individual scrutiny, but one of the most
noteworthy is the frankness with which Farwell describes the nudity he
observed, including his use of the word *breasts*. To actually name a gender-
specific body part was considered indelicate at best, as many people at this
time still euphemistically referred even to gender-neutral appendages as
"limbs." Thus, Farwell's reference to feet and legs was also relatively explicit
for the time as well. One would certainly not expect such candor from an
elderly man who had such misgivings about nudity. Farwell's disapproval of
the nudity he observed evidently related to the assertiveness of the display.
He noted, for example, that women danced during the production. As I have
already suggested, certain kinds of movement signal a performer's desire
and/or desirability and thereby heighten sexual dynamics within the audi-
ence-performer relationship. Conversely, Ziegfeld, you will recall, felt that
nude women who stood passively for audience members to gaze upon were
not sexually provocative.[81] While certainly a debatable point, the stillness of
these performers distanced viewer from viewed, figuratively speaking, and
thereby fostered the sense that the performance was indeed "art."

In his letter to the police chief, Farwell specified the location of the Auditorium Theatre building as though this were also an important reason to censor *Aphrodite*. In his query as to what the side street theaters of Chicago
might resort to if the prestigious Auditorium Theatre condoned such shows,
he alludes to local socioeconomic class prejudices. Further, Farwell's patriarchal attitude seems clear when he refers both to the police chief as a protective father to his daughter and to the city of Chicago itself as a guardian of
its citizens.

Farwell sent copies of his meticulously crafted letter to Mayor William
Hale Thompson as well as to Corporation Counsel Samuel A. Ettelson.[82] A

referee, Assistant Corporation Counsel James W. Breen, was called upon to settle the "squabble" over *Aphrodite* and, to do so, attended a performance. Asked by a news reporter how he liked the show, Breen reportedly answered: "Well, I was disappointed. It wasn't half as [l]urid as these fellows made out. I went there with my wife. Neither of us was shocked."[83] Notably, even Breen's comparatively liberal views contained an allusion to the well-worn belief in women's heightened moral sensibilities. In the end, Breen decided in favor of the play's continuation and, although he belittled Farwell's concerns about *Aphrodite*, the two men would meet again in less than two years, when the reformer initiated a complaint against *Ladies' Night*. Compared with his reaction to *Aphrodite*, however, Breen's judgment against *Ladies' Night* would seem harsh.

Ladies' Night opened at the Woods Theatre in March 1922, only sixteen months after Farwell's letter to Garrity about *Aphrodite*. The Woods was one of at least two Chicago theaters A. H. Woods owned in 1922.[84] It was quite new—only three years old when *Ladies' Night* came to town—and it was conveniently located in the heart of the Chicago "Loop" theater district.[85] The Auditorium Theatre, where *Aphrodite* played, was just six blocks to the south of the Woods, also in the theater district. The comparable, although by no means equal, status of these theaters is indicated in part by the fact that both were listed in a 1922 publication provided for the guests of the exclusive Drake Hotel, which included diagrams and locations for only twenty Chicago theaters.[86] Chicago had scores of theaters by this time, but as Farwell's comments indicate, an address in the downtown theater district signified to some extent that the theater attracted a monied clientele. The location of the Woods Theatre thus suggests the socioeconomic status of the audience base that presumably supported it, and it is a means by which to situate a show like *Ladies' Night* within the context of other theatrical venues available in the city of Chicago at that time. Although the Ziegfeld *Follies* performed practically next door to the Woods Theatre, for example, a burlesque theater, the Star and Garter, was not located in the Loop at all; and the Columbia Burlesque Theatre, though in the Loop, was a considerable distance away from the Woods.[87]

Tickets for *Ladies' Night* cost $1.50, a price that was comparable to the more elite entertainments offered in the city at the time. The ballet star Anna Pavlova appeared with the Chicago Symphony Orchestra at the Auditorium Theatre the week after *Ladies' Night* opened. Ticket prices for this event ranged from $1.00 to $2.50. In contrast, the going rate for burlesque shows at the Columbia was a mere fifty cents.[88] Still, because it was a relative newcomer to the theater district and perhaps because of the reputation of its owner and the shows it presented, not everyone accepted the Woods as a "legitimate" theater. An editorialist for the *Chicago Tribune*, for one, described the experience of attending *Ladies' Night*: "Realizing as we found

FIG. 37. Advertisement for *Ladies' Night*, Chicago, 1922.
Chicago Tribune, 19 March 1922, sec. 8. Courtesy of the
Library of Congress.

our seats that this was the first time we had been in this particular theatre,
although it had been open for more than three years, we wondered why. We
recalled such names as 'Up in Mabel's Room,' 'Parlor, Bedroom, and Bath,'
'Getting Gertie's Garter.' There was the answer."[89]

Chicago newspapers heralded *Ladies' Night* as the "feministic farce-frolic"
that had enjoyed a long run in New York the previous season. The cast of the
original production was expected in Chicago, except for John Cumberland,
whom John Arthur replaced in the role of Jimmy Walters. Advertisements
for *Ladies' Night* showed cartoon profiles of two curvaceous women in form-
fitting, one-piece bathing suits—Annette Kellerman's no doubt—poised to
dive off the edge of diving boards (fig. 37).[90] Perhaps this image alerted Farwell to what he felt were the morally suspect intentions of this production.
The newspapers carried notices for many other shows that were undoubtedly
as risqué and that attempted to highlight this quality in advertising. In one
newspaper, for instance, directly below an ad for *Ladies' Night* was a none too
subtle ad for performances at the Star and Garter burlesque theater.[91] But
because the Woods Theatre stood in the Loop theater district, Farwell probably felt especially obliged, as with *Aphrodite* at the Auditorium, to target
Ladies' Night for censorship. Besides, Farwell surely knew, as did almost
everyone else, that this play was co-authored by the same person who wrote

the now notorious *Demi-Virgin*. In any event, just eight days after it opened, Chicago newspapers (and the *New York Times* as well) announced that Farwell hoped to end the run of *Ladies' Night*.[92]

In spite of this initial flurry of attention the censorship of *Ladies' Night* received, later news coverage of the event was sketchy. The information that remains is as follows. Farwell apparently did not attend *Ladies' Night* but said that a man in whom he had "implicit confidence" had informed him that the play was "not fit to be shown." On this basis and perhaps supported by the biting critical assessments of Stevens, Collins, and Butler, Farwell asked Mayor Thompson to send city police to curtail the production. Thompson deferred to the city's Law Department, where the case was given over to James W. Breen, by now a seasoned arbitrator in such matters. Breen summoned the managers of the production to appear before him on Tuesday, 28 March 1922, at 11:00 A.M. They were charged to "show cause why the license of the theater should not be revoked." Furthermore, said Breen, "If the facts warrant it, we will permit the theater owners to take their choice of losing their license or closing the show voluntarily."[93] Breen's initial posturing in this instance was decidedly more stern than one would expect given his laissez-faire attitude toward Farwell's complaints against *Aphrodite*.

News reports do not name the Woods Theatre representatives who appeared for the eleven o'clock summons. Woods himself had just recently appealed an unfavorable judgment handed down in the *Demi-Virgin* case in New York and now awaited a court date.[94] In light of his personal notoriety, that Woods's name does not appear in reports about the Chicago production of *Ladies' Night* suggests that he was not directly involved in defending it against censorship. His infamy and his evident tendency to be litigious may, however, explain Breen's initially punitive attitude toward the *Ladies' Night* case.

In spite of his austere warnings, Breen did not, in the end, close *Ladies' Night*. He first assigned a "censor board" to attend the play and report back to him with recommendations.[95] The board comprised Rev. John P. Brushingham, secretary of the Morals Commission of Chicago, and two assistant corporation counsels, William Saltiel and Eugene O'Sullivan.[96] When the three censors returned with recommendations for "certain cutouts," Breen concurred. The managers of the production then agreed to comply with the decision, and the matter was apparently settled with no further ado.[97] Although Chicago accounts did not include the following information, the *New York Times* quoted Farwell as saying that the play—and again, he had *not* seen it— was "unfit for human eyes." The unnamed representatives of the Woods production declared this criticism unjustified, as the play had "run nearly a year in New York, where it was the fad of the better class of New Yorkers." A statement was also issued on behalf of the Woods Theatre: "There is nothing objectionable either in the book or the cast."[98]

Except for limited news coverage of the incident, little additional evidence remains of the censorship of *Ladies' Night* in Chicago. My extensive investigation of extant court records and consultation with city archivists did not yield specific information about what parts of the play were edited.[99] The Chicago Law and Order League, which operated jointly with the Hyde Park Protective Organization, met only irregularly. Sometimes months would pass between meetings, and members' activities were only briefly mentioned in official minutes, if mentioned at all.[100] The minutes of these meetings do not refer to Farwell's efforts against *Ladies' Night*.

The primary goal of these jointly run organizations in which Farwell figured so prominently, put simply, was to uphold the laws of the city and the nation. A motto printed in bold lettering at the top of League stationery asserted: "Obedience to Law is Liberty."[101] Indeed, to examine the censorship of *Ladies' Night* from a legal perspective is instructive. Chicago ordinances, as would be expected, prohibited immoral exhibitions and, as Farwell's attacks indicate, lent ardor to his crusades against artistic indecency. However, relevant codes were quite vague as to what constituted indecency. A 1911 ordinance did prohibit "[i]ndecent or lewd books, pictures, plays, etc.," but it was accompanied only by the explanation that "[n]o person shall exhibit, sell or offer to sell or circulate or distribute any . . . thing whatever of an immoral or scandalous nature, or shall exhibit or perform any indecedent [*sic*], immoral or lewd play or other representation."[102]

By 1922, when a revised edition of Chicago ordinances was published, this code was somewhat expanded. The expansion, though not extensive, is telling nonetheless. The new ordinance remained unchanged from 1911 except for the addition of a clause stating that immoral exhibits might not appear "in any place where the same can be seen from the public highway, or in a public place frequented by children which is not connected with any art or educational exhibition." The revised code also included in its scope "any picture representing a person in a nude state."[103] Thus, it would seem that in the interim between 1911 and 1922, legal definitions of and probably public perceptions as to what constituted indecency became somewhat more discriminating. Certainly artistic and/or educational functions might justify what would ordinarily be "immoral," a word that was also defined more specifically, at least in part, by depictions of nudity.

The evolution of these codes also underscores the fact that the notion of public display itself was multifaceted, even slippery. "Public" loosely defined virtually any situation in which one person was in the presence of another. It encompassed but did not necessarily include commercial performances and artistic exhibitions. This legal ambiguity raises questions about how codes that regulated display were enforced. For example, in reference to the exhibition of "indecent" forms of art and/or literature, the 1922 code explicitly prohibited such works near public highways or public places frequented by children unless educational purposes were being served. Presumably then, educational works could contain elements that would in other instances seem lewd, indecent, immoral, and scandalous, even if in full view of a public thoroughfare that children frequented.

Some 1911 codes related to body display were eliminated altogether by 1922. An ordinance had prohibited the exposure of "diseased, mutilated or deformed portions of [the] body" and stated further: "[a]ny person who is diseased, maimed, mutilated or in any way deformed so as to be an unsightly or disgusting object, or an improper person to be allowed in or on the streets, highways, thoroughfares or public places in this city, shall not therein or thereon expose himself to public view."[104] As this ordinance does not reappear in the 1922 manual, we may again justifiably conclude that in the intervening years the norms governing the display of the body changed considerably and, in fact, became less conservative. That this code ever existed and was still in place as late as 1922, however, substantiates the relationship between aesthetically based censorship and body shame and the combined power of both to effect body compliance.

This Chicago code is especially striking because it exacts legal compliance on the basis of aesthetic standards—standards that one would expect to be and indeed were defined and imposed by other social agencies. The mainstream entertainment industry, for example, then as now, exerted a profound influence on cultural definitions of beauty, in part by keeping deformity and disease away from public view and featuring almost exclusively those deemed attractive by current industry standards. That public "unsightliness" was declared to be *illegal* thus illustrates as well that cultural institutions often work collusively, their operant values intertwining, overlapping, and reinforcing one another to create a powerful network by which to exert influence on society as a whole.

How might such legally inscribed codes against body display and against the display of certain bodies have conditioned audiences to respond to popular entertainments of the 1920s? More important, how did these ordinances *reflect* the way in which performative behaviors involving body display, including but not limited to those classified as entertainment, were perceived? Did the deformity ordinance apply, for example, to an overweight person who dared to reveal what might to someone else have been "unsightly" or "disgusting"? If so, how might Louise Rosine have fared on Chicago beaches? And how was Fat Woman's submission to the obesity machine interpreted by an audience watching *Ladies' Night*?

While we cannot know for sure the answers to these specific questions, we can be certain that, by the time *Ladies' Night* came to Chicago in early 1922, the "official" position on body display did include both moral and aesthetic considerations. Aesthetic values, in fact, were morally laden by means of legal sanction. Ordinarily, to transgress an aesthetic principle is an altogether different matter than to transgress the law. But what of the situation where the law is itself based on the aesthetic principle? This layering and blending of valuing processes confounds a definitive explanation of the censorship of plays like *Ladies' Night* and other artistic censorship as well. Artistic censorship always represents a struggle between multiple cultural paradigms, many of which are insidious. But when we carefully probe the manifest contradictions between such paradigms and inspect the points at which operant values clash as well as bolster one another, we at least begin to understand the ways in which human beings within the social structures represented are themselves valued.

Conclusions

I have discussed the power of *performance* to remediate otherwise transgressive or brazen femininity throughout this book. And although viewers' perceptions that a woman was performing did not always legitimize her transgressive behaviors, these perceptions nonetheless marked a distinction between art and reality and, in general, made the latter more susceptible to censure. In other words, "public" display behaviors that were not sufficiently performative were more readily targeted as transgressive because they did not qualify as art or even entertainment. Certainly, these performances also frequently lacked the kinds of clear boundaries on which actors and audiences usually depend to define their relationship to one another. No proscenium, stage curtains, or rows of seats marked the territory between observer and observed, for example, when women went swimming. But to the extent that even a woman outside the commercial theater acknowledged by her actions the *performative* nature of her relationship to others—that is, when she treated the world as her audience, carefully measuring out the appropriate distance between herself and those who watched her—the greater her chances to escape censure.

For this reason, a daringly costumed "sea nymph" who paraded daintily before admiring eyes as a bathing beauty was celebrated. But a woman who, dressed identically so as to swim unfettered by superfluous clothing and unconscious of her impact on those nearby, was often punished. By the same token, a "Ziegfeld Girl," wearing almost nothing at all, could grow wealthy— for a time—as the glorious symbol of youthful American femininity staged within the luxurious trappings of enterprising American capitalism.[105] And a "flapper" who playfully posed in the controversial styles of the day was more easily dismissed than when she dared to embrace the life of freedom her new clothing symbolized.

Although *Ladies' Night* played in a clearly marked performance space, careful analysis of norms of public display, even legally coded ones, suggests that one reason that some audience members disliked the play was that it essentially invaded their privacy. *Ladies' Night* violated unwritten yet powerful codes of personal intimacy by the close proximity in which it figuratively situated audience relative to performer, using nudity or frank talk about nudity to include both groups within the same performance frame at a fundamental human level. Even the fact that, as a genre, the bedroom farce had moved one step closer to raw humanity by being set in a bath was threatening. That *Ladies' Night* was staged in a new Loop theater, having played to the "better class of New Yorkers," also may have created an expectation among some audience members that the bawdiness of the play's humor shattered.

These discrepancies altered the very definition of the theater experience, leaving some viewers hard put to classify it as an artistic, let alone a morally conscionable, one. It became virtually impossible to separate the moral infractions of *Ladies' Night* from the aesthetic ones, particularly since the play so flagrantly trespassed in both arenas. To all appearances, *Ladies' Night* did not expressly violate nudity standards, certainly not when compared with other entertainment venues of the time, even those that played practically next door. Nevertheless, the play disturbed many who came to see it, if the opinions of critics and censors are any measure of audience response. Preferences and prejudices linked to gender, sexual orientation, socioeconomic class, education, and geographic location intertwined to evoke an incongruous reaction of audience fascination and fury. Such a paradoxical response perhaps best symbolizes the transgressive nature of *Ladies' Night in a Turkish Bath*.

Afterword

The American 1920s were an era in which a curious mixture of laxity and censure prevailed. This was a society at odds with itself. Both pleasure-seeking and punitive, Americans found themselves either redressing or attempting to justify the sources of their greatest satisfaction. In this climate of paradox, leisure activities abounded, but appropriate boundaries of self-expression within the context of leisure were unclear. While some people seemed eager to test boundaries and explore newly discovered freedoms, others resented what they viewed to be a "too much too fast" approach. Landmark events, from World War I to the success of the suffrage movement, showed how changeable a world it was. Within the entertainment industry itself the explosion of commercial radio and cinema was cause for exhilaration as well as anxiety. And as entertainment, art, and leisure expanded as well as overlapped, society's arbiters struggled with how to appropriately manage complicated issues that resulted from their growth and merger, and by whose standards. It was to be expected that the clashing values embedded within and comprising these struggles occasionally surfaced and often did so in poignant ways.

On 10 September 1921, New York's Delmonico's restaurant was the site of a "charity fete" to aid chorus girls, many of whom were unemployed due to what one report described vaguely as "chaotic conditions in the theatre business." Several prominent members of the theatrical profession attended this "impromptu revue," including delegations from the Ziegfeld *Follies*, George White's *Scandals*, and the Greenwich Village *Follies*. Doraldina, the well-known star of motion pictures, and popular chorines from some of the larger revues also appeared on behalf of their needy colleagues. The *New York Times* stated that the sum raised on behalf of chorus girls was "substantial" but did not specify the amount.

Anyone who read this story in the *Times* was likely to notice an equally brief account below it that announced the selection of the "queen of New York beaches." Seventeen-year-old Madge Merritt, the newly designated queen, was one of twenty young women who paraded along Brighton Beach before a crowd of five thousand people who had gathered to watch the contest. Judges for this event included two artists, a Professor Herman M. Barnelot Moens of Holland who was described as an "authority on beauty," and Hope Hampton of "motion picture fame."[1]

In retrospect, the juxtaposition of these two events was, of course, anything but coincidental. Taken together, these moments of one ordinary day in the early 1920s in New York depict what we may now recognize as the essential features of an insidious double bind in which many women of the post-suffrage era were enmeshed. No longer struggling to attain the minimum rights of citizenship, as human beings, American women still found themselves less than full participants in society. Whether in pity or admiration, they were the objects of intense scrutiny, their worth assessed largely on the basis of the degree to which they adhered to highly codified standards of behavior and appearance. By intentionally entering public arenas where she might more easily be viewed—that is, by staging herself, mindful of the pleasure of others—a woman might be well compensated. If not, even the role of pitiable chorus girl was clearly not without its own recompense. Similarly, a young woman, otherwise a low-status member of society, could assume a demeanor that proved her willing submission to the evaluations of more powerful others and be accorded a measure of worth that was understandably appealing to her. These fleeting references to two seemingly unrelated events of a September day in 1921 in New York, like the many other instances noted in this book, are a window through which to view the juncture of several social quandaries whose negotiation had profound consequences on generations to come.

The Comaroffs explain that "history involves a sedimentation of micropractices into macroprocesses, a prosaic rather than a portentous affair in which events mark rather than make the flow of existence."[2] The narrative layering of events is part and parcel of the sedimentation process of history. The performances examined here, though distorted by time, culture, and the narrative process itself, still provide entry to a time and culture not our own and, in the process, enlarge our capacity to understand more about "home" than we did before. The resonance of these performances dissuades us from engaging in historical tourism, treating valuable artifacts as souvenirs. We become resistant to static notions of history, sure of nothing except that history as recorded is no more nor less than a draft to be written and rewritten and rewritten again, our own struggle for words a fitting tribute to the muted voices of the past that once struggled to be heard and still deserve to be.

When the last of Nellie and Roy Latham's seven children left home to go to college, Nellie explained to her husband that she intended to resume her career as a teacher. Decades later, my grandfather still expressed bewilderment at her insistence on this point: "Why, she didn't need to do that. I had a good job." Nellie was emphatic, however. "Why what am I supposed to do? Sit here and twiddle my thumbs?" In spite of his inability to comprehend his wife's determination to pursue the dream she had postponed once upon a time when she married him, there was an unmistakable note of pride in my grandfather's voice as he shook his head and said: "Sure enough, she went back to teaching. She taught five more years. She taught till she couldn't stand up. It took the fire department to put her out!"[3]

I vividly remember the time when I was only seven or eight years old and my grandmother took me to her bedroom, reached into the top of her closet, and took down a shoe box. She removed the lid of the box, and there, much to my surprise, lying like a corpse in a coffin, was a long, carefully kept braid of hair. The hair, she explained, was her own. It was dark, however, not gray as hers was by then. Although the significance of her story escaped me at the time, as she surely knew it would, she told me anyway that she had used this "switch" to fool her employers and keep her job. She knew that at some later point I would be able to recognize the gift her story was to me. No less poignant than her desire to teach the fundamentals of education to the children of her community was my grandmother's desire to tell me about her own willfulness, her opposition to those who would rescind her right to choose for herself the nature of her contribution to society.

Stories about passionate women, such as Nellie Latham, Crystal Eastman, Frances Kennedy, Louise Rosine, Allyn King, and others who inspired but also exasperated those around them, help us to interpret the enigma that was the American 1920s. Their experiences, when properly contextualized, teach us a great deal about the nature of human desire, transgression, and the way performance itself comprises, transforms, and ultimately transcends the experiences of our own lives.

Notes

Introduction (pp. 1–4)

1 Caryn Shinske, "A Century of Memories," *Brazil (Indiana) Times* 10 February 1996.

2 For a detailed discussion of the impact of and controversy over hair bobbing, see Paula S. Fass, *The Damned and the Beautiful: American Youth in the 1920s* (New York: Oxford University Press, 1977), 280–81, 456–57 nn. 35–37. Other works that explore the relationship between the self-styling of women and pervasive cultural values are many but certainly include Martha Banta, *Imaging American Women: Idea and Ideals in Cultural History* (New York: Columbia University Press, 1987); Lois W. Banner, *American Beauty* (Chicago: University of Chicago Press, 1983); and most recently, Kathy Peiss, *Hope in a Jar: The Making of America's Beauty Culture* (New York: Metropolitan Books, Henry Holt and Co., 1998). For a perspective that explores the idea of female presentation in the more narrowly defined realm of theatrical performance, see Faye E. Dudden, *Women in the American Theatre: Actresses, Audiences, 1790–1870* (London: Yale University Press, 1994).

3 The trials of being a rural teacher were described by one woman in this way: "The rural teacher's clothes, friends, actions, and even her telephone conversations and mail are closely observed and freely criticized. She is expected to attend the popular church, have no views on anything debatable, be an example in all things, and stand ready to serve as entertainer, refreshment committee, decorator, speaker, seamstress, stage hand or musician at any local celebration." Quoted in John H. Finley, "What Is the Matter with Teaching?" *Delineator* 108 (June 1926): 8.

4 Nellie Latham, my grandmother, told this story to me. The issue of a married woman's right to work in the 1920s is discussed in many print sources as well. See, for example, Hortense M. Lion, "The Boycott on Wives," *Outlook* 135 (12 December 1923): 628–30; "Married Women to Lose Jobs in Railroad Office," *Chicago Evening Post*, 27 September 1920. An essay that refers to the impact of marital status on teachers is named in the previous note. A secondary source that discusses this issue is Maurine Weiner Greenwald, "Working-Class Feminism and the Family Wage Ideal: The Seattle Debate on Married Women's Right to Work, 1914–1920," *Journal of American History* 76 (June 1989): 118–49. Kathryn Oberdeck also refers to the dilemma with which married women were faced in "Not Pink Teas: The Seattle Working-Class Women's Movement, 1905–1918," *Labor History* 32 (spring 1991): 229.

5 For a succinct summary of the varying uses of the term *performance*, including the way it is defined in this study, see Marvin Carlson, *Performance: A Critical Introduction* (New York: Routledge, 1996), 1–9.

6 Without specifically referring to the look of the flapper as a "performance," Anne Hollander, for example, notes that by 1920 the fashionable mode was in part determined by "new relaxed postures and gestures" and that "impulsive movements once thought to be lacking in any hope of style became the elements of chic." "Women and Fashion," in *Women, the Arts, and the 1920s in Paris and New York*, ed. Kenneth W. Wheeler and Virginia Lee Lussier (New Brunswick, N.J.: Transaction Books, 1982), 116.

7 In her analysis of fashion, Kim Sawchuck also states that "one must be careful in transferring paradigms from film theory, which tends to concentrate solely on the notion of the look, and on the eye as the primary organ of experience. Clothing, the act of wearing fabric, is intimately linked to the skin, and the body, to our tactile senses." "A Tale of Inscription/Fashion Statements," *Canadian Journal of Political and Social Theory* 11 (1987): 59.

8 The term *display* is sufficiently commonplace and vague as to merit elaboration. By far the most helpful definition of the word relative to this research is found in Erving Goffman's *Gender Advertisements* (Cambridge, Mass.: Harvard University Press, 1979). It is impossible to do justice to Goffman's astute discussion of human display as a sociological phenomenon in abbreviated form, but to describe the essence of his analysis assists the present study. Goffman places the relevance of human display in direct correlation with its ability to signal a person's social alignment. Without serving as specific or narrow symbols of communication, displays instead suggest or indicate social relationships in a diffuse manner. They vary in levels of formality and are often so inherently a part of our ordinary dealings that we take them for granted. This understanding of human display acknowledges it as a significant, observable, yet subtle means by which to recognize the nature of human alliances within social surroundings. It defines as well as validates the term *display* as utilized here. I contend that display, as Goffman defines it, is in fact a subset of the more inclusive concept of performance as defined by Carlson, noted earlier, in that Carlson also emphasizes recognizable and culturally coded patterns of human behavior presented with a consciousness as to their enactment (pp. 1–3). See also Carlson, *Performance*, 1–9.

1. *Starting Points (pp. 7–16)*

1 Kenneth A. Yellis, "Prosperity's Child: Some Thoughts on the Flapper," *American Quarterly* 21 (spring 1969): 46.

2 Estelle B. Freedman, "The New Woman: Changing Views of Women in the 1920s," *Journal of American History* 61 (1974): 393.

3 Ibid., 373.

4 Carroll Smith-Rosenberg, *Disorderly Conduct: Visions of Gender in Victorian America* (New York: Oxford University Press, 1987), 17.

5 Ethan Mordden, *That Jazz! An Idiosyncratic Social History of the American Twenties* (New York: G. P. Putnam's Sons, 1978), 217, 227.

6 Frederick Lewis Allen, *Only Yesterday: An Informal History of the Nineteen-Twenties* (New York: Harper and Row, 1931), 49.

7 Lois W. Banner, *American Beauty* (Chicago: University of Chicago Press, 1983), 275; Paula S. Fass, *The Damned and the Beautiful: American Youth in the 1920s* (New York: Oxford University Press, 1977), 280–81. Part of this discussion is also derived from my article "Performance, Ethnography, and History: An Analysis of Displays by Female Bathers in the 1920s," *Text and Performance Quarterly* 17 (April 1997): 170–81.

8 Elaine Showalter, ed., *These Modern Women: Autobiographical Essays from the Twenties*, rev. ed. (New York: Feminist Press, City University of New York, 1989), 9–10.

9 Nancy F. Cott, *The Grounding of Modern Feminism* (New Haven, Conn.: Yale University Press, 1987), 8.

10 Lary May, *Screening Out the Past: The Birth of Mass Culture and the Motion Picture Industry* (Chicago: University of Chicago Press, 1983), 200.

11 Ibid., 211–12.

12 Lewis A. Erenberg, *Steppin' Out: New York Nightlife and the Transformation of American Culture, 1890–1930* (Westport, Conn.: Greenwood Press, 1981), 70.

13 Ibid., 214.

14 Alison M. Jagger and Susan R. Bordo, eds., *Gender/Body/Knowledge: Feminist Reconstructions of Being and Knowing* (New Brunswick, N.J.: Rutgers University Press, 1989), 4; Joan Wallach Scott, *Gender and the Politics of History* (New York: Columbia University Press, 1988), 20, 22–23.

15 A very useful discussion of what might loosely be termed "body scholarship" but one that especially advocates our attentiveness to the presence of the body in history is Roy Porter, "History of the Body," in *New Perspectives on Historical Writing*, ed. Peter Burke (University Park, Pa.: Pennsylvania State University Press, 1991), 206–32.

16 Susan R. Bordo, "The Body and the Reproduction of Femininity: A Feminist Appropriation of Foucault," in *Gender/Body/Knowledge: Feminist Reconstructions of Being and Knowing*, ed. Alison M. Jaggar and Susan R. Bordo (New Brunswick, N.J.: Rutgers University Press, 1989), 13.

17 The December 1997 issue of *Theatre Journal* is, in fact, devoted entirely to the topic of "historicizing bodies."

18 John Comaroff and Jean Comaroff, *Ethnography and the Historical Imagination* (Boulder, Colo.: Westview Press, 1992), 17.

19 James C. Scott, *Domination and the Arts of Resistance: Hidden Transcripts* (London: Yale University Press, 1990), 3–4.

20 Ibid.

21 John Van Maanen, "An End to Innocence: The Ethnography of Ethnography," in *Representation in Ethnography*, ed. John Van Maanen (Thousand Oaks, Calif.: Sage Publications, 1995), 4–5.

22 Dwight Conquergood, "Rethinking Ethnography: Towards a Critical Cultural Politics," *Communication Monographs* 58 (June 1991): 180. Conquergood's early calls for the use of performance ethnography in performance studies include "A Sense of the Other: Interpretation and Ethnographic Research," in *Proceedings of the Seminar/Conference on Oral Traditions*, ed. Isabel Crouch and Gordon Owen (Las Cruces: New Mexico State University, 1983), 148–55. Conquergood

affirmed this approach more recently in "Ethnography, Rhetoric, and Performance," *Quarterly Journal of Speech* 78 (May 1992): 80–97.

23 Comaroff and Comaroff, *Ethnography*, 11, 16

24 Ibid., xi.

25 Victor Turner, *On the Edge of the Bush: Anthropology as Experience*, ed. Edith L. B. Turner (Tucson: University of Arizona Press, 1985), 207.

26 Ibid., 227–28. Time is a rather slippery matter in ethnography in that written accounts of fieldwork have often anachronistically characterized subject cultures. One of the greatest challenges ethnographers face is to remain contemporaries with their cultural informants when interpreting fieldwork experiences, avoiding tendencies, for example, to portray other cultures as less advanced. On this point, see Conquergood's "Rethinking Ethnography," 182–83. Also, the method of ethnography, despite its usual present-tense application, concedes to history, as it were, when the researcher attempts to convey the ethnographic experience to those outside the culture. Even if devoid of anachronistic insults, descriptions and interpretations usually become past-tense narratives by grammatical imperative. These issues also ultimately commend performance as remedial to ethnographic research.

27 One of the recognized predicaments of ethnography is, in fact, an overreliance on vision (literally, *seeing*) as a means of knowing. Conquergood, in particular, names this dilemma in "Rethinking Ethnography" (p. 183). Similarly, Paul Stoller, in *The Taste of Ethnographic Things: The Senses in Anthropology* (Philadelphia: University of Pennsylvania Press, 1989), describes sight as the "privileged sense of the West" and stresses the importance of *all* the senses to a more complete ethnographic experience (p. 5). In historical research, one often cannot rely solely or even primarily on evidence that supplies a visual image anyway. Photographs or illustrations simply may not exist. The method of historical performance ethnography is not unduly hindered by this reality in that it inherently fosters attentiveness to all the sensory elements of the performed events of history, not just those that "meet the eye."

28 Stoller, *Taste of Ethnographic Things*, 5.

29 Comaroff and Comaroff, *Ethnography*, 11. The Comaroffs use this phrase but do not specifically name cultural performances as the primary focus of the historical ethnographer's investigation. They do, however, imply a performative focus by their dedication to "processes that make and transform particular worlds— processes that reciprocally shape subjects and contexts, that allow certain things to be said and done. . . . The phenomena we observe may be grounded in everyday human activity . . . involved in the making of wider structures and social movements" (pp. 31–32).

30 Crystal Eastman, "Mother-Worship," in *These Modern Women: Biographical Essays from the Twenties*, ed. Elaine Showalter (New York: Feminist Press, City University of New York, 1989), 91. Eastman's essay first appeared in a series carried by the *Nation* in 1926 and 1927, titled "These Modern Women."

31 Comaroff and Comaroff, *Ethnography*, 34.

32 In fact, the matter is much more complicated than this quotation would indicate. Lincoln and Guba delineate several varieties of generalization. Admirably, they

do not use this rather fluid view of the concept to endorse a lack of investigative rigor. Their emphasis, like my own, is more on a sensitivity to the precise variables within a context and how best to exploit the realities of that context. See chapter 5 in Yvonna S. Lincoln and Egon G. Guba, "The Only Generalization Is: There Is No Generalization," in *Naturalistic Inquiry* (Newbury Park, Calif.: Sage Publications, 1985), 110–28.

33 Conquergood, "Rethinking Ethnography," 187 (emphasis mine).

34 Comaroff and Comaroff, *Ethnography*, 40.

2. Fashionable Discourse (pp. 18–62)

1 John Roach Straton, "Mary's Little Skirt," *New York Times*, 27 June 1921.

2 Numerous primary sources substantiate the fact that women were relentlessly scrutinized for evidence of moral insubordination. See, for example, "College Girl and Minister Debate on Flapper," *New York World*, 25 January 1925, sec. 2; Bruce Bliven, "Flapper Jane," *New Republic* 44 (9 September 1925): 65–67.

3 Bliven, "Flapper Jane," 65. Ethnic and racial stereotypes were, unfortunately, often employed to depict the demeanor of flappers (fig. 9).

4 This photograph accompanied a very informative article about a number of fashion-related issues entitled "Is the Younger Generation in Peril?" *Literary Digest* 69 (14 May 1921): 1.

5 "Corsets and the Mode," *Good Housekeeping* 75 (October 1922): 48.

6 Mary Ogden White, "Good Health—Your Job," *Woman Citizen* 5 (21 May 1921): 1239.

7 Of course, the very fact that the "look" of the flapper was portrayed with so little variation is itself a study in conformity.

8 Christina Simmons also points to the influence of a "new discourse on sexuality that appeared in the writings of white liberal commentators on sexual life in the 1920s and 1930s." She contends that from this discourse emerged a "myth" of Victorian repression that also strategically framed alternatives to this mythologized antisensualism. "Modern Sexuality and the Myth of Victorian Repression," in *Passion and Power: Sexuality in History*, ed. Kathy Peiss and Christina Simmons (Philadelphia: Temple University Press, 1989), 157.

9 Ibid.

10 Charlotte Perkins Gilman, for example, although aware of the reasons that women chose to focus on their appearance, clearly disdained the emphasis she felt most women placed on their looks. "Do Women Dress to Please Men?" *Century Magazine* 103 (March 1922): 651–55.

11 Unfair labor practices in the garment industry were also a concern of earlier feminists. I address this matter at a later point in the discussion.

12 "Is the Younger Generation in Peril?" 12.

13 Dorothy Dunbar Bromley, "Feminist—New Style," *Harper's Monthly* 155 (October 1927): 552. *Harper's* had been established before the Civil War, and although it had flourished as a forum in which works by popular novelists were featured, by the 1920s it had also begun to include articles of opinion on current topics.

According to Frank Luther Mott, this new editorial policy "spared" the life and influence of the magazine. *American Journalism: A History of Newspapers in the United States through 260 Years: 1690–1950*, rev. ed. (New York: Macmillan Co., 1950), 321, 731.

14 Nancy Cott, *The Grounding of Modern Feminism* (New Haven, Conn.: Yale University Press, 1987), 150–51.

15 Fred Davis, *Fashion, Culture, and Identity* (Chicago: University of Chicago Press, 1992), 104–7.

16 Notably, Kennedy also argued that an "actress can't appear in old models. The public looks to her for the styles." Clearly, performance and fashion were inextricably linked in a number of ways.

17 "Women Jurors Rule in Favor of Own Sex," *Chicago Daily News*, 21 March 1922.

18 "Actress Wins Legal Clash over Gown," *Chicago Evening American*, 22 March 1922.

19 "Old-Fashioned Even before Made, Verdict," *Chicago Herald and Examiner*, 23 March 1922.

20 "Women Jurors Rule."

21 "Woman Called for Jury Duty," *Chicago Daily News*, 20 March 1922.

22 William H. Stuart, *The Twenty Incredible Years* (Chicago: M. A. Donohue and Co., 1935), 150; Claude O. Pike, "New Delay for Small Looms in Jury Attack," *Chicago Daily News*, 3 April 1922.

23 Pike, "New Delay."

24 I do not mean to ignore the fact that Kennedy also had a socioeconomic advantage in this instance. Presumably, by having her husband defend her, she would have had no attorney fees and may even have had the benefit of her husband's professional reputation working for her.

25 This is not to deny the possibility that Small's request may indeed have been a stall tactic. The answer to that question lies outside the scope of this study. However, sincere or not, the issue Small raised was worthwhile. "Request Denied for Women," *Chicago Daily News*, 6 April 1922.

26 Davis, *Fashion, Culture, and Identity*, 104–7.

27 Paul H. Nystrom, *Economics of Fashion* (New York: Ronald Press, 1928), 29.

28 Many sources document specific fashion features of women's clothing in the 1920s. See, for example, Diana de Marly, *The History of Haute Couture, 1850–1950* (New York: Holmes and Meier, 1980), 143–72; Shirley Miles O'Donnol, *American Costume, 1915–1970* (Bloomington: Indiana University Press, 1982), 33–70. Because of the availability of these kinds of resources and because of the ideological bent of this study, I do not unduly emphasize literal aspects of fashion. As is necessary in any cultural analysis of fashion, however, I do address some specificities of style, both material and theoretical; but the precise lengths to which skirts rose and fell, for example, is by no means my primary consideration.

29 "The Story of the New Paris Mode: In Which It Will Be Seen that the Day of Democracy in Dress Is Past," *Vogue* 72 (13 October 1928): 68.

30 In her study of dieting in the 1920s, Margaret A. Lowe offers an intriguing and painstakingly researched account of how young women of the 1920s—at least the Smith College women on whom her study focuses—were acutely aware of

body image and wished especially to comply with the "look" of the flapper. She notes the importance of advertising, movies, and stores' use of live models to display flapper fashions. According to Lowe, "[s]tudents relished the new consumerism and avidly followed flapper fashions." Moreover, the "flapper image . . . encouraged student dieting." Clearly, the flapper look took great effort to achieve as well as to maintain. The work of manipulating one's image, from posturing to dieting, further substantiates my claim that to be "in style" was to perform. "From Robust Appetites to Calorie Counting: The Emergence of Dieting among Smith College Students in the 1920s," *Journal of Women's History* 7 (winter 1995): 49. Ann Douglas also mentions the rise of dieting in the 1920s in *Terrible Honesty: Mongrel Manhattan in the 1920s* (New York: Farrar, Straus and Giroux, 1995), 52–53.

31 J. C. Flugel, *The Psychology of Clothes* (London: Hogarth Press, 1930), 155–56, 161–62.

32 Robert S. Lynd and Helen Merrell Lynd, *Middletown: A Study in American Culture* (New York: Harcourt, Brace and Co., 1929), 159.

33 Quoted in Anne Rittenhouse, "Paul Poiret's Ten Short Precepts," *The Well-Dressed Woman* (New York: Harper and Brothers, 1924), 204.

34 Hugh A. Studdert Kennedy, "Short Skirts," *Forum* 75 (June 1926): 829–36. I will discuss the contents of this essay more fully in the "Fashion and Morality" section, below.

35 Carrie Chapman Catt, "How Many Yards in Your Skirt?" *Woman Citizen* 11 (August 1926): 10.

36 As was typical in most fashion debates, morality based or not, appeals to women to make choices independently of fashion propaganda were usually paired with one or more additional rationales. In Catt's case, the other primary antifashion plea was an economic one. She was dismayed that France so monopolized the clothing market. I will address her argument on this point later. For now though, it is sufficient to acknowledge that women were criticized on many levels when they appeared to comply with the fickle requirements of fashion. The inevitable but unstated assumption was, of course, that women *should* obey instead the particular alternative advanced by the persuader.

37 Advertisement for Butterick patterns, *Delineator* 98 (May 1921), 46–47.

38 Diana de Marly, *History of Haute Couture*, 146–47. The subject of French fashion in the post–World War I era, including the "boyish" look so popular during this time, is analyzed in considerable depth in Mary Louise Roberts, *Civilization without Sexes: Reconstructing Gender in Postwar France, 1917–1927* (Chicago: University of Chicago Press, 1994), esp. chap. 1, pp. 17–45.

39 Gabrielle Chanel, "Fait Expres—by Chanel," *Ladies' Home Journal* 46 (June 1929): 30. The caption under a "Chanel Creation" displayed beside the copy from which this quote is excerpted specifies not only the sizes for which the dress was designed but also the age range of women intended to wear it—fourteen- to twenty-year-olds.

40 "Corsets and the Mode," 48.

41 Rittenhouse, *Well-Dressed Woman*, 210.

42 Ibid., viii.

43 Ibid., ix.

44 Ibid., x–xi.

45 Hugh A. Studdert Kennedy, "Shorter Than Ever: Being an Answer to Mrs. Catt's Question, 'How Many Yards in Your Skirt,'" *Woman Citizen* 11 (October 1926): 19, 37

46 Mrs. Booth Tarkington, "We Needn't Be Robots in Our Dress," *Ladies' Home Journal* 45 (April 1928): 20.

47 Ibid.

48 Mary Alden Hopkins, "Do Women Dress for Men?" *Delineator* 98 (July 1921): 3.

49 Ibid.

50 Ibid., 49.

51 For an in-depth and fascinating account of women's participation in the commercialization of beauty, especially the growth of the cosmetic industry in the late nineteenth and early twentieth centuries, see Kathy Peiss, *Hope in a Jar: The Making of America's Beauty Culture* (New York: Metropolitan Books, Henry Holt and Co., 1998.)

52 A wealth of the former kinds of information appears in Nystrom, *Economics of Fashion*.

53 Catt, "How Many Yards in Your Skirt?" 10–11.

54 Ibid., 11.

55 Carrie Chapman Catt, "The Chemise Problem," *Woman Citizen* 11 (July 1926): 10.

56 Ibid.

57 "Who Makes Your Clothes?" *Woman Citizen* 4 (19 April 1920): 1112–13.

58 These concerns had been on feminists' reform agendas since before the turn of the century. Florence Kelley, for example, had struggled with these issues even before she was general secretary of the National Consumers' League, a position she held between 1899 and 1930. See Kathryn Kish Sklar, *Florence Kelley and the Nation's Work: The Rise of Women's Political Culture, 1830–1900* (New Haven, Conn.: Yale University Press, 1995), xvi, 140, 265. An address devoted to the perils of the tenement industry was delivered by Ida Van Etten at the American Federation of Labor national convention in 1890. Her speech, entitled "The Sweating System, Charity, and Organization," is included in Nancy F. Cott, ed., *Root of Bitterness: Documents of the Social History of American Women* (Boston: Northeastern University Press, 1986), 327–32.

59 In her explanation of the presence of high levels of generational tension in the 1920s, Ann Douglas refers to Catt and other feminists of the Progressive Era as "matriarchs." Douglas notes as well that "moderns aimed to ridicule and overturn everything the matriarch had championed." Moderns usually exaggerated matriarchal authority. Still, such women were, in fact, "the ascendant cultural force in late-Victorian America," a force whose influence did not disappear after the Great War. Granted, matriarchal momentum was reduced, especially after the singular, unifying issue of suffrage was gone, but there were other scores yet to settle. Douglas, *Mongrel Manhattan*, 6–7.

60 Crystal Eastman, "Suffragists Ten Years After," *New Republic* 35 (27 June 1923): 118.

61 Ranging in age from fourteen to eighteen, these women were generally family wage earners. They turned their paychecks over to parents, who then would help them purchase necessary clothing items.

62 Hattie E. Anderson, "Clothes, Money and the Working Girl," *Survey* 58 (15 July 1927): 417–18.

63 In real money, these percentages represent from $145 to $421.

64 "Clothes and the Working-Girl," *Literary Digest* 95 (24 December 1927): 24.

65 Ibid.

66 Ruth Shonle Cavan, *Business Girls: A Study of Their Interests and Problems* (Chicago: Religious Education Association, 1929), 72. See also Elizabeth Lyon and Adella Eppel, "Cost of Clothing among Missouri College Girls," *Journal of Home Economics* 21 (June 1929): 429.

67 This is perhaps especially true when one considers the findings of the Religious Education Association study: among women whose income was between $660 and $1,096 per year, 27 percent of it was spent on clothing and 25.3 percent on room and board. Cavan, *Business Girls*, 72. Perhaps it was no wonder that young employed women or those still training for careers were so conscious of their appearance, however. Mary Brooks Picken, who in 1923 supervised over 500 women in one of the largest correspondence schools in the country, was congratulated for having had "a mirror put in every room" of her school. The influence of this practice had, to her, "been decidedly for the better." Frank Crane, "How I Like a Woman to Look," *American Magazine* 96 (November 1923): 43.

68 Henriette Weber, "Silk Stockings and Sedition," *North American Review* 225 (January 1928): 83.

69 Nystrom, *Economics of Fashion*, 97.

70 Ibid., 99.

71 "The Battle of the Skirts," *Outlook* 132 (18 October 1922): 276. Nystrom also acknowledged Veblen, *Theory of the Leisure Class* (New York: Macmillan Co., 1917).

72 For a discussion of the advertising industry and its relationship to other mass entertainment venues in the 1920s, see Douglas, *Mongrel Manhattan*, 64–72.

73 Mary Alden Hopkins, "Woman's Rebellion against Fashions," *New Republic* 31 (16 August 1922): 332.

74 Ann Devon, "Will the Women Wear Them?" *Outlook and Independent* 153 (6 November 1929): 372.

75 Ibid.

76 "Doctors Dislike New Dress Styles," *Literary Digest* 104 (4 January 1930): 30. This point was also clearly articulated by some representatives of the YWCA. Dr. Sara Brown, a staff member for the organization, felt that shorter skirts were "not only sanitary" but that they removed the "age-old handicap which impedes woman's action in walking and climbing stairs." Lester A. Walton, "Y.W.C.A. Stamps Short Skirt with Seal of Approval," *New York World*, 18 January 1925.

77 "Is the Younger Generation in Peril?" 10.

78 "The Pope's Appeal to Men to Reform Women's Dress," *Literary Digest* 92 (29 January 1927): 27–28. The essayist, Bruce Bliven, expressed a more cynical view of just such an "emergency." In reference to the dress of "Flapper Jane," the

fictional character noted earlier whose identity was, presumably, a composite of the young women Bliven observed around him, he remarked wryly: "It is cut low where it might be high, and vice versa. The skirt comes just an inch below her knees, overlapping by a faint fraction her rolled and twisted stockings. The idea is that when she walks in a bit of a breeze, you shall now and then observe the knee (which is *not* rouged—that's just newspaper talk) but always in an accidental, Venus-surprised-at-the-bath sort of way ("Flapper Jane," 65–67).

79 Edward D. Tittmann, "Morality and Clothes—to the Editor of *The Nation*," *Nation* 121 (29 August 1925): 234.

80 "A New Crusade for Longer Skirts," *Literary Digest* 88 (16 January 1926): 31.

81 Reese Carmichael, "The Ladies, God Bless 'Em, Their Frocks and Frills," *Ladies' Home Journal* 38 (August 1921): 45.

82 Crane, "How I Like a Woman to Look," 43.

83 "The Catholic Crusade for Modesty," *Literary Digest* 82 (30 August 1924): 25–26.

84 Studdert Kennedy, "Short Skirts," 835.

85 "What Is Jazz Doing to Our Boys and Girls?" *Atlanta Constitution*, 15 January 1922, Sunday magazine, p. 2.

86 Mary Gray Peck, "Young People's Manners," *Woman Citizen* 5 (21 May 1921): 1245.

87 Mary Alden Hopkins, "What Shall the Poor Girl Wear?" *New Republic* 28 (23 November 1921): 377–78.

88 Clovis G. Chappell, *Christ and the New Woman* (Nashville, Tenn.: Cokesbury Press, 1928), 69.

89 Hopkins, "What Shall the Poor Girl Wear?" 377–78. For a less impassioned discussion of working women, see Harriet Mooney Levy, "The Woman in Business: Assets and Liabilities," *Jewish Woman* 10 (April–June 1930): 1–2.

90 Gilman, "Do Women Dress to Please Men?" 651–55. Gilman also discussed her views on these matters in *Women and Economics* (Boston: Small, Maynard & Co., 1898). This work is generously excerpted in *The Feminist Papers: From Adams to de Beauvoir*, ed. Alice S. Rossi (New York: Bantam Books, 1974), 572–98.

91 William Bolitho, "The New Skirt Length," *Harper's* 160 (February 1930): 293.

92 Ibid., 294–95.

93 Walter G. Muirheid, "Fashion Follies Follow War," *Mentor* 9 (1 September 1921): 32.

94 Fitzgerald's *Tales of the Jazz Age* (1922) is credited as the source of the term now commonly used to refer to the 1920s. F. Scott Fitzgerald, "Echoes of the Jazz Age," *Scribner's Monthly* 90 (November 1931): 459–60, 464–65.

95 From the standpoint of fetishism, all the attention devoted to these particular articles of apparel, even under the banner of health reform, seems symbolic. While undertaken with an awareness of the potentially much deeper psychological implications of these controversies, my analysis will generally concede the benefit of the doubt on such matters. That is, the opinions shown here will, more or less, be taken at face value. Naïveté, at least in this instance, involves less conjecture than cynicism. In any case, more than one book has already been devoted to the subject. See Valerie Steele, *Fetish* (New York: Oxford University Press, 1996),

33–142; David Kunzle, *Fashion and Fetishism: A Social History of the Corset, Tight-Lacing and Other Forms of Body-Sculpture in the West* (Totowa, N.J.: Rowman and Littlefield, 1982), 14–20, 181–83.

96 Emily Burbank, *The Smartly Dressed Woman: How She Does It* (New York: Dodd, Mead and Company, 1925), 104.

97 The history of the YWCA "shoe movement" or "shoe campaign" is described in Jane Bellows, *Feet and Shoes* (New York: Woman's Press, 1928), 33–35.

98 Young Women's Christian Associations (YWCA), *The Girl Reserve Movement: A Manual for Advisers* (New York: Woman's Press, 1923), 281–84. World Young Women's Christian Associations, *The Girl Reserve Movement: A Manual for Advisers* (New York: Young Women's Christian Association, 1921), 328. The Girl Pioneers of America and the Girl Scouts organizations published similar propaganda against fashionable styles of shoes. See Lina Beard and Adelia B. Beard, *The National Organization, Girl Pioneers of America, Official Manual: Pioneering for Girls*, 4th ed. (New York: Girl Pioneers of America, 1923), 122–23; Girl Scouts, Inc., *Scouting for Girls: Official Handbook of the Girl Scouts*, abridged ed. (New York: Girl Scouts, Inc., 1927), 164–65.

99 Walton, "Y.W.C.A. Stamps."

100 Florence A. Sherman, "Hygiene of Clothing," *Journal of Home Economics* 17 (January 1925): 25.

101 Carmichael, "The Ladies," 45.

102 Woods Hutchinson, "Health and Sports Suits," *Saturday Evening Post* 198 (8 August 1925): 20.

103 "A War against Tight Shoes," *Literary Digest* 74 (15 July 1922): 23.

104 Nystrom, *Economics of Fashion*, 147.

105 "The Bare-Neck Evil," *Literary Digest* 65 (3 April 1920): 116.

106 In case her warnings against unhealthy apparel were insufficiently persuasive, however, she added that "the fact that she wears practically no underwear is one of the crowning sins of the 'flapper.'" Once again, morality was thrown into the rhetorical mix, as if arguments against unhealthy apparel were incomplete without at least a passing reference to fashion's sinful qualities. Katherine Taylor Cranor, "Clothing and Health," *Journal of Home Economics* 15 (August 1923): 427.

107 Sherman, "Hygiene of Clothing," 22–23.

108 Marion Harland also noted the change from the corset's status of "indispensable" to "optional" in the 1920s. Lynd and Lynd, *Middletown*, 159–60.

109 Elizabeth Macdonald Osborne, "Some Like 'Em Cool," *Collier's* 80 (13 August 1927): 37.

110 Ibid., 19. One source that graphically represents the changing fashions in women's underwear is Nystrom, *Economics of Fashion*, 434 (fig. 19).

111 Catt, "How Many Yards in Your Skirt?" 11.

112 "Hats vs. Undies," *Woman Citizen* 11 (August 1926): 32.

113 "Doctors Dislike New Dress Styles," 30.

114 Freda Kirchwey, ed., *Our Changing Morality* (New York: Albert and Charles, 1924), v–vi.

3. *Fashionable Display (pp. 65–96)*

Earlier versions of parts of this chapter appeared in "Performance, Ethnography, and History: An Analysis of Displays by Female Bathers in the 1920s," *Text and Performance Quarterly* 17 (April 1997): 170–81, and in "Packaging Woman: The Concurrent Rise of Beauty Pageants, Public Bathing, and Other Performances of Female 'Nudity,'" *Journal of Popular Culture* 29 (winter 1995): 149–67. Used by permission.

1 Richard Martin and Harold Koda, *Splash! A History of Swimwear* (New York: Rizzoli, 1990), 43.
2 Charles E. Funnell, *By the Beautiful Sea: The Rise and Times of That Great American Resort, Atlantic City* (New York: Knopf, 1975), 130–31.
3 A. R. Riverol, *Live from Atlantic City: The History of the Miss America Pageant before, after and in spite of Television* (Bowling Green, Ohio: Bowling Green State University Popular Press, 1992), 9.
4 Martin and Koda, *Splash!* 43.
5 Funnell, *By the Beautiful Sea*, 140.
6 Atlantic City was certainly not the only resort town to hold bathers' revues, however. Many resort towns began to hold these "parades" by the early 1920s (see fig. 24).
7 Lena Lencek and Gideon Bosker, *Making Waves: Swimsuits and the Undressing of America* (San Francisco: Chronicle, 1989), 36.
8 "Pageant to Be Clean, Writes Mayor Bader," *Atlantic City Daily Press*, 2 June 1921.
9 Information provided by the Atlantic City Clerk's Office about bathing suit regulations that were in effect at this time does not indicate that the codes were this specific in proscribing beach attire for women. Apparently such specifications were enforced by other means. *Public Ordinances of Atlantic City, Compiled by Authority of City Council* (Atlantic City: Globe Company, 1916), 279–80; City of Atlantic City, *Atlantic City Ordinances* (City of Atlantic City, N.J., 1922), 9.
10 "'Copettes' Will Spot Beach 'Lizards' Who Annoy Girls," *Atlantic City Daily Press*, 2 June 1921.
11 "One Piece Suits Given a Welcome at Somers Point," *Atlantic City Sunday Gazette*, 5 June 1921; "Now the Rotarians Ask One-Piece Suit," *New York Times*, 8 June 1921.
12 "Defend 1-Piece Suit," *Atlantic City Daily Press*, 7 June 1921.
13 "This 'Doc' Sees a Bather's Strike over Nude Limbs," *Atlantic City Daily Press*, 17 June 1921.
14 "1-Piece Suits—or Nothing!" *Atlantic City Daily Press*, 8 June 1921.
15 "Now the Rotarians Ask One-Piece Suit."
16 "1-Piece Suits with a Skirt on the Beach," *Atlantic City Daily Press*, 13 June 1921; "No Objection to Suits Viewed," *Atlantic City Evening Union*, 13 June 1921. Note the presence of a member of the Beach Patrol, wearing the number 3 on his suit, lower right corner of fig. 26.
17 Lencek and Bosker, *Making Waves*, 36.

18 The title of this advice column is also quite useful for its descriptiveness, "New Bathing Suits Practical and Simple in Style—Beach Capes of Rubber and Brushed Wool—Stockings Invariably Rolled Down from the Knee Know [sic]—Tassels on Bathing Suits," *Atlantic City Sunday Gazette*, 12 June 1921.

19 Martin and Koda also suggest that beach codes varied from one location of the United States to another. *Splash!* 60.

20 One of the few sources I was able to locate that attempted to compare bathing suit regulations nationally is "Bathing-Suits and Bathing-Beach Regulations," *American City* 28 (June 1923): 569–70. This article is by no means thorough, however. In my research it has proved more effective to rely on newspapers and other documents of local history.

21 "H2 Oh Boy! City's Beaches Open Tomorrow," *Chicago Evening Post*, 15 June 1921; "Says Women Bathers Have No Conscience," *New York Times*, 17 June 1921.

22 Ione Quinby, "Chicago Nereids Are Sewed in by Beach Tailoress," *Chicago Evening Post*, 18 June 1921. The employment of "tailoress-censors" on Chicago beaches was also noted in "Sew Up Chicago Bathers," *New York Times*, 19 June 1921.

23 "Chicago Nereids."

24 "Chicago Sizzles under Heat Wave," *Chicago Evening Post*, 18 June 1921; "H2 Oh Boy!"

25 Photo captions, *Chicago Herald and Examiner*, 21 June 1921, photo section.

26 Photo caption, *Louisville Courier-Journal*, 19 March 1922, "Pictorial News" section.

27 "Now the Rotarians Ask One-Piece Suit."

28 "Bare Legs are O.K. for Bathers in Cleveland," *Chicago Herald and Examiner*, 19 June 1921.

29 *The Chicago Code of 1911*, revised and codified by Edward J. Brundage, Corporation Counsel (Chicago: Callighan and Co., 1911), 645.

30 *The Chicago Municipal Code of 1922*, revised and codified by Samuel A. Ettelson, Corporation Counsel (Chicago: T. H. Flood and Co., 1922), 764–65.

31 "Bathing-Suits and Bathing-Beach Regulations," 569–70. Martin and Koda describe the distinction between swimwear and underwear as crucial in the early phases of the development of bathing costume styles (*Splash!* 54).

32 "H2 Oh Boy!"

33 "Bars Beach 'Lizards,'" *New York Times*, 27 May 1921.

34 "'Copettes' Will Spot Beach 'Lizards' Who Annoy Girls."

35 Alexis Miller, a lifeguard, although equally cynical toward the bathers who frequented the beach, viewed their misdeeds more phlegmatically. He had placed danger signs on the beaches but said, "If the bathers run true to form, I expect to see them use these signs as coat . . . hangers. . . . It will be just like them." Victor Jagmetty, "Beach Combers," *Atlantic City Daily Press*, 9 June 1921.

36 "Beach Censors Will Be Named in July—Bader," *Atlantic City Evening Union*, 10 June 1921.

37 "Somers Point Women Ignore Surf Suit Row," *Atlantic City Daily Press*, 7 June 1921; "At 70 Wants Job as Bathing Girls' Censor," *New York Times*, 7 June 1921.

38 It was typical, for example, that all bathers, regardless of gender, were required to wear shirts that came no lower than a line level with the armpit. This rule was adopted by the American Association of Park Superintendents in 1917. Martin and Koda, *Splash!* 138.

39 See for example, "Zion Alderman Rebels against Lake 'Trousers,'" *Chicago Evening Post*, 20 August 1921; "Skirts for Men Bathers," *New York Times*, 21 August 1921.

40 "Zion Alderman."

41 "Hundreds in One-Piece Suits," *New York Times*, 13 June 1921.

42 "One Piece Suits Given a Welcome."

43 "Barelimbed Sea Nymphs Lure Crowds to 'Point,'" *Atlantic City Daily Press*, 6 June 1921.

44 "Somers Point to Have Bath Houses Soon," *Atlantic City Evening Union*, 9 June 1921; "Real Bath Houses," *Atlantic City Daily Press*, 9 June 1921.

45 "Barelimbed Sea Nymphs."

46 "Now Mayor 'Bob' Says He Never Saw One-Piece Suit," *Atlantic City Daily Press*, 8 June 1921.

47 "Even Staid Boston Shivers over Somers Point Bathing," *Atlantic City Daily Press*, 9 June 1921.

48 "Somers Point Draws Movies," *Atlantic City Sunday Gazette*, 26 June 1921.

49 Photo caption, *Chicago Tribune*, 26 March 1922, rotogravure section; "Calls 'Em Harmless despite Cry of 'Purities' for Ban," *Chicago Herald and Examiner*, 18 March 1922.

50 "Atlantic City Limits Suits," *New York Times*, 13 June 1921.

51 "Law Orders Drapery for Hawaiian Bathers," *New York Times*, 30 May 1921; "Propriety at Sea in Honolulu," *New York Times*, 31 May 1921.

52 One photograph of bathers on Chicago's Oak Street beach taken in 1930, for example, shows many women wearing one-piece suits with no stockings, knickers, or skirts. Martin and Koda, *Splash!* 73.

53 Two valuable sources on the impact of film in shaping images of women in the 1920s, including women's choices in fashion, are Maureen Turim, "Seduction and Elegance: The New Woman of Fashion in Silent Cinema," in Shari Benstock and Suzanne Ferriss, eds., *On Fashion* (New Brunswick, N.J.: Rutgers University Press, 1994), 140–58; Lary May, *Screening Out the Past: The Birth of Mass Culture and the Motion Picture Industry* (Chicago: University of Chicago Press, 1980), esp. chap. 8, pp. 200–36.

54 Unless otherwise noted, the details of this story are taken from "Authoress Goes on 'Attire Strike' in City's Hoosegow," *Atlantic City Daily Press*, 3 September 1921. Incidentally, Rosine's arresting officer, Edward Shaw, had been reassigned earlier in the summer to patrol the South Carolina Avenue beach rather than the Virginia Avenue beach that had formerly been his territory. For some reason, however, he was at the latter location when Rosine decided to "test the waters." Victor Jagmetty, "Beach Combers," *Atlantic City Daily Press*, 14 June 1921.

55 The four newspaper accounts are as follows: "Roll Up Stockings? No! Not Even in Jail," *New York Herald*, 4 September 1921; "Jail or Roll 'Em Up, Woman Chooses Jail," *New York World*, 4 September 1921; "Woman Bather Prefers Jail

to Rolling 'Em Up," *New York Tribune*, 4 September 1921; "Bather Goes to Jail; Keeps Her Knees Bare," *New York Times*, 4 September 1921.

56 "Jail or Roll 'Em Up."

57 In some ways, this "rupture," as it were, parallels an example drawn from George Eliot's *Adam Bede* and used by James C. Scott to illustrate the occasional open declaration of defiance "in the face of power" by subservient people. Texts of such defiance are based on "hidden transcripts" that are well rehearsed and widely circulated among subordinate groups and, at certain moments, "storm the stage." *Domination and the Arts of Resistance: Hidden Transcripts* (New Haven, Conn.: Yale University Press, 1990), 5–8.

58 Victor Jagmetty, "Beach Combers," *Atlantic City Daily Press*, 18 June 1921.

59 "Modesty for Bathers," *Chicago Daily News*, 22 March 1922.

60 Elaine Tyler May recounts the story of a 1920 divorce that effectively suggests the cultural paradox that women, though often attractive to men as flappers before marriage, were expected by those same men to give up the behaviors that label represented once married. *Great Expectations: Marriage and Divorce in Post-Victorian America* (Chicago: University of Chicago Press, 1980), 1.

61 "Death for Millions in 1921's Record Heat Wave," *New York Herald*, 4 September 1921, sec. 7.

62 "7 Prostrated As Heat Hits Record for Sept. 2," *New York Herald*, 3 September 1921.

63 "Local Weather Records," *New York Herald*, 4 September 1921.

64 "Authoress Goes on 'Attire Strike.'"

65 The following discussion is based on information found in several articles, all of which appeared on p. 1 of the *Atlantic City Daily Press*, 3 September 1921, the day Louise Rosine was arrested. The specific articles are entitled, "Beachfront Is Making Ready for Pageant," "Organizations May Enter If Bathing Costume Worn," and "Sell Tickets for Pageant."

66 Winners in several other categories were also awarded Annette Kellerman swimsuits.

67 Riverol, *Live from Atlantic City*, 7–8.

68 Lois W. Banner, *American Beauty* (Chicago: University of Chicago Press, 1983), 249

69 Riverol, *Live from Atlantic City*, 1.

70 Ibid., 6–7.

71 Banner, *American Beauty*, 250; Riverol, *Live from Atlantic City*, 7.

72 Riverol, *Live from Atlantic City*, 7–9; Banner, *American Beauty*, 255–57.

73 Banner, *American Beauty*, 258–61.

74 Frank Deford, *There She Is: The Life and Times of Miss America* (New York: Viking, 1971), 108–10.

75 Lencek and Bosker, *Making Waves*, 52.

76 Deford, *There She Is*, 111–12.

77 Photo, *Atlantic City Evening Union*, 8 September 1921

78 Photo caption, *Atlantic City Daily Press*, 9 September 1921.

79 "Gorgeous Beauty Feature of Climaxing Spectacles in City's Great Pageant," *Atlantic City Daily Press*, 9 September 1921. The obvious infractions against city

ordinances prohibiting the display of bare limbs during the pageant is also noted by Deford, who states, however, that the Atlantic City constables merely joined "in the spirit of the promotion" and appeared not to notice such infractions on the part of the bathing beauty contestants (*There She Is*, 61).

80 Funnell, *By the Beautiful Sea*, 147; Lois W. Banner, *Women in Modern America: A Brief History*, 2nd ed. (New York: Harcourt Brace Jovanovich, 1984), 176.

81 The production history of this play is described in Carol M. Ward, *Mae West: A Bio-Bibliography* (New York: Greenwood Press, 1989), 15–16, 140–41, 142. A recent in-depth analysis of this play, particularly in terms of its position within the broader context of West's career may be found in Emily Wortis Leider, *Becoming Mae West* (New York: Farrar Straus Giroux, 1997), 173–83. Interestingly, as Leider points out, by 1927, Atlantic City had suspended its pageant and did so for several years, at least in part because the contest had lost some respectability due to a scandal associated with a former contest winner. My own analysis of this play is based on my reading of a copy of the manuscript as retained in the Library of Congress. Mae West, *The Wicked Age*, or *The Contest*, 1927, Mae West Collection, Manuscripts Division, Library of Congress. As this is the only play discussed in this chapter, subsequent citations will omit the title and refer the reader simply to the appropriate act and page numbers as indicated on Library of Congress copy of manuscript.

82 1.3.

83 3.3, 11, 26.

84 1.4.

85 1.37, 1.18.

86 1.18–19.

87 3.22.

88 Florence M. Peto, "Swim—for Health, Youth and Beauty," *Outing* 75 (December 1919): 161.

89 Ibid.

90 Ibid., 182.

91 Ibid., 161.

92 Ibid., 162.

93 Ibid.

94 Ibid., 181–82.

95 The paradoxical nature of burlesque is discussed by Robert C. Allen, *Horrible Prettiness: Burlesque and American Culture* (Chapel Hill: University of North Carolina Press, 1991), 281–89.

96 See, for example, the nearly euphoric claims about the implications of women's new clothing styles in Woods Hutchinson, "Health and Sports Suits," *Saturday Evening Post* 198 (8 August 1925): 20–21, 137. Also, Marie Beynon Ray, "Sheer Modernism," *Collier's* 84 (17 August 1929): 19, 46.

97 Donald J. Mrozek, "The 'Amazon' and the American 'Lady': Sexual Fears of Women as Athletes," in J. A. Mangan and Roberta J. Park, eds., *From "Fair Sex" to Feminism: Sport and the Socialization of Women in the Industrial and Post-Industrial Eras* (London: Frank Cass and Co., 1987), 286–87.

98 Ibid., 289.

4. The Right to Bare (pp. 99–120)

I wish to thank John Rouse for his helpful comments on this chapter, an earlier version of which was published in *Theatre Journal* 49 (December 1997): 455–73. Used by permission of Johns Hopkins University Press.

The unidentified vice investigator was quoted in John Roach Straton, "The Trouble with the Modern Theatre," *Theatre Magazine* 31 (February 1920): 74.

1 Jack F. Sharrar, *Avery Hopwood: His Life and Plays* (Jefferson, N.C.: McFarland and Co., 1989; reprint, Ann Arbor: University of Michigan Press, 1998), 111; Ronald H. Wainscott, *The Emergence of the Modern American Theater, 1914–1929* (New Haven, Conn.: Yale University Press, 1997), 1–6, 72–73.

2 Susan Duffy and Bernard K. Duffy elaborate more fully on the identities and affiliations of pre-1920s reformers. In particular, they argue a "social-housekeeping" theater reform tradition in keeping with their position that the animus for the theater reform movement came from "well meaning, middle class women intent upon upholding standards of *taste* and *decency* outside the home" (emphasis mine). Indeed, I contend as well that this dual focus was present in most attacks on theater. In my review of censorship in the 1920s, however, I have found the most vocal and publicly recognized proponents of theater reform were male clergy. Still, these men also usually represented an ongoing reform tradition that had its roots in the Progressive era. See "Watchdogs of the American Theatre 1910–1940," *Journal of American Culture* 6 (spring 1983): 52–53, 58–59.

3 Billy Sunday, "Theater, Cards and Dance," in *The Best of Billy Sunday: 17 Burning Sermons from the Most Spectacular Evangelist the World Has Ever Known*, ed. John R. Rice (Murfreesboro, Tenn.: Sword of the Lord Publishers, 1965), 118–19. The editor of this collection does not make clear how many times Sunday preached this sermon but only that he presented it in Omaha, Nebraska, in 1915.

4 The similarity between theater reform efforts and Prohibition was noted repeatedly in the heated sparring over theatrical censorship carried on in various public forums throughout the decade. "Reforming the Stage from Within," *Literary Digest* 89 (17 April 1926): 32.

5 "Mary's Little Skirt," *New York Times*, 27 June 1921.

6 An excellent example of such logic is an essay written by Judge Charles A. Oberwager, entitled "Heaven Help the Modern Boy!" *Liberty* 4 (23 July 1927): 15–18.

7 Victorianism was, of course, a far more complex ideological framework than I imply here. My emphasis relates to the expectation, generally associated with the Victorian era, that a woman's influence should be within and through the home environment she created. She affected social morality by setting a virtuous example for her children and husband. See, for example, Matthew Schneirov, *The Dream of a New Social Order: Popular Magazines in America, 1893–1914* (New York: Columbia University Press, 1994), 37. Certainly, by the late nineteenth century, especially, many felt a woman's moral influence might properly extend to "social housekeeping." Whether within or outside the home, however, the Vic-

torian ideal for women did not include a concession to their sexual needs. A helpful discussion of this subject is found in Michael Mason, *The Making of Victorian
Sexual Attitudes* (New York: Oxford University Press, 1994), 215–23.

8 See, for example, Abe Laufe, *The Wicked Stage: A History of Theater Censorship and Harassment in the United States* (New York: Frederick Ungar, 1978),
60–61; Allen Churchill, *The Theatrical 20s* (New York: McGraw-Hill, 1975), 232.

9 Ronald H. Wainscott's discussion of women's roles in popular sex farces of this
era is useful in this regard (*The Emergence of the Modern American Theatre*,
chap. 4). Also, Robert C. Allen's *Horrible Prettiness: Burlesque and American
Culture* (Chapel Hill: University of North Carolina Press, 1991) insightfully critiques the ways in which burlesque shaped the image of women in American
culture.

10 Francette Pacteau, *The Symptom of Beauty* (Cambridge: Harvard University
Press, 1994), 100, 113.

11 Anne Hollander, *Seeing through Clothes* (New York: Viking Press, 1978), 87.

12 Faye E. Dudden, *Women in the American Theatre: Actresses, Audiences, 1790–
1870* (London: Yale University Press, 1994), 2.

13 Lewis A. Erenberg makes a similar claim in *Steppin' Out: New York Nightlife
and the Transformation of American Culture, 1890–1930* (Westport, Conn.:
Greenwood Press, 1981), 219.

14 Ted Shawn, "Is Nudity Salacious?" *Theatre Magazine* 40 (November 1924): 12.

15 "The Comic Slant on Stage Nudity," *Theatre Magazine* 38 (November 1923): 7.

16 James Whittaker, "Extra! A Ziegfeld Follies Girl Need Not Be a Raving Beauty,"
Chicago Tribune, 26 March 1922, sec. 8.

17 Richard Dana Skinner, "The Play: When Ziegfeld Stumbles," *Commonweal* 10
(24 July 1929): 316.

18 Others have noted Ziegfeld's powerful influence on ideals of female beauty as
well. See, for example, Erenberg, *Steppin' Out,* 218–19, and Allen, *Horrible
Prettiness,* 272. Although ideals in feminine beauty have fluctuated considerably
throughout American cultural history and although there have been many influences on these ideals, I contend that Ziegfeld must nevertheless be recognized as
a primary force in this regard if for no other reason than that never since the
Ziegfeld Girl has the popular American ideal of feminine beauty included heavy
women. In short, after Ziegfeld, to be counted among the "beautiful," a woman
must at the very least be thin.

19 Walter Tittle, "Ziegfeld of the Follies," *World's Work* 53 (March 1927): 567.

20 Florenz Ziegfeld, "How I Pick Beauties," *Theatre Magazine* 30 (September
1919): 158.

21 Florenz Ziegfeld Jr., "Picking Out Pretty Girls for the Stage," *American Magazine* 88 (December 1919): 34, 125.

22 Ziegfeld, "How I Pick Beauties," 159.

23 J. Brooks Atkinson, "Exploration Unrewarded," *Boston Evening Transcript,* 1 May
1922. For a more expansive account of burlesque at this point in its slow but eventual demise, see Allen, *Horrible Prettiness,* 241–49.

24 Carl Van Vechten, "A Note on Tights," *American Mercury* 2 (August 1924):
428–32.

25 R. L. Lurie, "Burlesque," *New Republic* 42 (8 April 1925): 180–81.

26 Leon Whipple, "Not Art and Not Model," *Survey* 55 (1 March 1926): 632.

27 John Bakeless, "The Anatomical Drama: Burlesque Shows and Lesser Wickedness," *Outlook and Independent* 156 (December 1931): 698. For a discussion of the evolution of the runway and its appropriation within several performance genres, see Tara Maginnis, "Fashion Shows, Strip Shows and Beauty Pageants: The Theatre of the Feminine Ideal" (Ph.D. diss., University of Georgia, 1991).

28 Joseph Kaye, "The Last Legs of Burlesque," *Theatre Magazine* 51 (February 1930): 36.

29 Fanny Brice, for example, claimed to have begun her professional career within the ranks of the burlesque chorus. Fanny Brice, "The Feel of the Audience," *Saturday Evening Post* 198 (21 November 1925): 181.

30 Joseph Wood Krutch, "Of Revues," *Nation* 122 (13 January 1926): 40–41.

31 Joseph Wood Krutch, "Bigger and Better," *Nation* 122 (2 June 1926): 616.

32 Rolphe Humphries, "Artists and Models: Through the Stereoscope, Right Eye: The Intellect," *New Republic* 54 (11 April 1928): 246–47.

33 Louise Bogan, "Artists and Models: Through the Stereoscope, Left Eye: The Senses," *New Republic* 54 (11 April 1928): 247.

34 Gilbert Seldes, "A Tribute to Florenz Ziegfeld," in *The American Theatre as Seen by Its Critics, 1752–1934*, ed. Montrose J. Moses and John Mason Brown (New York: W. W. Norton and Co., 1934), 242.

35 Gilbert Seldes, "The Theatre," *Dial* 73 (September 1922): 356–57.

36 Ann Douglas, *Terrible Honesty: Mongrel Manhattan in the 1920s* (New York: Farrar, Straus and Giroux, 1995), 98.

37 Francis Fergusson, "The Theatre: What Is the Revue?" *Bookman* 72 (September 1930): 409–10.

38 Ibid., 410.

39 Edmund Wilson, "The Finale at the Follies," *New Republic* 42 (25 March 1925): 126.

40 Erenberg, *Steppin' Out*, 255–57.

41 Four years later, Billie Burke married the man who specialized in women who bobbed about in curls and wore pretty frocks, Florenz Ziegfeld Jr. "Miss Burke Is Restless," *Chicago Record-Herald*, 9 October 1910, sec. 7.

42 In an otherwise impressive volume issued by the Women's News Service, for example, a discussion of "women and the stage" made no mention of the thousands of women employed in the nation's choruses. Although the book tried to compensate for the scant record of women's achievements as represented by the major newspapers of the day, Lillian B. Sheridan, author of the section on theater, continued in the tradition of overlooking vast numbers of women on whom the theater industry in no small way depended. "Women and the Stage," in *Women of Today: 1925 Edition*, ed. Ida Clyde Clarke (New York: Women of Today Press, 1925), 108–9.

    In later records of women's participation in the theater of the 1920s, information about the chorus also has been scant. Helen Krich Chinoy, for example, never refers to the theater professionals who comprised the choruses of the 1920s in her summary of the prominent participation of women in this decade of theater history. "Suppressed Desires: Women in the Theater," in *Women, the Arts, and the 1920s in Paris and New York*, ed. Kenneth W. Wheeler and Virginia Lee Lussier (New Brunswick, N.J.: Transaction, 1982), 126–31. Likewise, in the substantial text that Chinoy coedited with Linda Walsh Jenkins, an essay about Lydia Thompson and the British Blondes is the sole discussion of a female theatrical chorus. *Women in the American Theatre*, rev. ed. (New York: Theatre Communications Group, 1987).

43 Lois W. Banner also describes the fascination Americans had with chorus girls, noting that the stories and news columns devoted to women of the chorus were so common that one newspaper claimed that the chorus girl was a more popular topic of conversation than the president. *American Beauty* (Chicago: University of Chicago Press, 1983), 180.

44 "The Chorus Girl Irredenta," *Nation* 109 (20 September 1919): 391.

45 Whipple, "Not Art and Not Model," 632.

46 Tracy C. Davis, "Questions for a Feminist Methodology in Theatre History," in *Interpreting the Theatrical Past: Essays in the Historiography of Performance*, ed. Thomas Postlewaite and Bruce A. McConachie (Iowa City: University of Iowa Press, 1989), 69.

47 Marian Spitzer, "The Chorus Lady, Model 1924," *Saturday Evening Post* 197 (15 September 1924): 208. Hugh Leamy confirmed the comparatively high wages paid to chorus girls in "Toeing the Line," *Collier's* 86 (13 September 1930): 46.

48 Sophinisba P. Breckinridge, *Women in the Twentieth Century: A Study of Their Political, Social and Economic Activities* (New York: McGraw-Hill, 1933), 181–82.

49 Betty Van Deventer, "Lives of Chorus Girls," *Haldeman-Julius Quarterly* 2 (January–March 1928): 182.

50 Spitzer, "Chorus Lady," 210.

51 Erenberg, *Steppin' Out*, 215.

52 See, for example, "The College Girl vs. the Chorus Girl," *Publisher's Weekly* 116 (28 December 1929): 2924; Mary Day Winn, "Intelligentsia of the Chorus," *North American Review* 229 (June 1930): 701–4.

53 Ned Wayburn, the well-known *Follies* choreographer, claimed that, because of disciplined training, professional independence, and experience with the difficulties of real life, the women of the chorus were well equipped for matrimony. "Chorus Girls Make the Best Wives," *Collier's* 77 (27 March 1926): 20–21.

54 One unusually vitriolic essay was written by Samuel Marx, whose speculative and judgmental rantings about women of the theater are practically breathtaking. *Wild Women of Broadway Little Blue Book No. 1445*, ed. E. Haldeman-Julius (Girard, Kansas: Haldeman-Julius Publications, 1929), n.p.

55 These discussions almost always centered on *Follies* stars. For example, see Florenz Ziegfeld Jr., "What Becomes of the Ziegfeld Follies Girls?" *Pictorial Review* 26 (May 1925): 12–13, 48. Also consult the series featuring and written by the former *Follies* performer Lilyan Tashman, "Frolics and Follies," *Pictorial Review* 33 (October, November, December 1931), beginning on pp. 16, 17, and 22, respectively.

56 "Many Pretty Atlanta Girls Apply at Atlanta Theater for Opportunity to Shine in Big Chorus of Beauties," *Atlanta Constitution*, 6 January 1922.

57 Certainly, theater professionals did the most, in some cases, to perpetuate the lore. One exceptional source of inside information not only about the lives of chorus girls but about the whole of the system that employed them is Will A. Page, *Behind the Curtains of the Broadway Beauty Trust* (New York: Edward A. Miller Co., 1927). My thanks to Rodney Higgenbotham for bringing this source to my attention.

58 My thanks to Jack Sharrar, who generously provided me with a copy of the unpublished manuscript of this play.

59 Avery Hopwood, *The Gold Diggers*, Act 1, p. 9.

60 Ibid., 1.22.

61 Ibid., 1.23.

62 "A Naked Challenge," *Nation* 122 (23 June 1926): 229.

63 Arthur Hornblow, "League of Nations' Fifteenth Point," *Theatre Magazine* 44 (September 1926): 7. For nude or scantily clothed women to move about rather than remain still was often perceived as vulgar.

64 "Governor Smith Credited in Stage Clean-Up," *New York Times*, 7 April 1927.

65 Tittle, "Ziegfeld of the Follies," 567.

66 Lee Shubert, quoted in Hornblow, "League of Nations," 7.

67 Hornblow, "League of Nations," 7.

5. *The Transgressions of* Ladies' Night *(pp. 122–154)*

1 *The Gold Diggers*, discussed in chapter 4, opened the previous year and was still having a successful run. *Ladies' Night* premiered on 9 August, and *Spanish Love* and *The Bat* opened on 17 and 23 August, respectively. See "The Hopwood Hope," *New York Times*, 5 September 1920, sec. 6. An excellent biography of Hopwood discusses this pinnacle of his career in more detail. See Jack F. Sharrar, *Avery Hopwood: His Life and Plays* (Ann Arbor: University of Michigan Press, 1998), chap. 5, pp. 111–48.

2 Sharrar, *Avery Hopwood*, 135. In my 19 June 1996 telephone conversation with Sharrar, I learned that he had had difficulty locating a reading copy of *Ladies' Night*. In one of those quirks of historical research, my inquiries of the Samuel French publishing company, one of the places Sharrar had also contacted, led to the discovery of a 1920 carbon copy of the manuscript of *Ladies' Night*. A photocopy of this manuscript informs the present discussion. Hopwood and Charlton Andrews had apparently submitted the play to French, but it was never published by them in its original form. An adaptation by Cyrus Wood, *Good Night Ladies* (New York: Samuel French, n.d.) was published, but the date of this adaptation is not specified within it. Wood's version ran to great popular appeal— ironically, in Chicago—during World War II. See Sharrar, *Avery Hopwood*, 226–27, for further information about the Wood adaptation.

3 It is impossible to know to what extent *Ladies' Night* represents a true collaboration between Hopwood and Andrews, as neither was apparently inclined to discuss the subject. In this investigation, my analysis of authorial intentions is heavily influenced by the considerable commentary available on the subject by

Hopwood, whose notoriety provided him with many opportunities to discuss these matters in public forums. Andrews was a college professor and author of a text on dramatic writing called *The Drama To-day* (Philadelphia: J. B. Lippincott Co., 1913). *Theatre Magazine* noted Andrews's cryptic response alleging that the reason he joined Hopwood to create *Ladies' Night* was that A. H. Woods and John Cumberland, the actor who played Jimmy Walters in the New York production of the play, "needed a bath—to get them out of the bedroom." "Charlton Andrews," *Theatre Magazine* 32 (October 1920): 177. Andrews was not generally known as a comic playwright. Besides authoring books, he sometimes contributed to *Theatre Magazine*, as when he wrote a "Personality Portrait" of the actor Frank McGlynn, who was known for his portrayal of Lincoln. See vol. 31 (February 1920), p. 88.

4 Arthur Hornblow made a particular point of saying that the play was inferior to the abilities of its authors. "Mr. Hornblow Goes to the Play," *Theatre Magazine* 32 (October 1920): 185–86.

5 Alexander Woollcott, "The Play," *New York Times*, 10 August 1920.

6 Bernard Sobel, "Ladies' Night: Turkish Bath House Turns on Comedy Steam," *Dramatic Mirror* 82 (14 August 1920): 283.

7 Robert Bogdan discusses the history of the dime museum in America and notes that such attractions, which had specialized in the presentation of various "freak" exhibits, had, by the early twentieth century, been deserted by "respectable" citizens and left to "immigrants and country bumpkins." Between World War I and the 1930s, these museums became "vagabond shows" that still specialized mostly in freak exhibits. Even though they were considered disreputable by many people and were no longer as popular as they had been before the twentieth century, dime museums persisted even into the 1940s. *Freak Show: Presenting Human Oddities for Amusement and Profit* (Chicago: University of Chicago Press, 1988), 38.

8 Sheppard Butler, "In Memory of 'Ladies' Night'; News of Plays and Players," *Chicago Tribune*, 30 April 1922.

9 A disgruntled Fuzzy Woodruff, for example, unimpressed by New York theatrical imports to Atlanta, complained about comic bits that were often included in revues, bits that, in his view, had little appeal outside New York. Producers seemed not to realize that people in cities to which their shows toured would not be amused by references to New York's subways or popular restaurants. "Slow Curtain and Fast Music for Revue," *Atlanta Constitution*, 22 January 1922, Sunday magazine, p. 11.

10 For a thorough account of the remarkable fracas this production created, especially Woods's manipulation of the publicity over it, see Ronald H. Wainscott, "Attracting Censorship to the Popular Theatre: Al Woods Produces Avery Hopwood's *The Demi-Virgin*," *Theatre History Studies* 10 (1990): 127–40. See also the chapter derived from this article in Wainscott's *Emergence of the Modern American Theatre, 1914–1929* (New Haven, Conn.: Yale University Press, 1997), 75–90.

11 This was the name commonly used to refer to what we would today call a spa or health club.

12 In production, each of these women were given real names, but it is clear from reviews that viewers still perceived them as "types" (see fig. 34).

13 *Ladies' Night*, Act 2, pp. 5–6. All subsequent citations of this script will omit the name of the play. Interestingly, the exchange noted here mirrors a conversation in Act 1 of *The Demi-Virgin*. Two bathing beauties have been hired to appear in the movies. One woman says to the other, "Gee, I wish they'd give me a part where I could wear some clothes." The other woman later says, "Take enough off when you're young, and you'll have enough to put on when you're older!" Quoted in Wainscott, *Emergence of the Modern American Theatre*, 60.

14 2.9.

15 Ashton Stevens, "Everything but Speech Is Undressed in a Bath-House Farce at the Woods," *Chicago Herald and Examiner*, 24 March 1922.

16 2.11.

17 2.11.

18 2.10.

19 2.13.

20 1.1.

21 1.3–4.

22 1.2.

23 2.17.

24 A. H. Woods, "Why I Produce Bedroom Farces," *Theatre Magazine* 35 (June 1922): 352.

25 Avery Hopwood, "Is the Undraped Drama Unmoral?" *Theatre Magazine* 33 (January 1921): 6.

26 Ibid.

27 Jack F. Sharrar discusses, among other things, the autobiographical novel Hopwood wrote, as evidence of his homosexuality; *Avery Hopwood*, 199.

28 When Jimmy first spots Fred and Cort climbing through the window of the bathhouse, he calls out "Oh, boys! Oh, boys!" to get their attention (2.38). Dulcy also refers to the three men in this way (1.18, 3.16, 3.18).

29 George Chauncey, *Gay New York: Gender, Urban Culture, and the Making of the Gay Male World, 1890–1940* (New York: Basic Books, 1994), 290.

30 1.9.

31 3.5.

32 Chauncey, *Gay New York*, 288.

33 1.12–13.

34 Chauncey, *Gay New York*, 286.

35 Ibid., 290–91.

36 Ibid., 197.

37 1.42–43.

38 Chauncey, *Gay New York*, 54–55.

39 1.6.

40 James C. Scott, *Domination and the Arts of Resistance: Hidden Transcripts* (New Haven, Conn.: Yale University Press, 1990), 19.

41 Chauncey, *Gay New York*, 209.

42 Ibid., 223.

43 Chauncey quotes Thomas Painter, who described a Coney Island bathhouse steam room (*Gay New York*, 210–11).

44 1.46.

45 3.27.

46 Ann Douglas, *Terrible Honesty: Mongrel Manhattan in the 1920s* (New York: Farrar, Straus and Giroux, 1995), 288. I noted Van Vechten's favorable review of a burlesque show in chap. 4.

47 Sharrar, *Avery Hopwood*, 58.

48 Chauncey, *Gay New York*, 292.

49 3.11.

50 Avery Hopwood, "Why I Don't Write More Serious Plays," *Theatre Magazine* 39 (April 1924): 10, 56.

51 Ibid., 56.

52 2.45.

53 Robert C. Allen also makes this point in *Horrible Prettiness: Burlesque and American Culture* (Chapel Hill: University of North Carolina Press, 1991), 244.

54 2.10.

55 Ashton Stevens also referred to the preponderance of women in the matinee audience who attended this play. He interpreted their obvious enjoyment of the play as being a result of its lack of sexual appeal to them and felt that naturally "you would not expect an audience of women to be shocked by a bath-houseful of women draped for bathing" ("Everything but Speech").

56 Faye E. Dudden, *Women in the American Theatre: Actresses and Audiences, 1790–1870* (New Haven, Conn.: Yale University Press, 1994), 184.

57 Ibid.

58 Woods, "Why I Produce Bedroom Farces," 406.

59 That youth was itself often appropriated to legitimize sexually provocative displays may be illustrated in a variety of ways. It was not uncommon at this time, for example, for newspapers to run photographs of contestants for what amounted to baby beauty contests. The *Chicago Herald and Examiner* contained a series of such photographs in September 1920. Dorothea Norton was among the children pictured as contenders in the "Perfect Baby Show." Her published photograph was several times larger than most others that surrounded it. She appears naked but for a string of pearls and a bracelet, and she poses alluringly in partial profile, coyly looking into the camera over her shoulder. Unlike the other contestants, she is no "baby" but is almost six years of age. Aware of how the female body was routinely displayed in popular entertainment venues of the time, it is impossible to view Norton's photograph without recognizing that her pose alludes to these highly sexualized entertainments. This allusion highlights the inappropriateness of her nudity. Moreover, that a $1,000 prize was to be awarded to the winning "baby" also tellingly parallels the values of an entertainment system that placed so high a premium on the physical beauty of young females and their willingness to display themselves and, for that matter, still does. *Chicago Herald and Examiner*, 21 September 1920, sec. 3.

60 Ziegfeld was savvy enough to avoid giving the impression that he intentionally rejected older women when he selected choruses. Although he admitted that

almost all the women who comprised his choruses were between seventeen and twenty-two years of age, he carefully qualified this admission by saying: "We have very few older than that, for the simple reason that Cupid and Hymen claim them." Florenz Ziegfeld Jr. "Picking Out Pretty Girls for the Stage," *American Magazine* 88 (December 1919), 34, 125.

61 See, for example, Lois W. Banner, *American Beauty* (Chicago: University of Chicago Press, 1983), 278–79.

62 Richard Ziegfeld and Paulette Ziegfeld, *The Ziegfeld Touch: The Life and Times of Florenz Ziegfeld, Jr.* (New York: Harry N. Abrams, 1993), 301.

63 This information is found in a playbill and in news clippings from a scrapbook compiled by Mary Campbell Taylor, Playbills and Programs Collection, series 2, box 47, scrapbook 3, University of Chicago Library.

64 Lilyan Tashman, "Frolics and Follies," *Pictorial Review* 33 (November 1931): 27–28.

65 *Theatre Magazine* 32 (October 1920): 182.

66 Florenz Ziegfeld Jr., "What Becomes of the Ziegfeld Follies Girls?" *Pictorial Review* 26 (May 1925): 48. Ziegfeld and Ziegfeld, *The Ziegfeld Touch*, 301.

67 Ziegfeld and Ziegfeld, *The Ziegfeld Touch*, 301.

68 The account in which Lilyan Tashman describes Allyn King is a good example of narratives written by or about women who were "discovered" by Ziegfeld and who became famous for it. Tashman was in a café when Ziegfeld spotted her. She later became an actress in the movies. Her story is featured in a three-part series called "Frolics and Follies," *Pictorial Review* 33 (October, November, December, 1931).

69 Amy Leslie, "'Ladies' Night' On with Violent Shocks," *Chicago Daily News*, 22 March 1922.

70 Stevens, "Everything but Speech."

71 "Good Night, 'Ladies' Night,'" *Chicago Tribune*, 25 March 1922.

72 Charles Collins, "'Ladies' Night' Is Farcical Orgy of Mixed Bathing," *Chicago Evening Post*, 22 March 1922.

73 Scott, *Domination and the Arts of Resistance*, 19.

74 Hopwood, "Is the Undraped Drama Unmoral?" 238.

75 John Clayton, "The Scourge of Sinners: Arthur Burrage Farwell," *Chicago History* 3 (fall 1974): 68. This article provides a great deal of information about Farwell's reform activities but does contain some inaccuracies as well. Farwell's son, Stanley Farwell, wrote a letter to the editor of *Chicago History* that addresses and corrects these mistakes, which are mostly genealogical. A copy of this letter and other biographical information about Farwell is kept on file under Arthur Burrage Farwell's name in the library of the Chicago Historical Society.

76 These agencies include Chicago Law and Order League (president), Hyde Park Protective Organization (secretary), Illinois Vigilance Association (vice president), the Night Church (unspecified rank). Farwell was also on the council of the World's Purity Federation (WPF), a Wisconsin-based organization whose motto was "The White Slave Traffic and Public Vice Can and Must Be Annihilated." Farwell's affiliations with the Night Church and the WPF are confirmed by the stationery used by these organizations, the originals of which are found in

a publicity mailing dated 31 December 1920 and in a letter from Steadwell to Bell, 14 July 1925, respectively; Ernest Bell Collection, box 2, folder 2–3. The Illinois Vigilance Association affiliation is referred to in a letter from Hallam to Fitzpatrick, 1 October 1917; John Fitzpatrick Collection, box 6, folder 32. Copies of the minutes of the Chicago Law and Order League and the Hyde Park Protective Organization, which substantiate Farwell's crucial role in both organizations, are filed jointly in the Chicago Law and Order League Collection. All of these collections are kept at the Chicago Historical Society.

77 The range of Farwell's influence during the early part of this century is reflected in the fact that by century's end, as artistic censorship was once again a national concern, the name of Arthur Burrage Farwell resurfaced. The conceptual artist Joseph Kosuth, for one, called attention to Farwell's censorious influence in a 1990 museum installation and in his subsequent book. *The Play of the Unmentionable*, the title of both of Kosuth's works, notes Farwell's vehement opposition to the Armory Show of 1913, which was presented in Chicago after showing in New York. Roberta Smith, "'Unmentionable' Art through the Ages," *New York Times*, 11 November 1990, sec. 2. See also Joseph Kosuth, *The Play of the Unmentionable: An Installation by Joseph Kosuth at the Brooklyn Museum* (New York: New Press, 1992), 74. The words of Farwell that Kosuth quotes in his collection are taken from Milton Brown, *The Story of the Armory Show* (New York: Abbeville Press, 1988), 206. Farwell was reported to have said of the Armory exhibit, "It is a grave mistake to permit these pictures to hang either here or elsewhere. Why the saloons could not hang these pictures! There is a law prohibiting it. The idea that some people can gaze at this sort of thing without its hurting them is all bosh. The exhibition ought to be suppressed." When quoting these words in his 1992 review of Kosuth's book, John Dorsey was naturally inclined to add: "The speaker is not Jesse Helms, and the works in question are not homoerotica by Robert Mapplethorpe or any other recently controversial art. The speaker was Arthur Burrage Farwell, president of the Chicago Law and Order League." John Dorsey, "Exploring the Culture of Intolerance Joseph Kosuth's New Book Features Art; Found Objectionable, Then and Now," *St. Louis Post-Dispatch*, 16 August 1992, "Everyday Magazine."

78 Farwell to Garrity, 7 September 1920, folder 1, item 11, copy kept in the Chicago Law and Order League Collection, Chicago Historical Society.

79 June Sawyers, "The Night That 'Salome' Shocked the Whole Town," *Chicago Tribune*, 30 August 1987, Sunday magazine. Although Sawyers states that this performance was the season opener for the Chicago Opera Company in 1910, I have searched in vain in Chicago newspapers of the late summer and fall of 1910 for verification of Sawyers's report of this incident. The story is verified in Emmett Dedmon, *Fabulous Chicago*, enlarged ed. (New York: Athenaeum, 1981), 306, but Dedmon fails to give any date for the performance. A playbill clip of this elusive production as it was performed 30 January 1909 in New York, again with Mary Garden starring, may be located in series II, box 50, scrapbook 1, Playbills and Programs Collection, University of Chicago Library.

80 Farwell to Garrity, 20 September 1920, copy in Chicago Law and Order League Collection, folder 1, Chicago Historical Society.

81 Arthur Hornblow, "League of Nations' Fifteenth Point," *Theatre Magazine* 44 (September 1926): 7.

82 In his report to the Law and Order League, Farwell noted that he did not send a copy of his letter to the press and emphasizes this point in capital letters. Undoubtedly, this was a reminder that journalistic coverage of complaints against plays had come to be viewed a way to advertise them.

83 Minutes of the Chicago Law and Order League Board of Directors Meeting, 14 September 1920, folder 1, copy in Chicago Law and Order League Collection, Chicago Historical Society.

84 He also owned the Apollo Theatre at the opposite corner of the intersection of Randolph and Dearborn Streets, where the Woods Theatre stood.

85 The Loop refers to the part of the city encircled by the elevated public transportation railways of Chicago.

86 "Chicago Theatre Diagrams," series 2, box 34, folder 3, Playbills and Programs Collection, University of Chicago Library.

87 "Chicago Theatres," in *The Daily News Almanac and Year-Book for 1922* (Chicago: Chicago Daily News Co., 1921), 897.

88 Advertisement for *Ladies' Night, Chicago Tribune,* 27 March 1922; advertisements for Anna Pavlowa and the Columbia Burlesque Theatre, *Chicago Daily News,* 18 March 1922.

89 "Good Night, 'Ladies' Night.'"

90 Advertisement for *Ladies' Night, Chicago Tribune,* 19 March 1922, pt. 8; "Stage Attractions for the Coming Week," *Chicago Daily News,* 18 March 1922; Leslie, "'Ladies' Night' On with Violent Shocks."

91 Advertisement for Star and Carter Burlesque, *Chicago Tribune,* 27 March 1922.

92 "Farwell Asks City to Stop Show at Woods," *Chicago Tribune,* 28 March 1922, sec. 2; "'Ladies' Night' Is Censored," *Chicago Daily News,* 28 March 1922; "'Ladies' Night' Assailed," *New York Times,* 28 March 1922.

93 "Farwell Asks City to Stop Show at Woods."

94 "Appeals Theatre License Decision," *New York Times,* 19 March 1922.

95 Although it would seem that Breen's chosen methods of censorship in this case bear an uncanny resemblance to the "jury system" that had been proposed in New York by this time, these methods in fact were commonly employed to censor films in Chicago. For example, Breen had enforced the censorship recommendations of a "censor board" against a film called *The Dregs of a City* in 1920, one in which, incidentally, Police Chief Garrity was an actor. "Censors Bar Movie in Which Chief Garrity Acts," *Chicago Herald and Examiner,* 26 September 1920.

96 J. P. Brushingham was a clergyman who, by this time was quite elderly. He had begun preaching in Chicago in 1875 and had pastored several churches in the Chicago area by the time he was appointed as secretary of the Morals Commission of Chicago in 1917. He was affiliated with the Methodist Episcopal denomination. William Saltiel was a young attorney, in the early years of his legal career at the time of this incident. He became a member of the bar association in 1918. He was a well-known public speaker, having been director of the public speaking department at Columbia College of Music and then becoming a Chautauqua and

lyceum lecturer in 1920. He went on to have a distinguished legal career and continued to speak professionally as well. Information about Breen is found in Albert Nelson Marquis, ed., *The Book of Chicagoans* (Chicago: A. N. Marquis and Co., 1917), 83. Saltiel is listed in the 1926 edition of the same publication, p. 132. The Chicago Historical Society also holds a collection of William Saltiel papers.

97 "'Ladies' Night' Is Censored."

98 "'Ladies' Night' Assailed."

99 In my 31 October 1996 conversation with the chief law librarian of the City of Chicago, Scott Burgh, I learned that most records of cases that were not part of a City Council meeting were routinely destroyed after a few years.

100 Significantly, as an indication of their economic privilege, the officers of these organizations, all of whom were male, usually held their meetings in the Narcissus Tea Room of Marshall Field's, an elite department store in downtown Chicago. This meeting location is noted in the minutes of almost every meeting held by the organizations as maintained in the files of the Chicago Law and Order League, Chicago Historical Society. Also of interest, there are numerous financial updates in these records showing that Farwell used substantial sums of his own money to advance the causes of the organization.

101 Farwell to MacVeagh, 9 August 1912, folder 2, copy in Chicago Law and Order League Collection, Chicago Historical Society.

102 *The Chicago Code of 1911*, revised and codified by Edward J. Brundage, Corporation Counsel (Chicago: Callighan and Co., 1911), 644–45. This ordinance carried with it a fine of up to $100. This was a fairly standard amount for these kinds of misconduct, although some fines were less.

103 *The Chicago Municipal Code of 1922*, revised and codified by Samuel A. Ettelson, Corporation Counsel (Chicago: T. H. Flood & Co., 1922), 762–63.

104 *Chicago Code of 1911*, 645.

105 Robert C. Allen also explains how important the idea of performance or "show" was to the acceptance of female nudity after the turn of the century and includes Ziegfeld productions as a primary example of this acceptance. See *Horrible Prettiness*, 245.

Afterword (pp. 157–158)

1 "Queen of Beaches Chosen" and "Charity Fete Aids Chorus Girls," *New York Times*, 11 September 1921.

2 John Comaroff and Jean Comaroff, *Ethnography and the Historical Imagination* (Boulder, Colo.: Westview Press, 1992), 38.

3 Roy Latham told me of his conversations with Nellie and his feelings about her desire to work when I visited him on 2 February 1997.

Bibliography

Allen, Frederick Lewis. *Only Yesterday: An Informal History of the Nineteen-Twenties*. New York: Harper and Row, 1931.

Allen, Robert C. *Horrible Prettiness: Burlesque and American Culture*. Chapel Hill: University of North Carolina Press, 1991.

Anderson, Hattie E. "Clothes, Money and the Working Girl." *Survey*, vol. 58 (15 July 1927).

Andrews, Charlton. *The Drama To-Day*. Philadelphia: J. B. Lippincott Co., 1913.

———. "Personality Portrait." *Theatre Magazine*, vol. 31 (February 1920).

Andrews, Charlton, and Avery Hopwood. *Ladies' Night*. 1920. Photocopy of unpublished playscript courtesy Samuel French Company.

Bakeless, John. "The Anatomical Drama." *Outlook and Independent*, vol. 156 (December 1931).

Banner, Lois W. *American Beauty*. Chicago: University of Chicago Press, 1983.

Banta, Martha. *Imaging American Women: Idea and Ideals in Cultural History*. New York: Columbia University Press, 1987.

"The Bare-Neck Evil." *Literary Digest*, vol. 65 (3 April 1920).

"Bathing-Suits and Bathing-Beach Regulations." *American City*, vol. 28 (June 1923).

"The Battle of the Skirts." *Outlook*, vol. 132 (18 October 1922).

Beard, Lina, and Adelia B. Beard. *The National Organization, Girl Pioneers of America, Official Manual: Pioneering for Girls*. 4th ed. New York: Girl Pioneers of America, 1923.

Bell, Ernest. Collection. Chicago Historical Society.

Bellows, Jane. *Feet and Shoes*. New York: Woman's Press, 1928.

Benstock, Shari, and Suzanne Ferriss, eds. *On Fashion*. New Brunswick, N.J.: Rutgers University Press, 1994.

Bliven, Bruce. "Flapper Jane." *New Republic*, vol. 44 (9 September 1925).

Bogan, Louise. "Artists and Models: Through the Stereoscope, Right Eye: The Intellect." *New Republic*, vol. 54 (11 April 1928).

Bogdan, Robert. *Freak Show: Presenting Human Oddities for Amusement and Profit*. Chicago: University of Chicago Press, 1988.

Bolitho, William. "The New Skirt Length." *Harper's*, vol. 160 (February 1930).

Bordo, Susan R. "The Body and the Reproduction of Femininity: A Feminist Appropriation of Foucault." In *Gender/Body/Knowledge: Feminist Reconstructions of Being and Knowing*. Edited by Alison M. Jaggar and Susan R. Bordo. New Brunswick, N.J.: Rutgers University Press, 1989.

Breckinridge, Sophinisba P. *Women in the Twentieth Century: A Study of Their Political, Social and Economic Activities*. New York: McGraw-Hill, 1933.

Brice, Fanny. "The Feel of the Audience." *Saturday Evening Post*, vol. 198 (21 November 1925).

Bromley, Dorothy Dunbar. "Feminist—New Style." *Harper's*, vol. 155 (October 1927).

Burbank, Emily. *The Smartly Dressed Woman: How She Does It*. New York: Dodd, Mead and Co., 1925.

Cades, Hazel Rawson. "Good Looks: 'What Men Don't Like.'" *Woman's Home Companion*, vol. 51 (October 1924).

Carlson, Marvin. *Performance: A Critical Introduction*. New York: Routledge, 1996.

Carmichael, Reese. "The Ladies, God Bless 'Em, Their Frocks and Frills." *Ladies Home Journal*, vol. 38 (August 1921).

"The Catholic Crusade for Modesty." *Literary Digest*, vol. 82 (30 August 1924).

Catt, Carrie Chapman. "The Chemise Problem." *Woman Citizen*, vol. 11 (July 1926).

———. "How Many Yards in Your Skirt?" *Woman Citizen*, vol. 11 (August 1926).

Cavan, Ruth Shonle. *Business Girls: A Study of Their Interests and Problems*. Chicago: Religious Education Association, 1929.

Chanel, Gabrielle. "Fait Expres—by Chanel." *Ladies' Home Journal*, vol. 46 (June 1929).

Chappell, Clovis G. *Christ and the New Woman*. Nashville, Tenn.: Cokesbury Press, 1928.

"Charlton Andrews." *Theatre Magazine*, vol. 32 (October 1920).

Chauncey, George. *Gay New York: Gender, Urban Culture, and the Making of the Gay Male World, 1890–1940*. New York: Basic Books, 1994.

The Chicago Code of 1911. Revised and codified by Edward J. Brundage, Corporation Counsel. Chicago: Callighan and Co., 1911.

Chicago Law and Order League Collection. Chicago Historical Society.

The Chicago Municipal Code of 1922. Revised and codified by Samuel A. Ettelson, Corporation Counsel. Chicago: T. H. Flood and Co., 1922.

"Chicago Theatres." In *The Daily News Almanac and Year-Book for 1922*. Chicago: Chicago Daily News Co., 1921.

Chinoy, Helen Krich. "Suppressed Desires: Women in the Theater." In *Women, the Arts, and the 1920s in Paris and New York*. Edited by Kenneth W. Wheeler and Virginia Lee Lussier. New Brunswick, N.J.: Transaction Books, 1982.

Chinoy, Helen Krich, and Linda Walsh Jenkins, eds. *Women in the American Theatre*. Rev. ed. New York: Theatre Communications Group, 1987.

"The Chorus Girl Irredenta." *Nation*, vol. 109 (20 September 1919).

Churchill, Allen. *The Theatrical Twenties*. New York: McGraw-Hill, 1975.

City of Atlantic City. *Atlantic City Ordinances*. Atlantic City, N.J., 1922.

Clarke, Ida Clyde, ed. *Women of Today: 1925 Edition*. New York: Women of Today Press, 1925.

Clayton, John. "The Scourge of Sinners: Arthur Burrage Farwell." *Chicago History*, vol. 3 (fall 1974).

"Clothes and the Working-Girl." *Literary Digest*, vol. 95 (24 December 1927).

"The College Girl vs. the Chorus Girl." *Publisher's Weekly*, vol. 116 (28 December 1929).

Comaroff, John, and Jean Comaroff. *Ethnography and the Historical Imagination*. Boulder, Colo.: Westview Press, 1992.

"The Comic Slant on Stage Nudity." *Theatre Magazine*, vol. 38 (November 1923).

Conquergood, Dwight. "Ethnography, Rhetoric, and Performance." *Quarterly Journal of Speech*, vol. 78 (May 1992).

———. "Rethinking Ethnography: Towards a Critical Cultural Politics." *Communication Monographs*, vol. 58 (June 1991).

———. "A Sense of the Other: Interpretation and Ethnographic Research." In *Proceedings of the Seminar/Conference on Oral Traditions*. Edited by Isabel Crouch and Gordon Owen. Las Cruces: New Mexico State University, 1983.

"Corsets and the Mode." *Good Housekeeping*, vol. 75 (October 1922).

Cosmopolitan, vol. 85 (August 1928): illustration, p. 28.

Cott, Nancy F. *The Grounding of Modern Feminism*. New Haven, Conn.: Yale University Press, 1987.

———. *Root of Bitterness: Documents of the Social History of American Women*. Boston: Northeastern University Press, 1986.

Crane, Frank. "How I Like a Woman To Look." *American Magazine*, vol. 96 (November 1923).

Cranor, Katherine Taylor. "Clothing and Health." *Journal of Home Economics*, vol. 15 (August 1923).

Davis, Fred. *Fashion, Culture, and Identity*. Chicago: University of Chicago Press, 1992.

Davis, Tracy C. "Questions for a Feminist Methodology in Theatre History." In *Interpreting the Theatrical Past: Essays in the Historiography of Performance*. Edited by Thomas Postlewait and Bruce A. McConachie. Iowa City: University of Iowa Press, 1989.

Dedmon, Emmett. *Fabulous Chicago*. Enlarged ed. New York: Athenaeum, 1981.

Deford, Frank. *There She Is: The Life and Times of Miss America*. New York: Viking, 1971.

Delineator, vol. 98 (May 1921).

de Marly, Diana. *The History of Haute Couture, 1850–1950*. New York: Holmes and Meier, 1980.

Devon, Ann. "Will the Women Wear Them?" *Outlook and Independent*, vol. 153 (6 November 1929).

"Doctors Dislike New Dress Styles." *Literary Digest*, vol. 104 (4 January 1930).

Douglas, Ann. *Terrible Honesty: Mongrel Manhattan in the 1920s*. New York: Farrar, Straus and Giroux, 1995.

Dudden, Faye E. *Women in the American Theatre: Actresses, Audiences, 1790–1870*. London: Yale University Press, 1994.

Duffy, Susan, and Bernard K. Duffy. "Watchdogs of the American Theatre, 1910–1940." *Journal of American Culture*, vol. 6 (spring 1983).

Eastman, Crystal. "Mother-Worship." In *These Modern Women: Biographical Essays from the Twenties*. Edited by Elaine Showalter. New York: Feminist Press, City University of New York, 1989.

———. "Suffragists Ten Years After." *New Republic*, vol. 35 (27 June 1923).

Erenberg, Lewis A. *Steppin' Out: New York Nightlife and the Transformation of American Culture, 1890–1930*. Westport, Conn.: Greenwood Press, 1981.

Fass, Paula S. *The Damned and the Beautiful: American Youth in the 1920s*. New York: Oxford University Press, 1977.

Fergusson, Francis. "The Theatre: What Is the Revue?" *Bookman*, vol. 72 (September 1930).

Finley, John H. "What Is the Matter with Teaching?" *Delineator*, vol. 108 (June 1926).

Fitzgerald, F. Scott. "Echoes of the Jazz Age." *Scribner's Monthly*, vol. 90 (November 1931).

Fitzpatrick, John. Collection. Chicago Historical Society.

Flugel, J. C. *The Psychology of Clothes*. London: Hogarth Press, 1930.

Freedman, Estelle B. "The New Woman: Changing Views of Women in the 1920s." *Journal of American History*, vol. 61 (1974).

Funnell, Charles E. *By the Beautiful Sea: The Rise and Times of That Great American Resort, Atlantic City*. New York: Knopf, 1975.

Gilman, Charlotte Perkins. "Do Women Dress to Please Men?" *Century Magazine*, vol. 103 (March 1922).

———. *Women and Economics*. Boston: Small, Maynard & Co., 1898.

Girl Scouts, Inc. *Scouting for Girls, Official Handbook of the Girls Scouts*. Abridged ed. New York: Girl Scouts, Inc., 1927.

Goffman, Erving. *Gender Advertisements*. Cambridge, Mass.: Harvard University Press, 1979.

Greenwald, Maurine Weiner. "Working-Class Feminism and the Family Wage Ideal: The Seattle Debate on Married Women's Right to Work, 1914–1920." *Journal of American History*, vol. 76 (June 1989).

Hale, Martha Evans. "New Styles for This Winter." *People's Home Journal*, vol. 35 (November 1920).

"Hats vs. Undies." *Woman Citizen*, vol. 11 (August 1926).

Hollander, Anne. *Seeing through Clothes*. New York: Viking Press, 1978.

———. "Women and Fashion." In *Women, the Arts, and the 1920s in Paris and New York*. Edited by Kenneth W. Wheeler and Virginia Lee Lussier. New Brunswick, N.J.: Transaction Books, 1982.

Hopkins, Mary Alden. "Do Women Dress for Men?" *Delineator*, vol. 98 (July 1921).

———. "What Shall the Poor Girl Wear?" *New Republic*, vol. 28 (23 November 1921).

———. "Woman's Rebellion against Fashions." *New Republic*, vol. 31 (16 August 1922).

Hopwood, Avery. *The Gold Diggers*. 1919. Photocopy of unpublished manuscript.

———. "Is the Undraped Drama Unmoral?" *Theatre Magazine*, vol. 35 (June 1922).

———. "Why I Don't Write More Serious Plays." *Theatre Magazine*, vol. 39 (April 1924).

Hornblow, Arthur. "League of Nations' Fifteenth Point." *Theatre Magazine*, vol. 44 (September 1926).

———. "Mr. Hornblow Goes to the Play." *Theatre Magazine*, vol. 32 (October 1920).

Humphries, Rolphe. "Artists and Models: Through the Stereoscope, Right Eye: The Intellect." *New Republic*, vol. 54 (11 April 1928).

Hutchinson, Woods. "Health and Sports Suits." *Saturday Evening Post*, vol. 198 (8 August 1925).

"Is the Stage like the Augean Stables?" *Literary Digest*, vol. 107 (25 October 1930).

"Is the Younger Generation in Peril?" *Literary Digest*, vol. 69 (14 May 1921).

Jagger, Alison M., and Susan R. Bordo, eds. *Gender/Body/Knowledge: Feminist-Reconstructions of Being and Knowing*. New Brunswick, N.J.: Rutgers University Press, 1989.

Kaye, Joseph. "The Last Legs of Burlesque." *Theatre Magazine*, vol. 51 (February 1930).

Kennedy, Hugh A. Studdert. "Short Skirts." *Forum*, vol. 75 (June 1926).

———. "Shorter Than Ever: Being an Answer to Mrs. Catt's Question, 'How Many Yards in Your Skirt.'" *Woman Citizen*, vol. 11 (October 1926).

Kirchwey, Freda, ed. *Our Changing Morality*. New York: Albert and Charles, 1924.

Kosuth, Joseph. *The Play of the Unmentionable: An Installation by Joseph Kosuth at the Brooklyn Museum*. New York: New Press, 1992.

Krutch, Joseph Wood. "Bigger and Better." *Nation*, vol. 122 (2 June 1926).

———. "Of Revues." *Nation*, vol. 122 (13 January 1926).

Kunzle, David. *Fashion and Fetishism: A Social History of the Corset, Tight-Lacing and Other Forms of Body-Sculpture in the West*. Totowa, N.J.: Rowman and Littlefield, 1982.

Latham, Angela J. "Packaging Woman: The Concurrent Rise of Beauty Pageants, Public Bathing, and Other Performances of Female 'Nudity.'" *Journal of Popular Culture*, vol. 29 (winter 1995).

———. "Performance, Ethnography, and History: An Analysis of Displays by Female Bathers in the 1920s." *Text and Performance Quarterly*, vol. 17 (April 1997).

———. "The Right to Bare: Containing and Encoding American Women in Popular Entertainments of the 1920s." *Theatre Journal*, vol. 49 (December 1997).

Laufe, Abe. *The Wicked Stage: A History of Theater Censorship and Harassment in the United States*. New York: Frederick Ungar Co., 1978.

Leamy, Hugh. "Toeing the Line." *Collier's*, vol. 86 (13 September 1930).

Leider, Emily Wortus. *Becoming Mae West*. New York: Farrar, Straus and Giroux, 1997.

Lencek, Lena, and Gideon Bosker. *Making Waves: Swimsuits and the Undressing of America*. San Francisco: Chronicle, 1989.

Levy, Harriet Mooney. "The Woman in Business: Assets and Liabilities." *Jewish Woman*, vol. 10 (April–June 1930).

Life, vol. 88 (18 February 1926, 15 July 1926, 26 August 1926): cover illustrations.

Life, vol. 88 (9 September 1926): cartoons, pp. 8, 25.

Lincoln, Yvonna S., and Egon G. Guba. "The Only Generalization Is: There Is No Generalization." In *Naturalistic Inquiry*, chap. 5. Newbury Park, Calif.: Sage Publications, 1985.

Lion, Hortense M. "The Boycott on Wives." *Outlook*, vol. 135 (12 December 1923).

Lowe, Margaret A. "From Robust Appetites to Calorie Counting: The Emergence of Dieting among Smith College Students in the 1920s." *Journal of Women's History*, vol. 7 (winter 1995).

Lurie, R. L. "Burlesque." *New Republic*, vol. 42 (8 April 1925).

Lynd, Robert S., and Helen Merrell Lynd. *Middletown: A Study in American Culture*. New York: Harcourt, Brace and Co., 1929.

Lyon, Elizabeth, and Adella Eppel. "Cost of Clothing among Missouri College Girls." *Journal of Home Economics*, vol. 21 (June 1929).

Maginnis, Tara. "Fashion Shows, Strip Shows and Beauty Pageants: The Theatre of the Feminine Ideal." Ph.D. diss., University of Georgia, 1991.

Marquis, Albert Nelson, ed. *The Book of Chicagoans*. Chicago: A. N. Marquis and Co., 1917, 1926.

Martin, Richard, and Harold Koda. *Splash! A History of Swimwear*. New York: Rizzoli, 1990.

Marx, Samuel. *Wild Women of Broadway. Little Blue Book No. 1445*. Edited by E. Haldeman-Julius. Girard, Kans.: Haldeman-Julius Publications, 1929.

Mason, Michael. *The Making of Victorian Sexual Attitudes*. New York: Oxford University Press, 1994.

May, Elaine Tyler. *Great Expectations: Marriage and Divorce in Post-Victorian America*. Chicago: University of Chicago Press, 1980.

May, Lary. *Screening Out the Past: The Birth of Mass Culture and the Motion Picture Industry*. Chicago: University of Chicago Press, 1983.

Mordden, Ethan. *That Jazz! An Idiosyncratic Social History of the American Twenties*. New York: G. P. Putnam's Sons, 1978.

Mott, Frank Luther. *American Journalism: A History of Newspapers in the United States through 260 Years: 1690–1950*. Rev. ed. New York: Macmillan Co., 1950.

Mrozek, Donald J. "The 'Amazon' and the American 'Lady': Sexual Fears of Women as Athletes." In *From "Fair Sex" to Feminism: Sport and the Socialization of Women in the Industrial and Post-Industrial Eras*. Edited by J. A. Mangan and Roberta J. Park. London: Frank Cass and Co., 1987.

Muirheid, Walter G. "Fashion Follies Follow War." *Mentor*, vol. 9 (February 1930).

"A Naked Challenge." *Nation*, vol. 122 (23 June 1926).

"A New Crusade for Longer Skirts." *Literary Digest*, vol. 88 (16 January 1926).

Nystrom, Paul H. *Economics of Fashion*. New York: Ronald Press, 1928.

Oberdeck, Kathryn. "Not Pink Teas: The Seattle Working-Class Women's Movement, 1905–1918. *Labor History*, vol. 32 (spring 1991).

Oberwager, Charles A. "Heaven Help the Modern Boy!" *Liberty*, vol. 4 (23 July 1927).

O'Donnol, Shirley Miles. *American Costume, 1915–1970*. Bloomington: Indiana University Press, 1982.

Osborne, Elizabeth Macdonald. "Some Like 'Em Cool." *Collier's*, vol. 80 (13 August 1927).

Pacteau, Francette. *The Symptom of Beauty*. Cambridge, Mass.: Harvard University Press, 1994.

Page, Will A. *Behind the Curtains of the Broadway Beauty Trust*. New York: Edward A. Miller Co., 1927.

Peck, Mary Gray. "Young People's Manners." *Woman Citizen*, vol. 5 (21 May 1921).

Peiss, Kathy. *Hope in a Jar: The Making of America's Beauty Culture*. New York: Metropolitan Books, Henry Holt and Co., 1998.

Peto, Florence M. "Swim—for Health, Youth and Beauty." *Outing*, vol. 75 (December 1919).

Playbills and Programs Collection. University of Chicago Library.

Playgoer: A Magazine for the Theatre, vol. 2 (19 February 1928); vol. 3 (31 March 1929).

"The Pope's Appeal to Men to Reform Women's Dress." *Literary Digest*, vol. 92 (29 January 1927).

Porter, Roy. "History of the Body." In *New Perspectives on Historical Writing*. Edited by Peter Burke. University Park: Pennsylvania State University Press, 1991.

Public Ordinances of Atlantic City. Atlantic City, N.J.: Globe Co., 1916.

Ray, Marie Beynon. "Sheer Modernism." *Collier's*, vol. 84 (17 August 1929).

"Reforming the Stage from Within." *Literary Digest*, vol. 89 (17 April 1926).

Rittenhouse, Anne. "Paul Poiret's Ten Short Precepts." In *The Well-Dressed Woman*. New York: Harper and Brothers, 1924.

Riverol, A. R. *Live from Atlantic City: The History of the Miss America Pageant before, after and in spite of Television*. Bowling Green, Ohio: Bowling Green State University Popular Press, 1992.

Roberts, Mary Louise. *Civilization without Sexes: Reconstructing Gender in Postwar France, 1917–1927*. Chicago: University of Chicago Press, 1994.

Rossi, Alice S. *The Feminist Papers: From Adams to de Beauvoir*. New York: Bantam Books, 1974.

Saturday Evening Post, vol. 199 (24 July 1926). Hosiery advertisement, 62.

Sawchuck, Kim. "A Tale of Inscription/Fashion Statements." *Canadian Journal of Political and Social Theory*, vol. 11 (1987).

Schneirov, Matthew. *The Dream of a New Social Order: Popular Magazines in America, 1893–1914*. New York: Columbia University Press, 1994.

Scott, James C. *Domination and the Arts of Resistance: Hidden Transcripts*. London: Yale University Press, 1990.

Scott, Joan Wallach. *Gender and the Politics of History*. New York: Columbia University Press, 1988.

Seldes, Gilbert. "The Theatre." *Dial*, vol. 73 (September 1922).

———. "A Tribute to Florenz Ziegfeld." In *The American Theatre As Seen by Its Critics, 1752–1934*. Edited by Montrose J. Moses and John Mason Brown. New York: W. W. Norton and Co., 1934.

Sharrar, Jack F. *Avery Hopwood: His Life and Plays*. Jefferson, N.C.: McFarland and Co., 1989. Reprint, Ann Arbor: University of Michigan Press, 1998.

Shawn, Ted. "Is Nudity Salacious?" *Theatre Magazine*, vol. 40 (November 1924).

Sheridan, Lillian B. "Women and the Stage." In *Women of Today: 1925 Edition*. Edited by Ida Clyde Clarke. New York: Women of Today Press, 1925.

Sherman, Florence A. "Hygiene of Clothing." *Journal of Home Economics*, vol. 17 (January 1925).

Showalter, Elaine, ed. *These Modern Women: Autobiographical Essays from the Twenties*. Rev. ed. New York: Feminist Press, City University of New York, 1989.

Simmons, Christina. "Modern Sexuality and the Myth of Victorian Repression." In *Passion and Power: Sexuality in History*. Edited by Kathy Peiss and Christina Simmons. Philadelphia: Temple University Press, 1989.

Skinner, Richard Dana. "The Play: When Ziegfeld Stumbles." *Commonweal*, vol. 10 (24 July 1929).

Sklar, Kathryn Kish. *Florence Kelley and the Nation's Work: The Rise of Women's Political Culture, 1830–1900*. New Haven, Conn.: Yale University Press, 1995.

Smith-Rosenberg, Carroll. *Disorderly Conduct: Visions of Gender in Victorian America*. New York: Oxford University Press, 1987.

Sobel, Bernard. "Ladies' Night: Turkish Bath House Turns on Comedy Steam." *Dramatic Mirror*, vol. 82 (14 August 1920).

Spitzer, Marian. "The Chorus Lady, Model 1924." *Saturday Evening Post*, vol. 197 (15 September 1924).

Steele, Valerie. *Fetish*. New York: Oxford University Press, 1996.

Stoller, Paul. *The Taste of Ethnographic Things: The Senses in Anthropology*. Philadelphia: University of Pennsylvania Press, 1989.

"The Story of the New Paris Mode: In Which It Will Be Seen That the Day of Democracy in Dress Is Past." *Vogue*, vol. 72 (13 October 1928).

Straton, John Roach. "The Trouble with the Modern Theatre." *Theatre Magazine*, vol. 31 (February 1920).

Stuart, William H. *The Twenty Incredible Years*. Chicago: M. A. Donohue and Co., 1935.

Sunday, Billy. "Theater, Cards and Dance." In *Best of Billy Sunday: 17 Burning Sermons from the Most Spectacular Evangelist the World Has Ever Known*. Edited by John R. Rice. Murfreesboro, Tenn.: Sword of the Lord, 1965.

Tarkington, Mrs. Booth. "We Needn't Be Robots in Our Dress." *Ladies' Home Journal*, vol. 45 (April 1928).

Tashman, Lilyan. "Frolics and Follies." *Pictorial Review*, vol. 33 (October, November, December 1931).

Tittle, Walter. "Ziegfeld of the Follies." *World's Work*, vol. 53 (March 1927).

Tittman, Edward D. "Morality and Clothes—to the Editor of *The Nation*." *Nation*, vol. 121 (29 August 1925).

Turim, Maureen. "Seduction and Elegance: The New Woman of Fashion in Silent Cinema." In *On Fashion*. Edited by Shari Benstock and Suzanne Ferris. New Brunswick, N.J.: Rutgers University Press, 1994.

Turner, Victor. *On the Edge of the Bush: Anthropology as Experience*. Edited by Edith L. B. Turner. Tuscon: University of Arizona Press, 1985.

Van Deventer, Betty. "Lives of Chorus Girls." *Haldeman-Julius Quarterly*, vol. 2 (January–March 1928).

Van Etten, Ida. "The Sweating System, Charity, and Organization." In *Root of Bitterness: Documents of the Social History of American Women*. Edited by Nancy F. Cott. Boston: Northeastern University Press, 1986.

Van Maanen, John. "An End to Innocence: The Ethnography of Ethnography." In *Representation in Ethnography*. Thousand Oaks, Calif.: Sage Publications, 1995.

Van Vechten, Carl. "A Note on Tights." *American Mercury*, vol. 2 (August 1924).

Veblen, Thorstein. *The Theory of the Leisure Class*. New York: Macmillan Co., 1917.

Wainscott, Ronald H. "Attracting Censorship to the Popular Theatre: Al Woods Produces Avery Hopwood's The Demi-Virgin." *Theatre History Studies*, vol. 10 (1990).

———. *The Emergence of the Modern American Theater, 1914–1929*. New Haven, Conn.: Yale University Press, 1997.

"A War against Tight Shoes." *Literary Digest*, vol. 74 (15 July 1922).

Ward, Carol M. *Mae West: A Bio-Bibliography*. New York: Greenwood Press, 1989.

Wayburn, Ned. "Chorus Girls Make the Best Wives." *Collier's*, vol. 77 (27 March 1926).

Weber, Henriette. "Silk Stockings and Sedition." *North American Review*, vol. 225 (January 1928).

West, Mae. *The Wicked Age*, or *The Contest*, 1927. Mae West Collection. Library of Congress.

Whipple, Leon. "Not Art and Not Model." *Survey*, vol. 55 (1 March 1926).

White, Mary Ogden. "Good Health—Your Job." *Woman Citizen*, vol. 5 (May 1921).

"Who Makes Your Clothes?" *Woman Citizen*, vol. 4 (19 April 1920).

Wilson, Edmund. "The Finale at the Follies." *New Republic*, vol. 42 (25 March 1925).

Winn, Mary Day. "Intelligentsia of the Chorus." *North American Review*, vol. 229 (June 1930).

Woman's Home Companion, vol. 51 (June 1924). Corset advertisement, 99.

Wood, Cyrus. *Good Night Ladies*. New York: Samuel French, n.d.

Woods, A. H. "Why I Produce Bedroom Farces." *Theatre Magazine*, vol. 35 (June 1922).

World Young Women's Christian Associations. *The Girl Reserve Movement: A Manual for Advisers*. New York: Young Women's Christian Associations, 1921.

Yellis, Kenneth A. "Prosperity's Child: Some Thoughts on the Flapper." *American Quarterly*, vol. 21 (spring 1969).

Young Womens Christian Associations (YWCA). *The Girl Reserve Movement: A Manual for Advisers*. New York: Woman's Press, 1923.

Ziegfeld, Florenz Jr. "How I Pick Beauties." *Theatre Magazine*, vol. 30 (September 1919).

———. "Picking Out Pretty Girls for the Stage." *American Magazine*, vol. 88 (December 1919).

———. "What Becomes of the Ziegfeld Follies Girls?" *Pictorial Review*, vol. 26 (May 1925).

Ziegfeld, Richard, and Paulette Ziegfeld. *The Ziegfeld Touch: The Life and Times of Florenz Ziegfeld, Jr.* New York: Harry N. Abrams, 1993.

Newspapers

Atlanta Constitution, January 1922.

Atlantic City Daily Press, June and September 1921.

Atlantic City Evening Union, June 1921.

Atlantic City Sunday Gazette, June 1921.

Boston Evening Transcript, May 1922.

Brazil (Indiana) Times, February 1996.

Chicago Daily News, March–April 1922.

Chicago Evening American, March 1922.

Chicago Evening Post, June 1921, August 1921, March 1922.

Chicago Herald and Examiner, September 1920, June 1921, March 1922.

Chicago Record-Herald, October 1910.

Chicago Tribune, March–April 1922, August 1987.

Louisville Courier-Journal, March 1922.

New York Herald, September 1921.

New York Times, August 1920, May–June 1921, August–September 1921, March 1922, April 1927, December 1929, November 1990.

New York Tribune, September 1921.

New York World, September 1921, January 1925.

St. Louis Post-Dispatch, August 1992.

Index

Note: Page numbers in *italics* refer to illustrations.

Sawchuck, Kim, 160n.7
Scandals, George White's, 156
Schoolteachers, norms for, 1–2
Schroeder, Werner W., 28
Scott, James C., 12, 132, 145, 173n.57
Scott, Joan Wallach, 11
Seldes, Gilbert, 111–12
Self-presentation: contested control of, 9,
    62–63, 97; and social context, 11
Self-sufficiency, 53
Selznick Film Company, 80
Sexual innuendo, 128, 135–36
Sexuality: as challenge to Victorian morality,
    100, 163n.8; and character, 100; and
    fashion interest, 36; and sexual trans-
    gression, 77, 154–55. *See also* Desire;
    Homosexuality
Sexual rights, and feminism, 26
Sharrar, Jack F., 133, 179nn.58, 2, and 3,
    181n.27
Shaw, Edward, 83, 84, 172n.54
Shawn, Ted, 104
Sheridan, Lillian B., 177–78n.42
Sherman, Dr. Florence A., 55, 57–59
Shoes: and health, 54–57, 56; and socio-
    economic status, 44
Showalter, Elaine, 9
Shubert, Lee, 119–20
Shubert revues (musicals), 111, *114*, 118,
    119
Simmons, Christina, 22
Skinner, Richard Dana, 107
Small, Len, 28, 29
Smith, George W., 72
Smith-Rosenberg, Carroll, 8
Sobel, Bernard, 124
Social housekeeping, 175–76n.7
Socioeconomic status, and clothing, 43–44,
    46
Somers Point, New Jersey, bathing costume
    and beach regulations in, 78, 79–81, 88
Spanish Love (Hopwood), 179n.1
Spitzer, Marian, 115, 117
Stance. *See* Posture
Stereotypes, false representations within, 7
Stevens, Ashton, 127, 143, 151, 182n.55
Steward, Roy T., 146
Stockings. *See* Hosiery

Stoller, Paul, 162n.27
Straton, Rev. John Roach, 18, 22, 62, 100,
    119
Striptease, 110, 137
Stultz, Rev. T. D., 78
Subordination, 12–13
Sullivan, Florence, 28, 29
Sunday, Billy, 62, 100
Survey magazine, 40
Swanson, Gloria, 98
Swimming: and morality, 67; popularity of,
    66; public nature of, 4, 94; safety of, 66–
    69. *See also* Bathing costumes
Swimwear. *See* Bathing costumes
"Switch" (braid of hair), 1, 2, 14, 158

Tableau, nudity in, 119
Tanguy, Commodore William, 78, 79
Tarkington, Booth, 35–36
Tarkington, Mrs. Booth, 35–36
Tashman, Lilyan, 139–41, 178n.55, 182n.68
Taste (good taste), appeal to, 49
Taylor, Ada, 72, 79, 90
Temporality, and ethnography, 14
Theater: beauty requirements in, 104–8;
    censorship of, 4–5, 100–1, 108, 122,
    144–54; nudity in, 105, 110, 111, 118–
    21, 137, 148; women's attendance at,
    135–36, 182n.55; women's bodies
    appropriated in, 10, 101–3, 136
Theater reform, 18, 99–100, 104
Theatre Magazine, 119, 120, 141, 180n.3
Thompson, Lydia, 177–78n.42
Thompson, William Hale, 148, 151
Tourism, motivation of, 65, 67–69, 80, 81, 88
Transformation, 103
Tuberculosis, 59
Turner, Victor, 14
Twelfth Night parties, 89

Underwear: as bathing costume, 76; and
    health, 57–62, *61*. *See also* Chemises;
    Corsets
Utah, dress codes in, 48

Van Deventer, Betty, 114–15, 117
Van Etten, Ida, 166n.58
Van Maanen, John, 13

ABOUT THE AUTHOR

Angela J. Latham is Director of Theater in the Department of Fine Arts at Triton College in the Chicago metropolitan area. Her previous publications have appeared in journals devoted to the study of theater, performance, and culture. She holds a Ph.D. in theater history from the University of Illinois, Urbana-Champaign.

LIBRARY OF CONGRESS CATALOGING-IN-PUBLICATION DATA
Latham, Angela J.
    Posing a threat: flappers, chorus girls, and other brazen performers of the
American 1920s
        p.   cm.
    ISBN 0–8195–6400–1 (cl. : alk. paper). — ISBN 0–8195–6401–X (pbk. : alk.
paper)
    1. Women—United States—History—20th century. 2. Women in popular
culture—United States—History—20th century. 3. Costume—United States
—History—20th century. 4. Costume—Social aspects—United States.
    5. Nineteen twenties.
    HQ1420.L38   2000
    305.4/0973/0904—dc21   99-45571